CONSOLIDATING COLLEGES
AND MERGING UNIVERSITIES

CONSOLIDATING COLLEGES AND MERGING UNIVERSITIES

New Strategies for Higher Education Leaders

James Martin, James E. Samels & Associates

Johns Hopkins University Press
Baltimore

© 2017 Johns Hopkins University Press
All rights reserved. Published 2017
Printed in the United States of America on acid-free paper
9 8 7 6 5 4 3 2 1

Johns Hopkins University Press
2715 North Charles Street
Baltimore, Maryland 21218-4363
www.press.jhu.edu

Library of Congress Cataloging-in-Publication Data

Names: Martin, James, 1948 January 14– author. | Samels, James E., author.
Title: Consolidating colleges and merging universities : new strategies for higher
    education leaders / James Martin and James E. Samels & Associates.
Description: Baltimore, Maryland : Johns Hopkins University Press, 2017. |
    Includes bibliographical references and index.
Identifiers: LCCN 2016017126 | ISBN 9781421421674 (hardcover : alk. paper) |
    ISBN 9781421421681 (electronic) | ISBN 1421421674 (hardcover : alk. paper) |
    ISBN 1421421682 (electronic)
Subjects: LCSH: Universities and colleges—Mergers—United States.
Classification: LCC LB2341 .M28955 2017 | DDC 378.73—dc23
LC record available at https://lccn.loc.gov/2016017126

A catalog record for this book is available from the British Library.

*Special discounts are available for bulk purchases of this book. For more
information, please contact Special Sales at 410-516-6936 or
specialsales@press.jhu.edu.*

Johns Hopkins University Press uses environmentally friendly book materials,
including recycled text paper that is composed of at least 30 percent post-
consumer waste, whenever possible.

Contents

V   CLOSURE: HIDDEN COSTS AND COMPLEXITIES

Preface

The chapters that follow offer fresh thinking about the reasons colleges and universities are building partnerships and alliances in growing numbers and describe how to design and sustain these new models of strategic collaboration. Beyond traditional, focused program affiliations, contributors also examine the rising interest in both full institutional merger and closure, and provide detailed action steps to accomplish both. All of these strategies constitute what we describe in this volume as the *consolidation* of American higher education, and they are examined by a group of leaders who have successfully designed and led them. Their discussions also take place against a new set of concerns, identified by Moody's Investor Services in 2015, that the rate of mergers among small colleges and universities will double in the next few years and the rate of closures among those institutions will triple.[1]

Two decades ago, we assembled a different group of writers to study, more narrowly, the concept of merging colleges for mutual growth.[2] Since the publication of that book, we have observed, advised, and consulted on dozens of strategic alliance, consolidation, and full merger plans. Over this period, we have noted that while complete mergers of colleges and universities are continuing to increase in number, new and creative forms of partnership and affiliation are beginning to reshape institutions of all sizes and histories, including those categorized as elite. Jonathan Cole, author of *Toward a More Perfect University*, highlights this point in his recommendations for more "coordinated academic efforts among prestigious universities to reduce duplication . . . an Ivy League of academic cooperation."[3]

While some of the chapters that follow explore partnerships to eliminate program duplication and expand budget capacity, there are also chapters that provide the action steps necessary to merge two institutions. Chapters 2 and 16 offer the only strategic plans of which we are aware to close a college or university; these are written by a former president and an attorney who have both completed closures. Additionally, chapters and sidebars within chapters provide several original contributions to the field:

- A new, expanded typology of institutional partnership, alliance, and merger agreements. This list builds on and extends one of the first ones to appear in the higher education literature by Martin and Samels in their book *Merging Colleges for Mutual Growth* (1994). (Chapter 2)

- A detailed description of "Systemness," the leadership model behind the State University of New York, the nation's largest higher education system, written by the current chancellor who designed it. (Chapter 4)

- A chapter by two administrators at an Ivy League institution explaining why even elite universities are now developing strategic alliances to leverage resources and serve students more effectively. This chapter incorporates an extended sidebar interview with the president of another elite university detailing why she is actively seeking multiple partners to strengthen the future position and competitiveness of her own institution. (Chapter 7)

- A first-time discussion from the president of Southern New Hampshire University, who was recently invited by President Barack Obama to collaborate in the design of several national program initiatives in the area of competency-based education. For his chapter in this book, he and the executive director of College for America at Southern New Hampshire University have explored some of the ways that competency-based education can facilitate partnerships between colleges and universities. (Chapter 10)

- A master plan on how new technologies are creating new kinds of partnerships from the executive dean for Arizona State University. His focus is on the concept of the "New American University," which his institution has implemented, and how new forms of technology are a make-or-break element in the university's recent partnerships. (Chapter 9)

- One of the only chapters in the literature that outlines the action steps leading to a formal partnership between public and private higher education institutions. These guidelines are provided by a chief academic officer who has designed and implemented a success-

ful public-private partnership between two higher education institutions in the state of Idaho. (Chapter 12)

■ An introduction to perhaps the nation's most influential nonacademic consortium, the Boston Consortium for Higher Education,
written by its current executive director. This association of sixteen
institutional members, founded in 1995, is dedicated to joint projects that achieve measurable quality improvement in business and
operational areas and is viewed as the national model for administrators seeking innovative methods to coordinate services and
significantly reduce costs. (Chapter 13)

■ Aside from accrediting association guidelines, two of the first strategic plans, with action steps, to close a college or university, written by a president and an attorney who have led and coordinated
closures. (Chapters 2 and 16)

■ Multiple sidebars in most chapters by professionals in various areas
of operations. Some sidebar contributors have been invited because
they hold views contrary to chapter authors. Finally, most chapter
authors have been asked to contribute at least one sidebar of lessons
learned in response to the questions: "Looking back, what is the
most important piece of advice or lesson learned you can offer to a
leader building a partnership today?"

Chapters are grouped into five parts. Part I, "The New Necessities to
Partner," provides an overview; an extended Part II, "Strategic Alliance:
A Model That Rarely Fails, and Why," discusses the primary forms of
partnership and co-venture now being developed nationally; new developments in higher education consortia, both traditional liberal arts
consortia and newer affiliations to achieve business and operational
efficiencies, are explored in Part III, "Consortium: New Benefits, Changing Purposes"; Part IV, "Merger: The Right Reasons to Consider One,"
gives a detailed look at recent full mergers in higher education and the
strategic plans to accomplish them; and the final section, Part V,
"Closure: Hidden Costs and Complexities," covers the reasons to close a
college or university accompanied by the key administrative decisions
that closure must include.

Part I opens with a chapter that updates and extends a conversation
that Martin and Samels have been credited with initiating twenty years
ago in their book *Merging Colleges for Mutual Growth: A New Strategy
for Academic Managers*, regarding the intentional decision to merge
two institutions to achieve economies of scale and eliminate unnecessary
program duplication. In chapter 2, Martin and Samels continue this

conversation by also providing an expanded version of their original typology of the most common models employed when universities and colleges decide to partner.

Part II opens with chapters by two national authorities on the subject of strategic alliances, R. Michael Tanner, chief academic officer and vice president at the Association of Public and Land-Grant Universities, and Nancy L. Zimpher, chancellor of the State University of New York (SUNY) system, the nation's largest. Tanner and Zimpher are both central to any national conversation about the future of our largest individual universities and state systems. In chapter 3, Tanner asks, "When does large become too large?" His focus is on the need for some of our larger higher education institutions to rethink their growth patterns and consider new kinds of internal affiliations and co-ventures to make more strategic and efficient use of their resources and personnel. Zimpher explains her philosophy of "systemness," which is also predicated on leveraging the institutional resources and personnel within the SUNY system. Zimpher has championed this approach, and chapter 4 details some of its successes as well as projects that did not go as planned, why, and how her team addressed those downturns.

In chapter 5, Pamela Eibeck, president of the University of the Pacific, outlines her entrepreneurial approach to institutional growth and brand development through strategic partnerships. Eibeck centers on the role of the president in developing a campus-wide vision that can drive a successful process.

In the chapter that follows, Vita Rabinowitz, overall chief academic officer for the City University of New York (CUNY) System, and James Stellar, provost of the University at Albany within the SUNY system, expand on Rabinowitz's initial comment when invited to write about the recent rise in strategic alliances within both CUNY and SUNY: "To put it simply, we never thought this way ten years ago." Rabinowitz and Stellar detail the reasons and methods with which faculty colleagues are now beginning to develop new models of affiliation that leverage the present curriculum and faculty resources within two of the nation's largest systems of higher education.

In chapter 7, the topic is how and why elite institutions are joining forces to more effectively serve their students and their communities. The authors, J. Matthew Hartley and Alan Ruby, are the leaders of the Alliance for Higher Education and Democracy at the University of Pennsylvania, an organization focusing on global partnerships among universities and colleges both nationally and internationally. Hartley is also associate dean of the University's Graduate School of Education.

Following this, the familiar and often undervalued partnership between a university and a local community college is reconsidered for
the ways it still enfranchises sometimes very large numbers of students
at very low costs. Chapter 8 is written by two long-serving Chicago-
based presidents, Charles Middleton of Roosevelt University and Kenneth
Ender of Harper College.

Chapter 9 focuses on how new advances in technology, both instructional and administrative, are creating a new category of education
alliances. For this conversation, the executive dean for university initiatives at Arizona State University and his chief of staff explain how
this "New American University" has, not without some controversy,
become a "comprehensive knowledge enterprise" by implementing
several dozen internal and external academic partnerships.

Chapter 10 focuses on the new emergence of competency-based education both as a "disrupter" of previous systems and as a dynamic driver
of institutional affiliations and even full mergers. In this chapter, one of
the most recognized advocates for the competency-based education
agenda nationally, Paul LeBlanc, president of Southern New Hampshire
University, and Kristine Clerkin, executive director of College for America
at SNHU, outline how this movement is changing the nature of collaboration among colleges and universities. In 2015, LeBlanc was appointed,
while continuing as SNHU president, as senior advisor to Ted Mitchell,
under secretary for the US Department of Education, by the Obama
administration and was in residence in Washington; his contribution
incorporates several observations from this national role.

This conversation is followed by a discussion in chapter 11 of the
benefits and challenges in partnering internationally, including the creation of branch campuses in other countries. Contributors are Michael
Jackson, emeritus vice president and executive director of international
advancement at the University of Southern California, and James Larimore, chief officer for the advancement of underserved learners at
American College Testing (ACT).

In chapter 12, the book's section on strategic alliances closes with one
of the only chapters in the literature of which we are aware that provides
specific action steps for a formal partnership between a public higher
education institution and a private one. Its author is John Ottenhoff, vice
president for academic affairs at the College of Idaho. Ottenhoff completed a partnership at his present institution, a private college, with Idaho
State University. This chapter also includes a sidebar on the benefits of
developing partnerships between traditional and for-profit institutions,
written by the former chief academic officer of a for-profit college.

Part III opens with a discussion contributed by Phillip DiChiara, executive director of the Boston Consortium of Higher Education (TBC). TBC was founded in 1995 by a group of chief financial officers to create multiple, interlocking working groups, called "communities of practice," to consider new models for more efficient business operations among its membership. As noted above, TBC has come to be viewed as one of the most influential nonacademic consortia in the nation, and this chapter by its current executive director is the first extended examination of its models of decision making and goal setting.

R. Owen Williams, president of the Associated Colleges of the South, follows in chapter 14 with new considerations of the purpose and value of traditional liberal arts college consortia. Williams focuses his comments on how ongoing curriculum and academic program development can produce both cost savings and revenue generation.

Part IV focuses entirely on plans and strategies for merger, and its chapter is contributed by Susan Resneck Pierce, president emerita of the University of Puget Sound and long-serving consultant on these transactions. Pierce provides an overview of merger activities over the past decade along with reasons why some plans have succeeded while others have failed. She also clarifies the critical steps that presidents, provosts, and board members need to follow to complete a full merger.

The book concludes with a set of specific action steps to close a college or university, contributed by a former president who closed one. Michael Hoyle, now the chief financial officer of Lasell College, served as the final president of McIntosh College in New Hampshire. McIntosh ceased operations in 2009 after more than 110 years of service to students following a closure plan developed by Hoyle and his colleagues.

The authors would like to thank several individuals who made key contributions to the final form of this book. Nancy L. Zimpher, from her perspective as head of the SUNY system; Vita Rabinowitz, academic head of the CUNY system and James Stellar, provost at the University at Albany, took the time to provide updates on breaking news among their many institutions. Thanks are also due to Jessica Fisher Neidl, senior writer and director of correspondence at SUNY, for her skill and good cheer in managing the constant news cycles in the nation's largest state system. Once again, we would like to express appreciation to Arlene Lieberman of Samels Associates, Attorneys at Law, for her many contributions to the updated typology of partnerships, alliances, and mergers in chapter 2.

In closing, we would like to thank three individuals at Johns Hopkins University Press for their significant contributions to this volume. Kathy

Alexander, the Press's former publicity manager, helped us realize the potential in partnering with the Press's marketing team, and Catherine Goldstead, assistant editor and senior editorial assistant, demonstrated her skills in anticipating what authors need to complete their work on schedule. Finally, Greg Britton, editorial director and our editor for this volume, is to be thanked for his guiding vision and for wisely focusing us on future trends rather than past precedents.

Notes
 1. Woodhouse, "Closures to Triple."
 2. Martin and Samels, *Merging Colleges for Mutual Growth*.
 3. Roth, "What Is a University For?"

I

The New Necessities to Partner

CHAPTER ONE

The Consolidation of American Higher Education

James Martin and James E. Samels

Contributors to this book agree that American colleges and universities are partnering, merging, and closing at rates higher than at any time in the past fifty years. More and more institutions are choosing to join forces rather than risk standing alone, and for those who do not choose a partner, the future may be grim indeed, as the conversations that follow detail.

While reports from the National Center for Education Statistics illustrate that over the past twenty-five years the number of colleges or universities closing annually has fluctuated between zero to ten, there are two additional studies from researchers at Vanderbilt University and Higher Education Publications Inc. that detail the number of "private four-year colleges that have closed, or were acquired, doubled from about five a year before 2008 to about 10 in the four years through 2011," and among all colleges, "37 merged in the three years through 2013, more than triple the number from 2006–2009."[1] These later statistics capture the destabilization that many presidents, provosts, and faculty have been experiencing since 2008. In fact, the national focus in 2015 on Sweet Briar's trauma, while intensifying general concerns about small college fragility, has simultaneously drawn attention away from a growing group of institutions, many entrepreneurial, now planning *intentional* forms of alliance and partnership.[2] While some leaders still contend that it is hard to "kill" a college or university, this view overlooks the fact that no matter how hard it may be to close an institution, it is *less hard* than it used to be, marking a critical difference for many presidents, trustees, and students.

We have observed that as presidents and board chairs face sometimes unprecedented challenges, they will default to considerations of full merger or a simple "death with dignity" closure plan without an awareness that there are creative alternatives. They also often proceed with little sense of the significant, if not overwhelming, financial and goodwill costs that accompany closing an institution. Yet, as William Tierney explains in "The Disruptive Future of Higher Education," "If learning, as the central activity of any post-secondary institution, is going to undergo revolutionary changes, then the infrastructure and administrative tasks and functions that support and surround learning of necessity will need to change."[3] Most of the chapters that follow focus squarely on how to manage these evolving infrastructure and administrative issues within a context of alliances, affiliations, and partnerships.

Let us also explain why the volume is titled *Consolidating Colleges and Merging Universities* and what the organizing principle of the study is. In an earlier book from Johns Hopkins University Press, *Merging Colleges for Mutual Growth: A New Strategy for Academic Managers*, we created a typology of merger and partnership classifications built on conventional structural models of the 1980s and 1990s, such as a pure merger in which Institution A goes into Institution B, for example. Since that study, we have observed in our research, writing, and consulting the emergence of a rising number of nonstructural, win-win partnerships and affiliations without the constraints of governance, campus culture wars, and the substantive change implications required by regional and specialty accreditation associations. Thus we have grouped all of these transactions under the umbrella term "consolidation" in the chapters that follow.

In these conversations, numerous forms of affiliation and co-venture are detailed that create a cross-subsidized business model that can provide long-term sustainability for the participating institutions. They can also achieve the following specific advantages:

- shared curricula and faculty development
- collective procurement
- consolidated human resources
- increased efficiencies in campus operations and administrative services
- leveraged assets, particularly among underdeveloped campus resources

By rethinking and avoiding various structural and legal complications, partnering institutions can still net a greater yield and return on investment through nonmerger transactions. While designing mutual-growth synergies, institutions need not commit to substantive change or to a change of ownership and control with the regulatory requirements that accompany these decisions. Such nonmerger options can help both institutions remain nimble while still gaining marketing and branding advantages going forward.

A number of the institutions profiled in depth in this book have grown significantly larger through these partnerships and affiliations, but growth is not an imperative for a consolidation to be judged a success. In 2009, Arizona State University (ASU) enrolled 1,200 students in its degree programs, but as Philip Regier, university dean for educational initiatives and coauthor of chapter 9, explains, even a 30,000 student enrollment goal is now "hardly enough." He acknowledges that the university "has set its sights on growing online enrollment to at least 100,000 students in the next five years."[4] Clearly, ASU's growth has not come without its detractors, but at the same time, as a steady number of small colleges struggle to maintain their enrollments and still lose their footings, ASU's partnership growth plan is one to be studied more seriously.

Perhaps as controversial, Southern New Hampshire University's high-profile advocacy for a new competency-based system for student educational credit assessment—which has earned the interest and backing of the Obama administration—has helped it also grow into a national model now being emulated. Paul LeBlanc, its president since 2003 and the coauthor of chapter 10, has led SNHU through a period of steady growth to more than 30,000 students by focusing not on the traditional cohort of 18- to 20-year-olds but rather on older students who want flexible scheduling, continuous online access, and majors that lead to immediate employment or advancement in current employment. In LeBlanc's view, "The business models implicit in higher education are broken. Public institutions will not see increasing state funding and private colleges will not see ever-rising tuition . . . We are super-focused on customer service, which is a phrase that most universities can't even use."[5]

We focused in *Merging Colleges for Mutual Growth* on proactively joining institutions as a master-planning strategy. Since then, as we have noted various forms of merger gradually increasing, we still believe that as a primary growth strategy formal merger will not overtake or displace strategic alliances and simple, opportunistic forms of partnership in frequency over the next decade. As the newly appointed secretary of education for the state of Massachusetts explained in a 2015 interview concerning system-wide solutions short of full merger, "We need to consolidate programs and administrative services and to create alternative pathways for students to acquire degrees at lower costs. We also need to eliminate duplicative programs from college to college to college and provide better trained guidance and college orientation counselors for greater numbers of students to succeed."[6]

Institutional Partnering Criteria

1. Increased assets
2. Potential net profitability
3. Better overall competitiveness
4. Harmonious campus cultures
5. Enriched student life
6. Enhanced academic reputation and brand
7. Strengthened preexisting institutional partnerships
8. Effect on future fundraising
9. Mission complementarity
10. Impact on primary stakeholders
11. New market penetration
12. Scaling of operational efficiencies
13. Nonduplication of program offerings
14. Upgraded educational technologies
15. Improved campus facilities and operations

In researching and advising on dozens of partnership, affiliation, merger, and closure transactions since the publication of *Merging Colleges for Mutual Growth*, we have developed an original list of *partnering criteria* that serve as key indicators of long-term, collaborative success. Skillful management of these fifteen factors helps to create communities that trust one another to larger degrees and that are willing to take greater risks for greater rewards.

Institutional Partnering Criteria
1. Increased Assets

Most institutional partnerships offer the lure of "increased assets" through a potential doubling of institutional resources; however, as mentioned above, successful consolidations do not need to increase size. Rather, academic quality should be the primary driver.

2. Potential Net Profitability

When applying profitability as a criterion, it is wiser to remain conservative in forecasting than to allow enthusiasm or sentiment to overvalue the potential in one or more attractive partnership components.

3. Better Overall Competitiveness

We learned two decades ago in some of our earliest merger and strategic alliance projects that transforming competitors into collaborators can have a dramatic impact on the joint bottom line. Whether in a full merger or a simple dual-enrollment agreement, the longer partners let individual competitiveness hold back the work of institutional trust building, the less likely large gains will be achieved.

4. Harmonious Campus Cultures

Failing to manage carefully and transparently the mixing of student cultures can affect efforts in other areas. Thus alliance and merger planners will not leave working with student leadership groups until the final stages, as these individuals are full stakeholders although not always enfranchised as such.

5. Enriched Student Life

Successful partnerships and mergers can contribute to student diversity enrollments as well as to the expansion of co-curricular programming and student support services.

6. Enhanced Academic Reputation and Brand

Strategic partnerships provide a legitimate opportunity to identify and preserve the academic programs that shape the brand on both campuses, or, in the case of a narrower program-based affiliation not driven purely by growth goals, to identify the faculty, curricular, and marketing strengths to be highlighted.

7. Strengthened Preexisting Institutional Partnerships

Many universities and colleges will already maintain multiple alliances with other institutions. Especially if a new partnership requires some form of exclusivity, the institution owes it to preexisting partners to assess its impact and implications.

8. Effect on Future Fundraising

The key issue that immediately emerges in the area of fundraising is the decision to share prospect research and any privacy rules surrounding this decision. Each institution will need to clarify whether it has a privacy regulation regarding prospect research, and attorneys may be asked to advise on a common procedure going forward. Early candid discussions about the agendas of the two fundraising operations, if implicated in partnership planning, will be advisable.

9. Mission Complementarity

Often in planning a partnership or alliance, *similarity* is confused with *complementarity*. Yet, in our experience, leaders who value creative differences, rather than sameness, between the two institutions have devised the strongest and most durable agreements. Partnering universities may not need or benefit from two full English departments or dental hygiene clinics. Complementarity instead allows for one partner to take the lead in areas such as instructional personnel and research and the other potentially to add strengths in fundraising and infrastructure. Planners may be encouraged in initial discussions by the existence of a similar set of departments and personnel at the other institution without realizing that the combined institution may not have the capacity or will to preserve all of its preexisting personnel and programs.

10. Impact on Primary Stakeholders

When the term *consolidation* is used, "right-sizing" sometimes accompanies it, with the implication that the future institution will be smaller and leaner. But consolidation, as noted above, may also describe a larger yet more efficient organization. So the focus in joining partners does not need to rise or fall on whether the eventual institution is larger or smaller; it should instead focus on the benefits to primary stakeholders in areas such as enhanced curricula, faculty professional development, and new instructional technologies.

11. New Market Penetration

A well-designed agreement will focus on building new models of market penetration rather than simply doubling recruitment strategies that may already be producing mixed results at both colleges.

12. Scaling of Operational Efficiencies

The Boston Consortium of Higher Education (TBC), discussed in chapter 13, has achieved exemplary scaling opportunities in its more than twenty Communities of Practice, which invite, as examples, human resources, payroll, or financial aid representatives from its fifteen member institutions to meet on a monthly basis and devise cost-saving plans for rapid implementation. TBC also convenes working groups in specialty areas such as internal auditors, career center directors, and risk managers.

13. Nonduplication of Program Offerings

Partnerships can provide unusual opportunities for faculty leaders to consider the revitalization, repackaging, or even elimination of aging, underenrolled majors. Faculty senate leaders can be invited to collaborate in the design of a more nimble structure for the college or university's academic organization.

14. Upgraded Educational Technologies

Planners should seek, and assess, whether a potential partner maintains a robust social media identity, as these new forms of technology are helping an increasing number of institutions to offer their programs and curricula to a new generation of educational consumers.

15. Improved Campus Facilities and Operations

The more important word in this final criterion is not "facilities" but "operations." Rather than fixating solely on the challenges of two campus infrastructures, sometimes planners need to look beyond the equipment to the effectiveness of the operational models and personnel. As one planner informally observed to us, while co-utilization can lead to "lower energy bills in higher energy times," unless the co-venture is based on a plan that is complementary, it may be accompanied by duplicative, high-maintenance facilities and no plans for their use or disposal.

Five Recommendations for Partnership Planners and Presidents

1. Merge without merging
2. Bridge the public-private divide
3. Partner for quality improvement in nonacademic areas
4. Create internal partnerships among divisions, departments, and programs
5. Move beyond traditional partnership barriers by using social media

Moving Forward: Five Recommendations for Planners and Presidents

For leaders now considering the potential in a partnership, we offer five summary recommendations. These transactions are less intrusive and less costly than merger or closure, and they can provide the partners with additional time and resources to preserve their individual identities while still remaining open to more permanent solutions in the future.

1. Merge without Merging

Although we believe that their number will gradually increase, full mergers challenge even experienced leaders. Full mergers produce one board, one provost, one CFO, and, finally, one president, and while this may be the wisest strategy for the institutions involved, it can also be a shock to both communities and their leaders. Still, it is also a moment that should often be seized, because letting it pass may produce fewer, less agreeable, choices as time passes.

When we have consulted on the feasibility of a merger, one of the most frequent questions asked by presidents and attorneys is: "If this doesn't work, can we change our minds and still back out?" To address this concern, we suggest a simpler, more streamlined structure for partnering: *joint venture with assets transfer*. This type of agreement, currently being considered as a growth strategy by various institutions, including the University of the Pacific (UOP), as one example, does not require as significant an upfront investment, can lessen potentially problematic differences in culture and perspective, and can work around typical gaps between budgeting and fund accounting models. Pam Eibeck, president of UOP, offers this view of the benefits of a joint venture: "At the University of the Pacific, developing partners is viewed as a creative way for even strong institutions to expand their reach and extend their missions since colleges need to serve future students on those students' terms, and strategic alliances can produce a diversity of programs, delivery models, and support services that few institutions can deliver on their own."[7]

These joint ventures can accommodate separate governance and boards of trustees while still achieving economies of scale and efficiencies in operation through shared services. There is a need for cross-representation on both boards, and a single president or chancellor will most often lead the new enterprise. While it can be an intricate agreement to negotiate, our experience has also shown that it can create an entity that harmonizes key academic programs and service delivery systems while leveraging state and federal resources where applicable.

2. Bridge the Public-Private Divide

Public institutional leaders are beginning to consider the benefits in partnering with private colleges and universities. Planners are discovering that the traditional barriers to these alliances have sometimes existed more in perception than reality and can be overcome with collaborative academic programming that anticipates local and regional workforce needs. In one recent example, the College of Idaho, a private institution, and Idaho State University collaborated on a Physician Assistant Studies Program on the college's campus in Caldwell.

As a driver of the affiliation agreement, the state of Idaho's Department of Labor had projected a 40 percent increase in the need for physician assistants by 2018, and while one of the university's planners admitted they had begun their work in "uncharted territory," the final result is viewed as a significant benefit to the students at both institutions as well as the state's workforce. In the opinion of John Ottenhoff, vice president for academic affairs at the College of Idaho and author of chapter 12, their public-private agreement was worth the long effort: "We compete for students, for reputation, and for funding. However, collaboration between institutions, such as ours between a small private college and a large public university, can be of great strategic benefit. Partnerships can thrive when partners emphasize complementary strengths and seize a moment of opportunity in the marketplace."[8]

3. Partner for Quality Improvement in Nonacademic Areas

By nonacademic areas, we are referring to the innovative work of an organization like the Boston Consortium for Higher Education. Created in 1995 by a group of CFOs, the fifteen-member TBC is not a classroom-focused enterprise. Since its inception, TBC has served as an external resource for its member deans, directors, and managers to collaborate in "the development and practical implementation of cost-saving and quality improvement ideas."[9]

Through more than twenty ongoing "communities of practice" in areas such as purchasing, benefits, human resources, internal audit, and risk management, these administrators have been able simultaneously to strengthen infrastructures and conserve key resources for second and even third generations of leadership. As Phillip DiChiara, the organization's managing director for the past seventeen years, explains, "While some accomplishments may come quickly, larger achievements usually have longer gestation periods. However, whatever the time period has been, we have learned that the inevitable ups and downs in any collaboration have helped us collectively become a stronger, more productive, and more resilient enterprise."[10]

4. Create Internal Partnerships among Divisions, Departments, and Programs

Wise planners are learning that sometimes the best partnerships are not with other institutions but with colleagues in their own buildings. Whether seen in examples within the massive City University of New York system outlined by Vita Rabinowitz and James Stellar in chapter 6 or within the small liberal arts colleges discussed in R. Owen Williams's contribution on consortia (chap. 14), sometimes the most innovative partnerships emerge when faculty from the same institution consider their futures together. As Richard DeMillo, author of *Revolution in Higher Education*, observes, "Improved classroom productivity means, among other things, that the structure of academic institutions will change . . . conquering the problem of scale will require new kinds of institutions."[11] It is fair to say that sometimes the collaborations that drive this institutional change will not come from the outside but from the joint efforts of colleagues who are creatively addressing the same departmental, divisional, or college-wide challenges.

5. Move beyond Traditional Partnership Barriers by Using Social Media

Finally, we urge planners to move beyond the traditional, structural barriers that destroy partnership potential. As a strategy, we suggest using various social media to help shape and drive their collaborations. As the educational process is increasingly digitized on student smartphones and tablets, there will emerge new ways to think about partnerships that go beyond merging campus buildings and faculty governance systems. DeMillo continues, "Now, you're seeing senior faculty members . . . coming back to the classroom and saying, 'How can we do this better? Can we make this more focused on data rather than gut feelings, for example? Is there a better way to use technology?'"[12]

To be sure, technology will be accompanied by the need for institutions to develop more sophisticated feedback mechanisms and support services to help their students and faculty improve, but we believe that future strategic alliances will move beyond simply combining bookstore operations by enhancing teaching and learning processes more comprehensively than either college could do alone.[13]

The models described in this book are often not driven by a goal of greater size or power but rather by the achievement of quality, coherence, and sustainability, and by a dedication to becoming more nimble and collaborative institutions. As more colleges and universities join forces, their students will benefit from shared resources, updated programs, enhanced learning systems, and more invigorated alumni networks, as examples. As partnerships continue to gain prominence, however, the provost of one elite university offers a word of caution to planners: "the external environment remains filled with rapid change, and continuous vigilance about the right way forward is needed. Can we change fast enough to survive but slow enough to do so wisely?"[14] It now falls to the designers of agreements like those profiled in the following chapters to answer that question.

Notes

1. Jacobs, "Here's How Many Colleges Have Closed"; McDonald, "Small U.S. Colleges Battle Death Spiral."

2. Martin and Samels, *Turnaround*.

3. Tierney, "Disruptive Future of Higher Education," 22.

4. Hensley-Clancy, "New American University."

5. Kahn, "Amazon of Higher Education."

6. James Peyser, Massachusetts secretary of education, interview by James Martin and James E. Samels, June 19, 2015.

7. Pamela Eibeck, e-mail to James Martin, November 28, 2015.

8. John Ottenhoff, e-mail to James Martin, August 12, 2015.

9. "Mission," Boston Consortium for Higher Education, accessed August 15, 2015, www.boston-consortium.org/about/mission.asp.

10. Phillip DiChiara, e-mail to James Martin, August 13, 2015.

11. DeMillo, "Gatekeepers No More."

12. Jaschik, "Revolution in Higher Education."

13. Warrell, "Students under Surveillance."

14. Robert Groves, "Low Trust in Institutions in a Churning Sea of Rapid Change," *Provost's Blog*, November 19, 2015, https://blog.provost.georgetown.edu/low-trust-in-institutions-in-a-churning-sea-of-rapid-change/.

CHAPTER TWO

Reader's Guide: The New Typology of Collaboration and Closure

James E. Samels and James Martin

What has changed in higher education over the last twenty-five years that makes these times tempestuous, even catastrophic, for many small colleges and large universities? There are many reasons, and they have emerged in all sectors of the profession: unforgiving competition, declining financial aid, escalating budgets, benefits costs, tuition discounts, family debt burden, employment gaps, growing governmental scrutiny, declining numbers of traditional students, a fickle student consumer market, open source and social media learning, and shifting accreditation and licensure priorities.

Perhaps more than at any time in the history of American higher education, the *value proposition* of higher education is being threatened. This precarious market position has placed trustees under a microscope to examine more closely the discharge of their fiduciary and stewardship responsibilities in preserving mission and exhausting all reasonable alternatives to pure merger, closure, or other irreversible structural change. In most cases, this *right-sizing* process brings about the discontinuance of outdated, low-enrollment academic programs and inevitable faculty and staff retrenchment. Though it will bring cold comfort to those who have lived through many of these developments, the silver lining is that institutions are now compelled proactively to assess institutional performance based on data-driven metrics for evaluating and predicting overall financial health, enrollment growth, conversion yield, endowment, return on investment, and peak financial performance.

In our first book, *Merging Colleges for Mutual Growth: A New Strategy for Academic Managers*, we predicted the coming consolidation of American higher education. Consequently, we have often been asked since then what are the clear and present pressures that push colleges and universities to merge, consolidate, retrench, or close?

We offer these six drivers as an overview:

1. *Debt levels.* Overall debt levels more than doubled from 2000 to 2011 at the more than 500 institutions rated by Moody's Investor Service. At the same time, the amount of cash, pledged gifts, and investments declined more than 40 percent relative to the amount owed.

2. *Declining revenues.* In 2015, Moody predicted that pockets of stress will persist, with roughly 20 percent of public and private universities experiencing weak or declining revenue growth owing to limited pricing flexibility and fundamentally challenged student demand. Stress will be highest at smaller, regional public universities with less than $500 million in revenue and at small, private universities and colleges with less than $200 million in revenue.[1]

3. *Need for change.* The need for change in higher education is clear and compelling given the emerging disconnect between ever-increasing aspirations and universities' ability to generate the new resources to finance them.[2]

4. *Tuition pricing.* In our early research, we wrongly anticipated that tuition pricing would begin to close the gap in line with prevailing consumer price index (CPI). Unhappily, this CPI indexing did not materialize for a significant number of tuition-dependent institutions.

5. *Challenging external environment.* Since 2008, significant changes were brought about by the market meltdown—that is, capital campaigns take longer than before and realistically yield less—in part attributable to rising student debt and daunting economic times. What has also changed are the external pressures of the bond market and bond rating services, placing institutions of higher learning under intense scrutiny by issuing daunting industry outlooks based on the several market forces and conditions.

6. *Less time to plan and execute.* In our earliest college merger consulting from the 1970s through the 1990s, we typically programmed and financed the transaction over a one- to two-year period. Today, the parties move more nimbly, in some cases executing preliminary letters of intent and memoranda of understanding (MOUs) in several months, not years.

A Typology of Partnership Models

Twenty-five years ago, the common cure, or at least hope, for an ailing institution was a pure merger and acquisition. Just as medicine has focused on prevention for chronic disease, the best way for an institution to ensure its health is to develop a proactive, creative strategic partnership plan for the future. These days, with the changing demographics of students, new competition, and declining enrollments, some fragile institutions may still wish to consider a merger, but be aware that there are other less drastic and risky options that should be explored first. These include *strategic partnerships*, *program transfers*, *joint ventures*, *co-branding*, and even *consortia*.

Joint Venture

A joint venture is one of the most productive approaches to the mutual-growth merger. This shared investment and campus-sensitive approach offers the distinct advantages of preserving the respective identities and governance structures of the participating institutions while promoting creative, specific collaborations in areas of academic programming, administrative efficiency, and complementary growth. A basic affiliation agreement may provide for mutual faculty exchange opportunities, joint enrollments, transfer articulations, shared library resources, joint externships, and other related advantages. The affiliated institutions may share the surplus proceeds generated from the joint educational endeavors and enrollment growth. A key advantage of affiliation agreements is that they offer the least intrusive impact on participating institutions, while offering a period of collegial confidence and trust building in preparation for potentially more permanent educational partnerships.

Unlike permanent mergers and consolidations, joint ventures leverage the mutual core strengths of the partners for a common and unified business purpose—with explicit shared risk investment and return on investment net-revenue reward. The practical advantage of joint ventures is that they require no major governance restructuring or even new corporate bodies. As one example, the University of the Pacific and Samuel Merritt University are exploring ways to leverage their distinctive yet complementary programs, market growth strategies, and combined bottom-line assets—paradoxical though it may seem, preserving separate faculty and separate accreditation. With increasing frequency, mission-complementary schools, colleges, and universities are developing major resource-sharing consortia designed to effectuate administrative

Successful Joint Ventures

A joint venture is a contract for association of two or more parties to a common enterprise. These ventures are typically limited in time and scope, and they are often focused on one solitary venture with benchmarks and milestones for contract extension and renewal. The key distinguishing characteristic of joint ventures is sharing of risk and reward—read as net profit.

Unlike mergers and consolidations, joint ventures may not necessarily require the creation of new corporate bodies and can arise from the negotiation of the parties directly—without implicating substantive change in governance, control, and policy making. Best-practice joint ventures include the following three examples.

1. DePaul University–Rosalind Franklin University of Medicine and Science

DePaul University and Rosalind Franklin University of Medicine and Science have established a unique, wide-ranging alliance to help address the expanding need for healthcare professionals prepared to meet the challenges of an increasingly collaborative and rapidly evolving field.

The Alliance for Health Sciences is designed to

- to establish curricular pathways for DePaul students to graduate professional degree programs at Rosalind Franklin;
- to expand and strengthen academic programs at both schools;
- to foster collaboration between faculties of the two institutions; and
- to create additional research opportunities for students.

The universities will collaborate to develop innovative, rigorous curricula that will benefit DePaul undergraduates pursuing health careers by preparing them for highly competitive professional programs and grounding them in the cross-disciplinary knowledge and broader perspectives on health that are required for success in today's healthcare environment. An early admission pathway will streamline qualified students' progress through undergraduate programs at DePaul into the highly competitive master's and doctoral programs at Rosalind Franklin, including medicine, pharmacy, pathologist assistant, podiatry, physician assistant, and physical therapy. Together, the two schools will seamlessly integrate a strong undergraduate and liberal studies foundation, contemporary professional health education, and state-of-the-art health and medical training facilities. Students enrolled in the jointly developed curricular programs may benefit from reducing, by one year, the overall time required to complete their professional degrees.

(continued)

As part of the agreement, DePaul hopes to expand its successful master's entry into the nursing program at the Rosalind Franklin campus in North Chicago. The program admits those with either science or nonscience bachelor's degrees, providing them with an accelerated path to becoming a registered nurse. Rosalind Franklin University will soon break ground on a new 53,000-square-foot education facility to accommodate this program and others with increasing enrollments.

"There's a natural fit between DePaul and Rosalind Franklin," said Dr. Wendy Rheault, vice president of academic affairs at Rosalind Franklin. "Both have growing enrollments, top-notch science and health facilities and well-established commitments to community needs." In recent years, DePaul also has expanded its education programs in the sciences, establishing the College of Science and Health and building two new state-of-the-art facilities dedicated exclusively to science instruction. It currently has more than 3,200 students enrolled at its College of Science and Health, and its recently established multidisciplinary health sciences degree is the university's fastest-growing undergraduate program with more than 440 students. "DePaul students will meet regularly with faculty and staff from Rosalind Franklin, a rare benefit for undergraduates in pre-professional programs," said Patricia O'Donoghue, DePaul's interim provost, in a news release from October 3, 2012. "They'll get academic and career advice from medical professionals and gain contacts who will give them an advantage as they apply to graduate health programs. They'll be prepared for the intensity of graduate study and gain first-hand experience in Rosalind Franklin's classrooms and laboratories."

The schools also will create a joint competitive research fund that will provide seed money for new areas of exploration. Those projects are expected to help secure external research grants from federal, state, and local governments as well as private foundations.

2. University of Medicine and Dentistry of New Jersey–Rutgers University

On July 1, 2013, the New Jersey Medical and Health Sciences Education Restructuring Act went into effect, integrating Rutgers, the State University of New Jersey, with all units of the University of Medicine and Dentistry of New Jersey, except University Hospital in Newark and the School of Osteopathic Medicine in Stratford. In an instant, Rutgers became a 65,000-student school with a $3 billion budget. It will rank among the top twenty-five research universities in the nation, with more research spending than Harvard, Yale, or Northwestern University.

3. University of the Pacific–Samuel Merritt University

The University of the Pacific and Samuel Merritt University (SMU) have come together to consider merger because of the attractiveness of achieving economies of scale, efficiencies in operation, and nonduplication of programs by combining two mission-complementary institutions.

- The parties share a deep commitment to quality education that is responsive to the needs of the students, the community, and the healthcare industry.
- As universities with similar missions and a complementary set of degree programs, the parties anticipate that a close affiliation could extend both of their visions and allow them to benefit from mutual growth, collaborations, and academic excellence. The parties share the intention that an affiliation between Pacific and SMU would maintain the culture and entrepreneurial spirit of SMU.

streamlining, expense reduction, cost avoidance, increased and net bulk discount rate, and other collective service and goods procurements.

Institutional Merger

Central to an informed understanding of higher education mergers is a familiarity with basic merger models and corporate restructuring terminology. When trustees consider legally available merger options, it is counsel's responsibility to explain the full range of alternatives, including advantages and risks to the institution in the near and long terms. At the core of collegiate mergers sits the legal framework of corporate charters, trustee bylaws, contracts, statutes, common law, and regulatory promulgations. Taken together, these legal authorities shape much of the merger plan and process. This legal component is predicated on the supposition that several other necessary elements are present in the merger plan: complementary educational missions, shared faculty scholarship aspirations, involved student bodies, flexible governance systems, and endowment and resource articulations.[3]

In considering merger as an academic management strategy, college and university trustees should start by closely examining the range of structural alternatives, including pure merger, consolidation, consortium, asset transfers, and educational affiliations. Trustees must try to preserve an institutional mission adaptable to the educational marketplace while also strengthening their institution's academic offerings. Academic managers and the members of the merger task force must consider risks and benefits with an eye to preserving each institution's distinctive name and reputation. The levels of risk will typically correlate with the up-front investment either institution is willing to make toward pure merger. If one institution assumes the major share of liabilities, the merger agreement will provide it with the bulk of surplus tuition and boarding fee revenues generated over the long term.

In past decades, many colleges and universities considered merging mainly in response to financial exigency or even insolvency. Endowment goals were often missed, and dedicated funds were utilized under the guise of interest-free loans for which repayment was unlikely over time. As fiscal matters deteriorated, senior administrators unavoidably delayed payments to product and service vendors, credit lines constricted, and payrolls and debt service obligations were deferred. Annual financial statements painted a steadily worsening picture as auditors began to look more closely at the financial underpinnings of an older, weakened institution or an up-and-coming college that suddenly found itself overextended.

In its purest form, mergers assimilate two or more institutions: $A + B = A+$.

In effect, the merged institution is dissolved, leaving the other institution as the sole survivor. In a best-case situation, the merging institution will devise a self-liquidating resolution of outstanding liabilities, with remaining assets dedicated to continuing the merged institution's programs according to mutually agreed-upon parameters.

In a traditional consolidation, the equation $A + B = C$ preserves the consolidated institutional name and niche. Higher education consolidations involve two or more institutions that are collapsed into one new college or university, usually with a different name, mission, and scale of operation. The new institution typically houses multiple schools or colleges and reflects a diversity of degree program offerings at undergraduate and graduate levels. Several variations of corporate governance structures are available to accommodate separate but coordinated or reconstituted trustee boards.

In the preponderance of cases, the merging institution seeks to accomplish economies of scale, efficiencies in operation, and nonduplication of programs and services. In some mergers, administrative operations are centralized, and the administrators and staff are merged into one entity using a combination of incentives such as attractive early retirement packages, reassignment, and layoffs. In other cases, the administrators and staff of the more weakly positioned institution are let go, while the administrators and staff of the stronger institution remain intact.

Building an Effective Partnership: The Process

The process for entering into partnerships involves the following action steps:

- Research, investigate, and interview potential partners.
- Conduct an environmental scan to identify high-demand programs and best-practice models.
- Identify motivated and impassioned leadership who will be committed to spearheading the process; the chief academic officer is often the most logical candidate.
- Hold introductory meetings to determine whether the parties think they can work with each other and whether working together would be mutually beneficial.
- Execute nondisclosure agreements.
- Enter into letters of interest or letters of intent.
- Do due diligence.
- Determine which programs should be the basis of the partnership.
- Align the curricula that will be central to the partnership.
- Convene faculty, staff, student, and alumni focus groups and field interviews.
- Prepare applicable academic licensing and accreditation notifications and applications.
- Draft and execute memoranda of understanding and affiliation agreements.
- Obtain state regulatory approval, as well as any applicable regional, specialty, or other required accreditation approvals.

Partnerships

Partnerships present institutions with an attractive alternative to merging. Partnerships enable institutions to leverage their existing programs and resources to significantly expand enrollment at minimal cost. Partnerships have the potential to turn a fragile institution into one that is not merely surviving, but thriving:

EARLY COLLEGE DUAL AND CONCURRENT ENROLLMENT

One partnership model involves the early college concept. In this format, undergraduate courses are provided to high school students who have dual or concurrent enrollment in the higher education institution. The higher education institution offers its courses on-site at the high school. The higher education institution can either send its faculty on-site or give joint appointment to existing high school faculty after vetting their credentials for conformity to the college's hiring policy. Families pay some tuition costs for participation in early college programs. Because the programs are pursued as part of the public high school curriculum, however, the costs are lower than regular college tuition.

This model has the advantage of accelerating the education process. Students who have exposure to higher education while in high school may have an easier transition to college. Early college may induce some students who might otherwise have chosen a different path to pursue higher education. There is lower family debt burden when college education is accelerated in this way, and the higher education partner can take advantage of existing facilities and resources at the high school. This enables the college to keep costs per credit down, while gaining increased revenue from expanded enrollment.

BACHELOR DEGREE COMPLETION AND TRANSFER ARTICULATIONS

Another model involves bachelor degree completion programs and transfer articulations. The advantage of this format is that graduates from one institution who meet specified eligibility requirements have guaranteed admission to the upper-level partner. In addition, under these agreements, students can often transfer with no loss of credit. When a cohort of students is involved, an institution may be able to offer a discount. The students get the benefit of lower costs, while the institution gets the benefit of having a reliable and effective feeder process.

There are three types of articulation agreements: mandated, statewide, and individual. Mandated articulation agreements exist as part of legislation and mandate credit transfer between programs. Statewide articulation agreements are voluntary plans usually developed through the collaborative effort of educators, regulators, legislators, and others. These agreements are between community colleges and public universities, but they may also include agreements between public and private institutions. In the absence of mandated articulation and statewide agreements, colleges and universities often work out individual school-to-school agreements.

Consortium

Some institutions have found that consortia offer an attractive solution for cutting nonacademic costs. Participation in a consortium is something that institutions should consider early on as a cost-saving means to greater administrative efficiency. By the time an institution has reached the point of fragility, the advantages of joining a consortium may not be significant enough to turn around the fate of a struggling institution. As Phillip

DiChiara, managing director of the Boston Consortium for Higher Education and author of chapter 13 in this volume, explains:

> Mergers between academic institutions have a role to play in the changing environment, but creation of a traditional academic consortium is not likely to provide a solution at that point of dysfunction. Ideally, consortia are in place long in advance of any crisis. They typically provide an alternative to operational redundancy, inadequate scale or limited financial capital. As consortia typically engage in a network relationship among several institutions, there is an implication of a democratic and mutually advantageous relationship. While it is not inconceivable that several institutions facing an existential crisis may be able to find fresh common ground that might enable continued operations, collaboration is a tool that requires ceding some decisional sovereignty to the group, not an individual school. Under threat of failure, it is difficult to imagine that being likely.[4]

Co-branding

When institutions consider mergers, consolidations, or strategic partnerships, they should take advantage of co-branding benefits. Co-branding brings an attractive, competitive edge to sharpen both institutions' focus and advantage in the higher education marketplace. This mutual-growth, win-win approach extends to hundreds of successful examples in widely diverse fields of study: professional sports, healthcare, telecommunications, agriculture, and the list goes on. Co-branding partnerships bring shared research, scholarship, and return on investment. As one example, the research and development process typically requires a significant number of bench-level laboratory workers to support every new PhD research fellow. Such collaboration adds new market share.

Program Transfer

An institution facing burdensome debt service and deferred maintenance, declining enrollments, increasing operating costs, and pending financial exigency may still be able to transfer its programs to another institution. A notable example is Goddard College's program transfer to Green Mountain.[5] Goddard transferred its full-time residential programs to Green Mountain. Goddard College retained its real estate and has been able to survive using a low-residency program model.

A second example of successful program transfer was the transfer of Boston University's undergraduate nursing program to Northeastern University.[6] At the time, Boston University foresaw the declining ability of even a large private research university to compete with the lower, publicly subsidized tuition of the public program at the University of Massachusetts, Boston.

When program transfer is not feasible, an institution may wish to consider curtailing outdated underenrolled programs before draining resources to the point where institutional closure becomes inevitable. Although closing even a single academic program may be controversial, this course of action constitutes a less radical option than the decision to close an entire college or university, as detailed below and in chapter 16 in this volume, by Michael Hoyle.

Institutional Closure: A Legal Handbook

A synthesis of case law reveals that a court is likely to examine at least four issues in analyzing a higher education closure decision: First, whether the board of trustees breached its fiduciary duties in arriving at a decision or in failing to arrive at a decision. This includes an examination of the process used to reach the decision, the information before the board, and the good faith or lack of fraud, ill will, or deceit. Second is whether the board followed the proper procedures as mandated by federal and state law, accreditors, and the institution's charter and bylaws. Liability exposure is minimized to the extent that the board obtains court approval ahead of litigation. Third, the effect of closure on faculty and student contract rights needs to be addressed proactively. Fourth, the court may examine the adverse impact on the public interest resulting from closure.[7]

Closing a college has now become a common enough set of decisions that regional accreditation agencies have issued guides to inform the process. The New England Association of Schools and Colleges promulgated its first version of closure guidelines in 1980, *Considerations when Closing an Institution of Higher Education*; the Northwest Commission on Colleges and Universities in 1982, *Considerations when Closing an Accredited and Candidate Institution Policy*; and the Southern Association of Colleges and Schools in 1995, *Closing a Program, Site, Branch or Institution*.[8] In 2013, Clay Christensen, Harvard Business School professor and architect of disruptive innovation, predicted that "a host of struggling colleges and universities—the bottom 25 percent of every tier—will disappear or merge in the next 10 to 15 years."[9] Financial difficulties, declining enrollments, and a shrinking number of United States high school graduates in multiple regions are putting increased pressure on colleges, especially small, tuition-dependent institutions.

In 2014, Moody's Investors Service issued a negative outlook for the higher education industry as a whole and found that one in ten public and private colleges suffers "acute financial distress" because of falling revenues and weak operating performance. Moody's also proclaimed that the 2015 outlook remains negative for four-year US colleges, universities, and community colleges that issue revenue bonds. Among the four-year colleges, a major pressure will be slow growth in tuition revenue, while declining enrollment is driving the negative outlook among community colleges.[10] For institutions that are facing the unfortunate fate of closure, there is often a way to ensure that some part of the institutional legacy lives on. This can be in the form of having the acquiring institution include the merged institution's name as one of its schools or colleges, as part of an institute or program name, or naming a building after the acquired college and displaying memorabilia of that institution in public areas.

Before deciding whether to close a college, an institution should perform a self-assessment unprecedented in its thoroughness. Although the process will be challenging and arduous, the ability to make difficult decisions may mean the difference between institutional survival and closure. As an initial guide, regional accreditation associations list these required steps as elements of a closure process:

- Planning and consulting with all affected constituencies
- Considering all available less drastic options (i.e., merger, consortium, partnerships, interinstitutional sharing, restructuring, program closure)
- Preferring a consultative process, with the final decision to be made by the governing board
- Acting before the institution has lost educational quality, integrity, and financial viability
- Designating a spokesperson
- Controlling flow of information
- Conducting due diligence
- Reviewing corporate status and determining necessary filings and actions
- Devising a teach-out plan, including:
  - contract with another institution to teach-out programs
  - transfer of federal or state grants as well as financial aid and scholarship monies
  - prior approval by accreditor of teach-out agreement

> ➤ designation of whether degrees of transferring students will be in the name of the closed institution, the institution performing the teach-out, or joint degrees

- Offering provisions for faculty and staff that may include severance agreements, assistance with outplacement, and relocation
- Paying out financial obligations
- Making agreements with or paying creditors
- Dispersing assets (i.e., physical plan, equipment, library, special collections, art, or other funds)
- Dispersing funds from donors, grantors, and other special funds
- Preserving student academic and other records and designation of record holder
- Notifying and issuing a final report to the state academic licensing authority
- Issuing a substantive change and final report to the accreditation agency
- Notifying federal and state agencies
- Performing a legal audit to ensure compliance and that all necessary steps have been taken[11]

The Legal Risks in Closing a College or University

Whether closure involves academic programs or the entire institution, the legal risks are similar:

- Displaced students may sue.
- There is the possibility of student fraud claims for being induced to enroll in a program or institution that was already slated for closure.
- Faculty layoffs can trigger legal complications related to collective bargaining agreements, tenure, and multiyear contracts.
- Institutional closure generates extensive negative publicity.
- An adverse effect on alumni relations is possible.
- Institutional reputation and legacy can face significant damage.[12]

Death and Resurrection: Colleges That Have Survived Closure or Apparent Closure

Antioch College

Antioch College is the epitome of the school that refuses to die. The college opened in 1853 and since then has closed four times: in 1863, 1881, 1919, and 2008. After many years of instability, Antioch had its peak years in the 1960s and 1970s, when the student body was around 2,400 and its finances were relatively healthy. Several graduate schools were opened around the country under the name Antioch University with Antioch College as a base. In the early 2000s, enrollment declined to around 600 students. Following implementation of a renewal plan for restructuring, enrollment fell to around 370 students. In 2007, the board of trustees voted to close, and closure took effect on June 30, 2008, in spite of alumni efforts to keep the college open. A task force was subsequently created out of university and alumni representatives to develop a plan for an independent Antioch College.

In 2009, the Antioch College Continuation Corporation (ACCC) and Antioch University agreed to an asset purchase agreement, which transferred the campus, endowment, and exclusive right to the name "Antioch College" to the ACCC, thereby enabling the college to operate as an independent corporation with its own board of trustees. In 2011, the Ohio Board of Regents gave the revived Antioch College provisional authorization for the bachelor of arts and bachelor of science degrees. In 2014, the Higher Learning Commission granted Antioch College candidacy status in pursuit of accreditation, thereby restoring federal financial aid eligibility. Antioch College is now a member of the Great Lakes Colleges Association, which means that Antioch students have the ability to transfer to any of the other thirteen consortium members if they choose.

Atlantic Union College

Atlantic Union College (AUC) in South Lancaster, Massachusetts, was founded in 1882 and was the oldest campus in the Seventh-day Adventist worldwide educational system. AUC was granted the right to confer the bachelor of arts degree in 1933, the bachelor of science degree in 1954, and the master of education degree in 1990. New England Association of Schools and Colleges (NEASC) accreditation was obtained in 1945. In the 1950s, the school served around 900 students and, until its closing, had one of the strongest nursing programs in Massachusetts. Following years of financial challenges, AUC lost its NEASC accreditation in 2011 and along with it federal financial aid eligibility. An attempt to continue as

(continued)

a Massachusetts branch campus of Washington Adventist University (WAU), a Maryland school, ended when WAU was unable to obtain Massachusetts Department of Higher Education approval in time for the following semester. AUC closed its doors in July 2011.

Four years later, the college obtained Massachusetts Board of Higher Education approval to offer two bachelor degree programs: the BS in health science/biology and the BA in theology/religion. The college is reopening without regional accreditation, which means AUC students will not be able to receive federal financial aid. The college reportedly plans to compensate by offering a discounted opening tuition of less than $18,000 per year, about $6,000 less than what students paid when the college last operated.

Sweet Briar College

Alumni are a powerful constituency in higher education. No one wants to say that she graduated from a defunct college. Just ask the students at Sweet Briar. Yet Sweet Briar, contrary to popular perception, never closed. Pamela DeWeese, the college's dean of faculty and chief academic officer, is interviewed in more detail about the situation in chapter 16 of this volume.

Founded in 1901, Sweet Briar College announced, after 114 years of operation, that its board of directors had voted to close because of "insurmountable financial challenges."* Among the cited causes were declining enrollment and an endowment insufficient to accommodate large-scale changes. The college had about $25 million in debt and was facing the possibility of default. Although the institution was technically solvent, some board representatives believed that insolvency was inevitable and that closing before the financial picture deteriorated further would allow the college to honor various financial obligations.

In response, Sweet Briar alumnae, students, faculty, and other supporters mobilized against the closure through legal action, social media, and a national fundraising campaign. Sweet Briar alumnae raised $12 million in pledges in approximately one hundred days. This concerted action resulted in an agreement that kept Sweet Briar from closing and allowed it to move forward as a community into the 2015–16 academic year. A new board and new president were appointed, and while the future understandably remains uncertain, if the new leadership can succeed in moving Sweet Briar onto solid ground, the decision will clearly be viewed as both bold and correct.

*Anderson and Svriuga, "Sweet Briar to Close Because of Financial Challenges."

The risk of student lawsuits can be minimized by continuing to offer the program through the expected graduation date of existing students; ensuring teach-out opportunities with nearby, comparable institutions; assisting students with transfer opportunities, including administrative and technical assistance and covering the cost of transfer applications, transcripts, and tuition differentials; designating an easily accessible communications person to keep students informed and the lines of communication open; and assisting students with the financial impact, including help with transferring financial aid and scholarships.

The source documents that need to be consulted include the following:

- Institutional constitutions, bylaws, and statutes

- Federal, state, and local constitutional provisions, laws, administrative procedures, and agency regulations

- Policies of regional accrediting or professional associations

- Debt instruments or other documents reserving decision-making power to outside entities, such as a founding religious order

- Faculty handbooks that reserve certain consultation or governance rights to faculty in closure situations

- Uncodified policies, board resolutions, or other "informal" reflections of past practice

- Collective bargaining agreements[13]

In addition, major sources of potential contractual or other obligations to individual constituencies should be reviewed at the outset of any closure deliberation. The most typical sources, some of which are referenced above, include:

- Faculty handbooks

- Student handbooks, and admission and financial aid materials

- Staff handbooks, benefit plans, and benefit descriptions

- Institutional, department, or program websites

- Endowments, donations, and grants restricted to the unit being considered for closure[14]

Finally, it is important that the college or university "consistently articulate its strong commitment to helping its students transfer. The spokesperson should communicate this message as soon as possible

Demographics, Market Share, and Religious Mission: A Snapshot of Recent Closures in New England

A college or university gives up much of the autonomy over its fate when the outcome is closure. Ultimately, that institution is accountable to the courts, to state agencies such as the Corporations Division of the Secretary of State, to the state higher education regulatory agency, and to accreditors and donors.

What follows is an illustrative list of examples of institutional closures in recent years simply from the six New England states:

Aquinas College (MA)	Marion Court College (MA)
Belknap College (NH)	McIntosh College (NH)
Bradford College (MA)	Mount St. Mary College (NH)
Burdett College (MA)	Nathaniel Hawthorne College (NH)
Castle College (NH)	Notre Dame College (NH)
Concord College (NH)	Stevens College (MA)
Franconia College (NH)	Windham College (VT)

Though religiously affiliated and faith-inspired institutions constitute a relatively small portion of postsecondary institutions, they tend to be strikingly overrepresented in accreditation actions and closures nationally. Perhaps it is not surprising that these religiously missioned institutions are subject to declining demographics, enrollment levels, and conversion yield rates as parochial secondary schools have become an endangered species.

after the closure decision is made . . . The institution's compassion for its students and willingness to commit institutional resources to facilitate transfer . . . will be the centerpiece of the closure plan. The institution's documents, as well as its public statements, should clearly convey and keep repeating this message."[15] Because of the traditional shared governance model in higher education, however, closure decisions may require consultation and involvement of "outsiders" in the usual trustee and administrative decision-making processes, and they will influence the various risk factors. Sometimes, creditors, corporate members of the institution, faculty, or even students have the right to participate in financial exigency or closure deliberations. Any consideration of a college or university closure must therefore begin with a diligent effort to identify all sources of procedural and substantive obligations on the part of the institution.

Seven Lessons about Closures

1. *Closures save money.* Contrary to popular misconceptions, closures are the most expensive choice a college can ever make based on the regulatory accreditation due diligence fiduciary, liquidation, and residual exposure associated with closure.

2. *Attorneys and accountants will do the due diligence.* Do your own due diligence, make your own phone calls, and filter your own information and co-sourcing from input received from attorneys and accountants.

3. *Closures are reversible.* Do not assume that you can undue a closure. It almost never works that way. Sunk costs in closure and potential liability exposure will, in the preponderance of cases, keep the coffin nailed down.

4. *Student records will not be an issue.* Wrong. In most states there are statutory and regulatory requirements about providing for student records, so pay attention early and often to the student and other educational records conservation.

5. *No free lunches.* The board needs to be prepared to dedicate resources to conducting the highest level of fiduciary responsibility and due diligence in considering the closure option.

6. *Consider consolidation.* Instead of merging permanently with another college or university, consider forming a partnership for the period that an educational program is effective and in high demand.

7. *Never let the other party write the deal.* Always move one step ahead with initial letters of interest, intent, memoranda of understanding, and other contractual documents.

Conclusion: The Changing Shape of Higher Education

Whether through merger, program transfer, or closure, it appears that some form of consolidation is reshaping a growing number of colleges and universities:

- *Enrollment declines.* Between 1966 and 2010, college student numbers doubled as baby boomers, and then their children, enrolled. The number of high school graduates peaked in 2011 and is projected to fall or flatten until 2024. That stagnation coincides with new lower-cost online alternatives, as the number of college students taking at least one online course nearly doubled, to 45 percent, between 2008 and 2013.

Common Mistakes Leaders Make in Closures

You do not need to go it alone. Engage the best and most experienced college closure experts. Choose a consulting and advisory partner who has a solid track record of experience in closures and, importantly, avoiding closures.

Plan for the worst and hope for the best. Be certain to outline a full range of scenarios based on best scenario, worst scenario, and likely scenario from the several perspectives of near-term liquidity, separating deficit, and long-term sustainability.

Develop a spending plan for the closing. Even though most uninitiated think that closures need no spending plans, just the opposite is true. Due diligence takes time, effort, and resources to get results.

Pay attention to board leadership and make no assumptions regarding levels of understanding. Map out a clear process and remember that, in matters of closures, the full board must be consulted even though an executive committee or other committee of the board may engage in the fact-finding due diligence process.

Be honest about your dashboard key performance indicators. Even if your endowment-to-operating ratio, debt service, conversion yield, and retention are challenged, there may still be collaborative solutions to be found.

Play out all reasonable options. Methodically consider all strategies from a simple program transfer to full merger.

Remember that tenure is not insulation from discontinued employment upon closure. Tenure is not an affirmative defense from discontinued employment as a result of enrollment-based program retrenchment.

Stay out in front of public information. The court of public opinion can foster a negative perception in the larger community. Create events that will influence outcomes.

- *Online competition.* In the opinion of some financial planners, approximately one-third of all colleges and universities in the United States are on an unsustainable financial path.[16] Small private schools are endangered by declining enrollments resulting from relatively flat high school graduation rates and increased competition from online competitors.[17]

- *Low tuition revenues.* For the 2015 fiscal year, public and private universities in the United States are expected to experience the slowest net tuition revenue growth in more than a decade.[18]

- *Cost-sharing consortia.* College affordability is one of the major factors at the heart of declining enrollments. As Jillian Berman explains, "About 40 million Americans are already saddled with student loan debt and the heightened attention on the issue has made college students wary of taking on more."[19] As a result, more and more colleges are searching for new levels of efficiency and joining consortia such as those detailed in chapters 13 and 14 of this volume.

Moving forward, it is imperative that challenged institutions candidly assess their viability and not hesitate to take proactive measures to ensure long-term institutional sustainability. At the same time, boards of trustees have a fiduciary obligation to take definitive action before institutions go bankrupt. In our view, the wiser course for an institution is often to reinvent itself through a consolidation involving program transfers, strategic alliance, consortial membership, or mutual-growth merger. If, after considering and pursuing all available options, institutional survival is imperiled, the institution should be proactive to preserve assets, transfer programs, and secure quality teach-out partners to ensure a *death with dignity*; that is, closing its doors while still a fully accredited, respected college or university remembered for generations of productive alumni and a legacy of teaching and learning.

Notes

1. Moody's Global Credit Research, *US Higher Education.*
2. Harvard University, *Harvard University Financial Report, 2012.*
3. Weeks, "Creative Options."
4. Phillip DiChiara, e-mail to Samels Associates, June 23, 2015.
5. Goddard College's program transfer to Green Mountain occurred in 2002.
6. The nursing program transferred to Northeastern University in 1987.
7. Johnson and Weeks, "To Save a College."
8. *Closing a Program, Site, Branch or Institution* was published jointly by the Southern Association of Colleges and Schools and the Commission on Colleges in August 2011; see http://www.sacscoc.org/subchg/policy/Closeprogramcampusinstitution.pdf.
9. "Clayton Christensen: Bottom 25 Percent of Colleges Will Disappear," *edSurge*, November 5, 2013, https://www.edsurge.com/news/2013-11-05-clayton-christensen-bottom-25-percent-of-colleges-will-disappear.
10. Tuby et al., *Slow Tuition Growth Supports Continued Negative Outlook.*
11. "Merging or Closing a Postsecondary Institution Program or Site," Middle States Commission on Higher Education, 2009, http://www.msche.org/documents/Closing-Merging-030311.pdf; "Considerations When Closing an Institution of

Higher Education," New England Association of Schools and Colleges Commission on Institution of Higher Education, April 2010, https://cihe.neasc.org/downloads/Pp13_Considerations_When_Closing_an_Institution_of_Higher_Education.pdf; "Considerations When Closing an Accredited and Candidate Institution Policy," Northwest Commission on Colleges and Universities, 2010, http://www.nwccu.org/Standards%20and%20Policies/Policies/PolicyDocs/Considerations%20When%20Closing%20an%20Accredited%20and%20Candidate%20Institution%20Policy.pdf; "Closing a Program, Site Branch or Institution: Good Practices," Southern Association of Colleges and Schools/Commission on Colleges, August 2011, http://www.sacscoc.org/subchg/policy/Closeprogramcampusinstitution.pdf; Lindquist and Hilmes, "Policy Statement on Considerations When Closing A Postsecondary Educational Institution," Council on Postsecondary Accreditation, April 1982, https://archive.org/stream/ERIC_ED473680/ERIC_ED473680_djvu.txt.

12. Babbit, Land, and Warner, "Anticipating and Managing the Legal Risks of Academic Program Closures."

13. Ibid.

14. Ibid.

15. Babbit, "Closing an Academic Program without Litigation."

16. Denneen and Dretler, "The Financially Sustainable University."

17. Susan Fitzgerald, a senior vice president at Moody's, discusses this issue in Berman, "Why More U.S. Colleges Will Go Under."

18. Moody's Global Credit Research, *US Higher Education.*

19. Berman, "Why More U.S. Colleges Will Go Under."

II

Strategic Alliance: A Model That
Rarely Fails, and Why

When Does Large Become Too Large? A View of Higher Education Partnerships and the Implications of Institutional Size

R. Michael Tanner

This book presents many arguments and examples of educational institutions that have found new strength in cooperative partnerships and alliances among institutions, and in the bigger leap to consolidation or merger of smaller organizations into a larger one under unified governance. As the visible cost of college has risen in comparison with median family incomes, and especially since the economic downturn of 2008, the driving rationale for these consolidations often is organizational effectiveness and efficiency in dealing with financial constraints. American four-year public universities experienced a 25 percent reduction in state and local appropriations per student and increased tuition revenues by 23 percent per student over the period 2006 to 2012.[1] The niche previously occupied by a college may no longer be viable, and the college has to find ways to expand its market, reduce its costs, and become attractive to a larger paying student clientele, or contemplate bankruptcy and closure. Consolidation and merger may offer an attractive and sensible path to a healthy new future. There are many sound reasons why larger entities have a competitive advantage in the context of current trends and technological changes, and a well-executed consolidation, or an alliance with finely tuned strategies for cooperation, will be better adapted to the present circumstances.

Growth poses many problems, however. Some growing pains persist. In strategic alliances, partnerships, and mergers, the promise of synergy usually looms large. The devil is in the details; I highlight places where the devil predictably appears.

In general, maintaining coherence, sense of direction, and responsiveness can be difficult in large organizations expected to be highly coordinated. Strong leadership must certainly articulate a compelling mission. Functionally, the information flows and decision-making processes have to be carefully structured to avoid overload, miscommunication, and clumsiness. In manufacturing, the concept of "economy of scale" is well known: the cost per unit of production (one automobile, one smartphone, etc.) can be much smaller when one design and one tooling for manufacture can be used to produce a high volume of units. Information puzzles, however, are subject to complexity that can make solving them much more difficult the larger they become, creating diseconomies of scale.[2] And much of the running of a large organization involves processing information and making decisions where scale can become an obstacle to effective action. Excessive centralization can lead to overload at the center, delays, and stultifying bureaucracy and inertia; excessive decentralization can lead to fragmentation, misalignment of goals, and failure of coordination. There is no simple universal prescription for success in operating on a large scale.

Universities are not at all alone in grappling with this challenge. The corporate world is full of examples of companies that grew large as a result of a successful business model for one era and then lost momentum, creative drive, and focus as the times changed. Some have struggled to reinvent themselves to overcome the complacency born of success and inertia, and others have moved to restructure to regain clarity of purpose and management. Boards of directors have rethought how the pieces of the business fit together and made the call to break apart one large entity into separate parts, or to articulate the parts into separate divisions to clarify the function of each and give greater freedom to the management of the divisions. Despite the many advantages of being large, particularly in a global marketplace, larger is not always better per se. The art is in knowing how, and even whether, being larger can be better. The decisions of Hewlett-Packard to separate into two companies, HP Inc. and Hewlett-Packard Enterprise, and of Google to form Alphabet are recent examples.[3]

Technology and Scale

When two organizations are combined, such diseconomies of scale can appear in many different guises. The ever-increasing power and speed of computer systems lull people into thinking that a more powerful computer can always extricate them from information snarls. It can come as an unpleasant surprise whenever complexity growth outstrips computer power. If two organizations merge, there is an apparent economy of scale in combining databases and simultaneously having a richer data set. Absent savvy database implementations, however, even a straightforward query can take twice as long to answer, and some conditional queries can be much more than twice as hard to answer. Performance as experienced by any individual user can be far worse than it was before.

As an example, in 2004, the University of Illinois (UI) completed a much-needed overhaul of multiple legacy computer systems in finance, human resources, registration, financial aid, and others by implementing an integrated enterprise system—a project called UI Integrate. The integration encompassed a financial system that for the first time simultaneously handled transactions and accounts for all three campuses of the university (Urbana-Champaign, Chicago, and Springfield). The conceptual beauty and simplicity of a single integrated system was initially contradicted by the performance degradations encountered by users trying to get financial reports, in part because the integrated system had to cull entries and transactions for Springfield, for example, from the mass of transactions and records generated at Urbana-Champaign and Chicago. Pooling all the data made individual queries more complex to execute. Complexity is the unwanted companion to organizational scale. Those consolidating have to seek ways of simultaneously simplifying processes to keep complexity growth in check.

In many ways, advances in both information technology and in transportation have been driving forces pushing for larger scale. Those surfing the Internet situate themselves in a bigger world, and the opportunities they can access online change their appetites and expectations. The mobility of people and goods is stunning compared to a half-century ago. Over that time, businesses that have been able to exploit the advantages of inexpensive and ubiquitous communications and lower cost of transportation have been gradually squeezing out smaller, locally based enterprises. Although higher education has been buffered from their full impact, the same technology and market trends that have caused individually owned movie theaters to close and small stores—even department stores—to struggle are altering the market for higher education.

Fortunately, colleges can adapt by capitalizing on the new ways of doing business. Even a small college can now get its message out almost instantaneously on the Web, and every institution has the potential for a larger sphere of influence and for attracting mobile college students over a bigger physical region, but at the same time they are sharing the space with more competitors. Being competitive in their bigger sphere may require larger scale and cooperation with new allies, some of which may even be current competitors.

Best Practices

- Perform due diligence, analyze the task, and make the commitment to work through all the academic and administrative elements required to meld two cultures into one before making the decision to consolidate.
- Describe and shape the new vision and test the buy-in before charting the course of action. Getting as many key players as possible on board through early involvement will pay welcome dividends later.
- Do not look to impose and enforce more coordination and cooperation among units than is essential for the principal advantages of consolidation to be achieved.

Consolidation: Appeal and Impediments of Greater Scale

I next analyze a series of considerations that arise when two entities are consolidated, giving for each a quick sketch of the appeal and then highlighting one or more impediments. Because many consolidations are motivated by the pressure to preserve or enhance quality while increasing market visibility and lowering costs, the focus is on phenomena that influence institutional competitiveness and efficiency. I note in passing that some consolidations are instigated as a result of shifts in the political winds or consolidations of power at another level that have only marginal connection to immediate institutional effectiveness, and I will not dwell on those dynamics.

Consolidations might be considered at many levels, for example, by combining departments, by merging schools within a college, or by merging separately governed institutions. Often the consolidation is prompted by a mismatch between the capacity of a unit and its expenses, and the demand for its services and associated revenues. Merging a department that has consistently low enrollments with another academically compatible growing department may be the least disruptive way to redress an imbalance. State budget cuts may force a college to operate with fewer instructional resources per student, without any loss of enrollments. Downsizing, merging, or closing departments that are too expensive for the reduced budget, despite the anguish this can provoke, may be the best strategy available.

Here I consider the more dramatic merging of two separate institutions. It is a moment of existential crisis for at least one of the two, and identities that may have been fixtures for years are going to be reshaped or lost. A new unified identity will hopefully rise. Multiple dimensions come into play. Despite the fact that academic institutions are not conventional businesses, I borrow the language of business to describe the phenomena and frame of analysis, because business analyses are typically the underlying drivers of consolidation.

Brand Strength and Customer Expectations
Appeal

All those who spend time in cyberspace are bombarded with advertisements and messages clamoring for attention. A result of all this clutter is that the task of establishing a brand and a market presence in any domain has changed. It requires more focused, creative, and sustained effort. In one higher education example, the University of Phoenix has demonstrated the avenues for branding and marketing at scale. In a comparatively short time frame with extensive well-positioned advertising, it has established a national brand and presence.

Consolidating two institutions can facilitate positive branding and improve visibility for the combined entity. One win is in the numbers game. It has more students, more majors offered, more scholars, more publications, more books in the library, more research dollars, and so forth. In rankings of various types, the combined entity automatically moves up. "Bigger" also conveys to many students that the combined institution is more successful and more stable for the future. Whether in selecting television channels, websites, or merchandise, students are accustomed to exercising freedom of choice. "Bigger" can mean that a student will have more choice, be it for majors, social experiences, or recreation. A consolidated institution can strengthen and promote a single brand with a combined marketing budget.

Impediments

The concomitant responsibility that comes with projecting a strong, unified brand is that the new organization has to live up to the implicit promises of the brand—and do so consistently across all its branches. In important respects, the two previously separate groups have to move swiftly to adopt a common culture, a similar way of interacting with students, faculty, and staff, as well as with vendors and outside parties. Forging a common culture—through propagating unified policies, providing education and training for employees, and developing a sense of community across the former boundary—can be an enormous challenge.

For the student, the simplification of interacting with one consolidated institution will not be fulfilled if the student has to jump through two different types of hoops at every turn. The promise of having a wide choice of majors will be undercut if a student has to get on a bus or drive twenty miles to a remote site every day to take the classes required for the chosen major. Classes that are supposed to be equivalent must be harmonized so that similar learning objectives are achieved.

Moreover, having uniform policy and practices across multiple sites is not entirely optional; in some instances it is imposed by law. Human resources practices that are different at different sites may become a vulnerability when employees experience unfair treatment in the workplace.

Nancy L. Zimpher in chapter 4 in this volume gives an excellent case study of the power of branding and the value it can create. The name of the State University of New York system's 2010 strategic plan, "The Power of SUNY," expresses the promise of a unifying brand that assures a quality learning experience for students. To live up to that promise, SUNY set out to harmonize experiences across sixty-four campuses in meaningful ways. One of the big challenges for SUNY is fulfilling the promise of "seamless transfer," allowing mobile students to move smoothly from one SUNY campus to another without experiencing frustrating academic setbacks. SUNY recognized that it is not enough just to have a common numbering system. The nub of the challenge is to have common course descriptions that lead to consistent learning outcomes. A huge effort was made to identify 15,000 courses that fit common descriptions and transfer successfully. Ongoing effort will be required to avoid unintended drift away from common descriptions and outcomes, so that students can transfer from one SUNY campus to another with confidence in their background and level of preparation.

A consolidation is particularly promising when the two institutions start with a considerable cultural compatibility. Melding the two cultures can be a big challenge, and it is not made any easier when the leadership is simultaneously striving to squeeze out needless redundancies and gain economies of scale.

Market Power
Appeal

The bigger new entity does command greater respect in the marketplace, and not just in terms of its visibility and branding. It is a bigger employer, and so in labor negotiations it will get more attention. It is a larger consumer of goods and services, so it can press vendors to get better prices. It can coordinate new combinations of capabilities to create more attractive and marketable programs. Its one centralized voice speaks with greater authority.

Impediments

Becoming a bigger player can be a mixed blessing. In some instances, such as labor negotiations, the new entity's greater impact on the market means it may face more aggressive opposition; it is worth drawing a battle line when a negotiation could set a tone or establish a precedent with other employers.

There is also the possibility of getting better pricing as a result of higher volume, but I offer two caveats. First, depending on the market in question and the size of the combined institution, there may not be as much leverage for better pricing as one would think. Major supply channels such as Amazon have become remarkably efficient and their pricing is established publicly, so suppliers may not have a lot of margin to negotiate away. Second, in negotiating a purchasing contract, one has to think carefully about the terms of delivery. There may be a substantial price break, relative to the commodity's price at local retailers, if a commodity is delivered in bulk to a college's central receiving dock. But having a delivery sitting on that central receiving dock does not mean satisfaction for the ultimate customer, who may be someone in a department on the other side of campus, or even at another campus. The institution has to arrange for timely and reliable delivery from central receiving to the customer's desktop. If one adds in the true costs of the internal delivery system, the final total price may not be that terrific after all. And, for good reason, many customers will go back to the high-touch local retailer if they are made to wait excessively. Amazon's extraordinary attention to delivery logistics has been crucial to its rapid growth, and a consolidated campus has to include a timely delivery solution in thinking about procurement cost savings.

Synergies and Organizational Effectiveness
Appeal

There can be authentic and justified excitement when two colleges are merged or consolidated under unified leadership, and one contemplates the many possibilities for synergies. Fitting together pieces from the strengths of each can make a new whole that is much greater than the sum of the parts. For instance, a recognized performing arts program at one might be paired with a creative MBA program at the other to articulate a new MBA in arts management appealing to digital natives.

All around, the old and maybe tired formulas can be reexamined to take advantage of the unaccustomed juxtapositions of variables. Approached with open minds and discerning eyes, rethinking the mosaic of college units and offerings can get creative juices flowing.

The greater effectiveness of a unified voice may not be restricted to just the top administration. It can carry down to many lower levels. A college may find it appropriate to have representatives in various settings, for example, from local architectural review boards to national associations, and a small college cannot afford to have a presence everywhere desired. The combined entity can expand its connections while clarifying its positions with a coordinated message. Partnerships of various stripes are an avenue to create greater value and enrich the activities of both partners when complementarity and compatibility amplify existing strengths and differential advantages.

Impediments

The allure of synergies must be balanced by analysis of what will be necessary to realize the benefits. What degree of cooperation and coordination in actions is required, and how hard is it to achieve? If two departments are going to offer a jointly constructed major, will that mean students will have to travel regularly between two distant sites? Will many more faculty have to spend time in joint meetings, or traveling between sites? The administrative burden of forging and maintaining relationships can quietly drag down the high-flying expectations for synergy. Aspirations for a merged department fall apart if there is not sufficient buy-in for its new recast mission. In the worst case, productivity is much less than the sum of parts because incompatible personalities forced into the same arena end up engaging in chronic combat.

In chapter 5 in this volume, "Presidential Vision and Partnership Development: An Evolving View," University of the Pacific President Pamela Eibeck gives a historical example of creating synergies through complementarity in the university's merger fifty years ago with an independent law school, the McGeorge School of Law, and what has become the Dugoni School of Dentistry. Incorporating these schools expanded the offerings under the University of Pacific umbrella. At the same time, she notes, the distances separating the three sites made it sensible for the schools to retain a high degree of independence and, as a result, the opportunities for economies of scale were limited.

Efficiencies and Economies of Scale
Appeal

Larger scale offers many opportunities to rethink the design and ambitions of an organization and the deployment of its resources in relation to its mission. At its inception, an institution may have had a mission well suited to that historical moment and context, but the evolution and renewal processes may not have kept up with changing times. The history of a university has usually visibly dictated its physical spaces; less visibly, it may have left administrative and academic lines that are not optimal for the future. With consolidation of two organizations, or even just substantial growth, there is an opportunity to rebalance and restructure for higher efficiency.

Higher efficiency and economies of scale are obtained when specialization and optimization of design and operation allow "fixed" costs to be amortized over many more units of production, resulting in a lower marginal cost per unit. In higher education, expected staffing requirements can easily drive up the operating cost per student at a small college: a college must have a designated Title IX officer, legal counsel, perhaps a hazardous waste disposal specialist, and so forth.[4] The costs of these skilled personnel rarely scale in direct proportion to the number of students enrolled; there often is a minimum threshold of expense. Employing someone with the requisite skill set incurs a premium when those skills are only applied a fraction of the time. Similarly, a dean of a small school is still a dean, and expects to be paid as a dean on equity grounds. That can imply higher cost per student of the dean function in that school, but it is overhead easily overlooked in the haze. The faculty component of instructional costs depends on faculty salary levels and the distribution of class sizes. Just mounting a comprehensive curriculum in a subject area requires that a suite of courses be offered with adequate frequency, and this alone can compel a small college using conventional instructional delivery to offer small sections with high costs per student. Although large universities must also keep a close eye on curriculum and scheduling to achieve the desired class size distribution, there are economies of scale to be achieved by doing so.

Pursuant to a consolidation, one looks to eliminate redundancies. To crystallize and simplify some issues, consider the following thought experiment. Two colleges, College A and College B, physically located side by side, have identical organizational structures, departments, and enrollments. One is just a copy of the other. Now the two are merged to form one new college with twice the size—and rife with redundancies. Ignoring the human resource dimensions and pretending it is merely a computer game, where should the redundancies be removed to achieve efficiencies, and what is the design of the new organization? If the challenge at one college was that uniformly every program was woefully undersubscribed, one can restructure at the faculty and staff level. In a stark version, all the students at College B are reenrolled in College A, and every employee at College B is dismissed (or vice versa, or some blend of the two extremes).

Relative to direct instruction, everyone at College A is expected to do twice as much as they were doing before: faculty teach twice the number of students (while also producing just as much research). A department chair still has the same number of faculty and the same curriculum, however, so the chair's personnel and curriculum duties are no more onerous. The deans have the same number of department chairs, and so forth. (One can certainly eliminate a redundant president from College B!) The human resources office has the same number of people on the payroll, so the workload there has not increased. With a modest increase in information technology (IT) expenses, new computer systems can handle the increased student load. Relative to class size, it might not be out of the question to see average class size double if the colleges were really undersubscribed.

Physical plant and maintenance, for one, are in a different boat. There are twice as many buildings and grounds. Without probing more deeply, the best one could hope for would be to have maintenance and ground crews work more efficiently with better equipment and more specialized functions, and they could be overseen by fewer supervisors with better job-tracking software and work assignment optimization.

The black-and-white simplicity of this thought experiment breaks up into many pixels and many shades of gray when one begins to grapple with more realistic conditions. Unless there is a great methodological leap enhancing teaching capacity, the faculty of College A will not be able to double their students. Maybe some terribly underenrolled sections could have double the students, but many could not. Colleges A and B will not have perfectly redundant curricula. Perhaps some departments can be comparatively smoothly merged with their counterparts and eventually staffed with fewer than the combined faculty and staff, but other times there will be complementarity that forces tough decisions, while also opening opportunities. For example, College A offers Scandinavian studies, whereas College B offers Serbo-Croatian studies, both expensive to mount. Will the combined college maintain both? It might if students from College A have been yearning to study Serbo-Croatian, and those from College B to study Scandinavia. By the time all the knotty curriculum design and faculty deployment issues are addressed, maybe the college can see a way to have a 25 percent or more increase in student-to-faculty ratio, lower the cost per student, and maintain educational quality.

Restructuring and rebalancing the curriculum have architectural implications. If class sizes double, rooms to accommodate the doubling are needed. One certainly cannot reasonably expect all the faculty to shuttle back and forth between the campuses of Colleges A and B and meet twice as many sections. Classrooms may have to be remodeled to get the necessary character and size distribution of the spaces.

Rethinking the physical plant raises the question of the efficiency of space utilization. The natural drift in classroom demand and allocation is toward overstuffed classes at the times both students and faculty find most attractive and empty rooms at off-hours. Most universities have a great many spaces sitting idle much of the time. To achieve efficiencies in the physical plant and reduce maintenance costs, a smaller number of buildings must be used more intensively, and those not used repurposed or eliminated. If one goal is to reduce the physical plant costs per student, the curriculum, the instructional spaces, and the scheduling of those spaces must be part of an integrated strategy.[5]

Impediments

Scrutinizing the places where running a larger bricks-and-mortar campus does not allow economies of scale begins to reveal some of impediments to size. It is easy on paper to say that cutting more grass with a bigger mower is more efficient, but when the time devoted to moving the bigger mower from place to place are included, the savings may be much lower than the paper estimate. Back-of-the-envelope calculations can glibly overestimate the cost savings of scale and underestimate the diseconomic logistic and complexity barriers.

Transportation and movement of people and goods can take a disproportionately greater toll when a large campus attempts to operate as a single integrated entity. Unconstrained scheduling of classes can result in students and faculty spending a larger fraction of their day in unproductive transit. This is the analog of the commuter clog penalty paid most visibly in urban environments, with many hours spent daily in traffic jams.

The Internet has shrunk distances and unquestionably facilitated operating at large scale. There is no perceptible added delay owing to distance of separation. But, as noted above, expectations for regular communication among all members of a group will be frustrated if the group becomes too large. A common manifestation of this is just the seemingly simple task of scheduling a meeting with good attendance by a set of independent participants. The greater the number of participants involved, the more difficult it is to find an acceptable time. Size becomes a drag.

The vexation of large meetings with too many people for everyone to speak and be heard is related to another observable phenomenon of scale, a manifestation of natural human behavior. If a department gets to be very large, say, fifty people, it eventually ceases to operate as a single department. At some point it will usually break up into smaller groupings to conduct serious business that involves dense interactions. The fifty people will form several caucuses of fifteen to twenty for most of the regular business and only come together as a department of the whole as needed to resolve major overarching policy issues. In principle, similar departments from Colleges A and B might be combined into one larger department, using efficient shared "back-office" services. In practice, however, the doubled department may prove difficult to hold together.

Administrative overhead can be attached to this phenomenon. The big department might have only one department head, earning a somewhat better salary commensurate with the importance of the new size, but then the subgroups have their own leaders who may be designated "associate heads" meriting a modest stipend. Add up the augmentations, and at the end of the day the reduction in administrative expenses is less than expected.

Many generic "back-office" functions can now be well done at distance. On the other hand, "efficient" services poorly executed lead to dissatisfaction with the lack of response and the bureaucratic lethargy and anonymity of the services provided. They can save money on one line of the accounting books, but beware when they impose inefficiencies on the employees served, where the loss of productivity is unaccounted.

In brief, many dimensions of productivity can experience an economy of scale when a versatile design can be used many times over and production optimized to lower the per unit cost. Computer chips are an outstanding example. The fantastic leaps in performance per price in IT are a chief factor in making feasible partnerships and mergers that would have been impossible long ago. At the same time, there are limits that must be recognized and taken into consideration—physical limits and human limits. Without close attention to the structuring of interactions, communications, and logistics, the alluring efficiency gains of scale may be thwarted by myriad microlosses from awkward design, information overload, complexity, and ambiguity.

Conclusion: Value versus Price

Without a doubt, technological evolution and especially the information revolution are making it feasible to coordinate much larger enterprises and reap the rewards. The infrastructure of communication makes physical distance much less important. Instantaneous messaging has brought people together and made active dialogue across distance commonplace, so much so that now many know friends on the other side of the nation much better than they do their next-door neighbors. High-bandwidth connections allow workable partnerships and intellectual communities to form in a fluid way, with scant regard to geography. Knowledge industries (e.g., finance and banking) thrive on the power of the information revolution.

At the same time, economics are pushing small enterprises to examine the market niche they inhabit and to ask whether they can remain small and stay competitive. In a number of sectors—including agriculture, manufacturing, and information technology—it has become harder to carve out a niche and a market at modest size without having strong partners in place. For instance, a handful of massive automobile companies dominate the global market in terms of the percentages of cars sold. In fact, digging into history reveals that many of them became massive through a series of partnership, mergers, and acquisitions. Small car companies generally must sell expensive cars, and they are part of larger supply chains or allied with top companies to keep component costs down.

While it is debatable whether higher education is an enterprise that shares the essential characteristics of industries dominated by giants, it is certainly not isolated from the trends to scale. Enthusiasts for massive open online courses (MOOCs) predicted that higher education would experience disruption and a great shakeout. Mercifully, the great disruption was oversold. Nonetheless, many smaller institutions can no longer count on a secure future in a regional market.

A key to a successful partnership is probing what substantive new value is added through partnership. Jonathan R. Cole and others observe that cooperative leagues emerged among research universities from the imperative for competition in athletics.[6] The Midwest's academic alliance called the Committee for Institutional Cooperation is not well known nationally, yet the Big Ten Athletic Conference from which it sprang has its own television channel. Ironically, competition, the *sine qua non* of athletic excitement, is the driving force that makes cooperation inevitable. Multi-institutional partnerships in research have made possible capital-intensive research projects, such as the W. M. Keck Observatory in Hawaii, or the Large Hadron Collider in Geneva, that would be well beyond the reach of any one of the partners. The Internet will facilitate exciting partnerships at a much lower threshold.

A merger is the all-consuming partnership, and the success of the merger depends heavily on the vision for how the merged institution will reengineer itself, not just the substantive offerings and programs of the new institution, but also how it will think: what its mission will be, how and by whom decisions will be made, what connections and communications protocols must be in place, where it will find its inspiration and new identity.

Beyond the question of whether new value can be created, the tougher question is whether the value achievable through a partnership will outweigh the price of the necessary coordination. In achieving coordination across the whole, independence and freedom of action by the parts are diminished. If coordination demands that a center or institute director ask permission before taking an action, for example, and the request must travel through multiple administrative layers, each pondering the question at length because the administrator does not have a basis for granting permission, the answer will be a long time coming. In the meantime, the opportunity for the center may be lost. Long delays are common in big organizations. They are one inspiration for the maxim "Better to ask forgiveness than permission."

A simple heuristic for organizational design is not to demand any tighter coordination than is necessary to create the value added. An organization can be nimble only if it can think and act quickly. Invariably, speed hinges on the exercise of local authority over locally controlled resources, while institutional coherence and integrity are sustained by respecting an institutional framework that shapes the context.

There are surely opportunities for a university to pursue ambitions opened up by growing larger or by entering into meaningful partnerships. At the same time, both growth and partnerships add a new set of complexities and burdens that attach to coordinating more pieces. There are limits that begin to impinge with size. The shrewd will design administrative structures to simplify and minimize their effects, and turn down a chance to become too big to succeed.

Notes

1. Johnson and Yanaguira, *How Did Revenue and Spending per Student Change?*

2. Brassard and Bratley, *Algorithmics.*

3. Bailey, "Hewlett-Packard Is Splitting into Two Companies"; Womack, "Google Rises after Creating Holding Company Called Alphabet."

4. Title 34 Education, §106.8 Designation of Responsible Employee and Adoption of Grievance Procedures, 20 U.S.C. §1681 and 1682 (2010).

5. As an example, see the Brigham Young University–Idaho story as recounted in Christensen and Eyring, *Innovative University*.

6. Cole, "Building a New Research-University System."

CHAPTER FOUR

"Systemness": A New Way to Lead and Manage Higher Education Systems

Nancy L. Zimpher

The State University of New York is the largest comprehensive public university system in the world. Owing to its composition and history, SUNY has a unique perspective on what we call *systemness*—that is, how public higher education systems work to make the most of strategic alliances and other forms of affiliation between central system administrations and component campuses. There is a purpose to cultivating systemness: to create a whole that is stronger than the sum of its parts. In the case of higher education, it is to create public university systems that serve a state and its citizenry more effectively than independent institutions can do on their own.

Creating effective systemness forces university leaders to ask themselves and their colleagues: "How can we do better?" This question is particularly urgent in the current era of intensifying specialization, expanding student services, and reduced state funding. In a book focusing on the value of developing partnerships and various co-ventures within university systems, this chapter provides a series of strategic, system-approach best practices and recommendations.

While some universities and systems have answered the question of how they can do better by consolidating, even merging, colleges or programs in order to save costs; in SUNY's case, the focus is more often on collaborative and less on consolidative approaches as a means to refine systemness to better serve students and the state.[1] In this chapter, I provide several action plans for systems to make best use of their structures and personnel to build alliances from the center out, strengthening from within.

Every state in the Union operates some kind of public higher education institution. Most states have systems, and these consist of anywhere

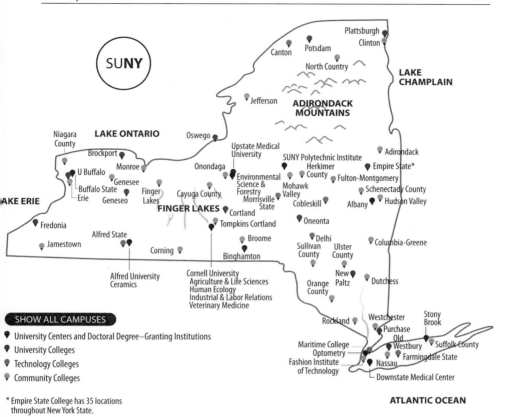

SUNY

LAKE CHAMPLAIN

LAKE ONTARIO

ADIRONDACK MOUNTAINS

AKE ERIE

FINGER LAKES

SHOW ALL CAMPUSES

- University Centers and Doctoral Degree–Granting Institutions
- University Colleges
- Technology Colleges
- Community Colleges

* Empire State College has 35 locations throughout New York State.

ATLANTIC OCEAN

The State University of New York system.

from 3 to 112 schools, the largest being the California Community Colleges system. Some states like California, Louisiana, Oklahoma, and Texas support multiple separate public systems. Some states like Iowa, Michigan, and New Mexico have public flagship universities from which branch smaller satellite campuses. Many states have two systems that separate public universities from community colleges. In the case of SUNY, it is the system's *comprehensiveness* together with its size that sets it apart from other states and systems in the country. SUNY is composed of sixty-four schools, including a mix of doctorate-granting research universities, liberal arts colleges, community colleges, specialized and technical schools, health science centers, and land-grant colleges. Each one of these institutions has a president, and a chancellor who reports to an eighteen-member board of trustees that oversees the system. Almost 100 percent of New York State residents live within thirty

What is the greatest challenge to developing a successful partnership between higher education institutions?

The great inhibitor to developing successful partnerships is funding channeled into silos. This tendency makes us competitive rather than collaborative and does not enable collective impact. Instead, we favor forms of fused funding to encourage all stakeholders to set common goals, evidence-based interventions, and sustainable change.

miles of a SUNY institution, and 93 percent live within fifteen miles of one.

Founded in 1948 and headquartered in Albany, the SUNY system administration pulled together under a unifying administrative umbrella thirty-two already existing schools that had been operating independently, some for more than a hundred years. At the outset, "the heart and face of the system," according to SUNY's historians, "were eleven State Teachers Colleges and six Agricultural and Technical Institutes."[2] The system also included four colleges at Cornell University—the New York State Colleges of Agriculture and Life Sciences, Human Ecology, Veterinary Medicine, and Industrial and Labor Relations—New York's land-grant institutions.

University systems, particularly comprehensive systems, have greater potential than individual institutions, public or private, to extend educational opportunities and resources to the widest possible body of students and thereby have the greatest potential to improve quality of life for individuals, in service of their state's economic strength. Although system comprehensiveness has particular, inherent possibilities for internal partnerships and strategic alliances, the strategies offered in this chapter can be developed by the leaders of any system, no matter what its size or structure.[3]

Partnering to Create Mobility and Student Success

In late 2014 and early 2015, I traveled to several SUNY campuses to meet and talk with groups of students about their college experience. I wanted to hear about their experiences with student services, registering for classes, selecting majors, and I wanted to know whether their needs were being met. If not, I wanted to hear what they suggested university system should do about it. The core message from these many conversations was that today's students expect a level of mobility in their education never seen until now. This expectation is rooted in the explosive acceleration and advancement in technology over the last two decades, reshaping both how students throughout the education pipeline learn and how faculty teach. There are several strategic partnerships the SUNY system is currently developing among its campuses and external stakeholders—including elected officials, national and local education organizations, and local governments—to enhance student mobility to speed time to degree. This chapter discusses four models of *system-driven* collaboration that other systems can adapt: (1) strategic enrollment management, (2) rational tuition policies, (3) student financial aid literacy, and (4) seamless transfer mechanisms.

1. Strategic Enrollment Management

In New York State, on average, only twenty-three of every one hundred ninth-graders will go on to graduate high school, enroll in college, and complete their degree on time or close to on time, that is, within six years. That number is even lower in our upstate urban centers, with only sixteen of every one hundred completing. Of those students who fall off, some will have some kind of post–high school college experience, but they do not complete a degree. This tells us that New York's education pipeline, from cradle to career, is not seamless, so that everyone, no matter where they are born or where they go to school, has an equal chance to succeed. At SUNY, we frame these and all our system-wide efforts around a formula: Access + Completion = Success. All strategic decisions as a system go toward improving results in each area for our 460,000 students, which requires building multiple all-university and cross-sector partnerships and alliances. To that end, grown out of our 2010 strategic plan, *The Power of SUNY*, is our concerted effort toward building Strategic Enrollment Management, or SEM.

SEM initiatives expand the funnel to encompass the complete student life cycle: recruiting, enrolling, retaining, and graduating. Toward our Access + Completion = Success formula above, *recruitment* and *enrollment* fit into the Access bucket, and *retainment* and *graduation* go into Completion. Across the system, SUNY's four-year graduation rate is 47 percent, fourteen points higher than our national public counterparts. Our six-year graduation rate of 65 percent is seven points higher than the national publics and rivals private colleges. Promising as these figures are, competitively speaking, they show that the system needs to do better still. We are compelled to shoot above the 60 percent mark because most jobs today that pay a middle-class wage or more require some sort of postsecondary training; by 2020, this will be true for nearly 70 percent of all jobs in New York.[4]

At SUNY, toward organizing SEM and student success efforts, we have built SEM partnerships with all of our campuses by establishing a centralized Strategic Enrollment Management Office, by creating a system-wide Completion Agenda, and by implementing new accountability measures toward meeting all agenda goals.

CENTRALIZED STRATEGIC ENROLLMENT MANAGEMENT OFFICE

Individual schools within systems often have their own strategic enrollment initiatives, but systems with central governing bodies and big-picture views have the potential to move these efforts to scale and to make a greater impact. Furthermore, comprehensive systems like SUNY are well positioned to serve an increasingly diverse citizenry and complex world of work. System-wide retention and completion initiatives require durable partnerships among units of each campus's academic and student affairs operations. The most effective structures for SEM take an integrated approach that links a centralized SEM office with designated campus-level retention officers who coordinate directly with any campus body involved in retention and completion: undergraduate admissions, financial aid, the registrar, new student orientation and first-year experience programs, enrollment data analysis, graduate and professional admissions, access and opportunity programs, career services, and any student services that troubleshoot impediments to student success.[5] In university systems, on far too many individual campuses, no one leader or division is responsible specifically for retention. To date, six of SUNY's campuses now have designated chief retention officers or someone of another title who fills that role, with more such developments in the works, as guided by the central SEM office. Having such an officer on every campus signals the importance of efforts to increase graduation and success rates and also creates a point person to interface with the system-level office. At its heart, SEM is an exercise in organization.

COMPLETION AGENDA

In early 2015, in response to the national call for the 60 percent college completion goal, we began developing SUNY's system-wide Completion Agenda, in which we committed to awarding 150,000 degrees per year by 2020; in 2014, we granted 93,000. This increase factors in the projected number of skilled graduates that New York State will need to make up a strong workforce and economy. To add an additional 57,000 degrees per year is a steep climb, and it cannot happen without collaboration and buy-in from our colleges. Empowering them to graduate more students has required the creation of new system-wide policies and supports that are driven by centralized management.

Once we set our goal of 150,000 completions per year, we convened an executive team within the system administration that included me, our provost, and support from our central project management office. Together, we intensively surveyed our system "strategy landscape," as it were, to see what individual institutions in our system were doing to drive completion and what we were doing as a system overall. We looked for opportunities for partnerships that could bring campus-driven projects to system scale. To date, we have identified twenty-three evidence-based initiatives and collaborations that are working to bring to scale across the system, including "Finish in Four" initiatives, applied learning, an online college-readiness tool, student financial literacy and early alert tools, and seamless transfer policies.

NEW ACCOUNTABILITY MEASURES

In July 2015, the system issued a request for proposals to our campuses to give them the opportunity to apply for grant funding to support these projects. It is from this point forward that the systemness approach, in terms of forming and meeting our Completion Agenda, will kick into gear as we engage campuses more deeply in collaborative initiatives to ensure their successes. The Office of Strategic Enrollment Management tracks our campuses' progress toward increasing the number of degrees they grant each year. Accountability for and assessment of progress toward completion goals are now built in to the annual presidential review process conducted by the chancellor.

2. *Rational Tuition Policies*

SUNY's tuition is the lowest among public colleges in the Northeast and is in the lowest quartile in the nation, but college in America is still not cheap. In the last three decades, the cost of college has tripled.[6] Mirroring this increase, nationally, the percentage of college graduates who borrow to finance their undergraduate education is up 20 percent over the last twenty-five years or so—from 49 percent in 1992 to 69 percent in 2013. Borrowing students today graduate with an average debt of $28,400, pushing the national student loan debt total up to an unprecedented $1.2 trillion.[7]

Historically, one of the biggest and most stubborn challenges SUNY faced was that its tuition-setting ability was tied to the state legislature's regulations and budget practices. When SUNY had been allowed to raise tuition in the past, it was sporadic and almost always dealt a blow to students and their families. In the course of sixty years, the state allowed the university to raise tuition only thirteen times—the smallest of these increases was 7 percent (2009–10), and the highest was 43 percent (1991–92). Seventeen times since 1963 (when SUNY first started charging tuition), a first-year student who entered SUNY never had to pay a tuition increase during his or her college career; nineteen entering classes saw one tuition increase; eight entering classes saw two tuition increases; and the class entering in 1989–90 saw three increases. The process was both unfair and impractical.

Beginning in 2009, we began to advocate at the system level for a rational, predictable tuition policy that would allow students and their families to plan for the cost of their college education over the course of five years. The process required multiple forms of collaboration to win over faculty and student governance groups, unions, and legislators. With careful, persistent work, we were successful in each of these areas, and it was recognized by many that these collaborations and partnerships were another illustration of what systemness could accomplish. Then, in 2011, Governor Andrew M. Cuomo signed into law the groundbreaking NY-SUNY 2020 Challenge Grant Act, which secured a five-year rational tuition policy allowing students to plan for pre-reported incremental tuition increases, never more than $300 per year, and provided the SUNY system with a reliable revenue source to maintain academic quality. Critically, the legislation also includes a maintenance of effort assurance of state support that the university can count on. Further, it codified SUNY's responsibility to maintain affordability for New York's students, for whom even the planned, incremental tuition increases would be a roadblock to college. As part of NYSUNY 2020, the system covers this tuition gap for New York's neediest students. The credit is applied to each individual New York State resident undergraduate student eligible for the Tuition Assistance Program (TAP) and funded from campus resources.

3. Student Financial Aid Literacy

If predictable tuition is one leg of SUNY's affordability strategy, promoting student financial literacy is the other because even though SUNY's tuition is comparatively low, a little more than half of SUNY students take out loans.[8] At 55 percent, SUNY's borrowing average is lower than the national level, as is the default rate among its students. Across the country, default rates for two-year public colleges are considerably higher than at four-year schools, and this is the same at SUNY.

As a result, SUNY has begun to implement a new financial aid system, Smart Track. Smart Track is a technology- and communications-driven

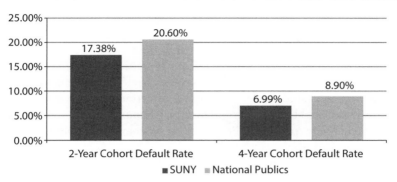

Cohort default rates for student loans: State University of New York versus national publics, 2011. *Source:* National Student Loan Data System, US Department of Education.

approach to educating students on loan borrowing, debt, default management, and academic success. Its twin goals are to lower default rates and increase retention and graduation rates.

Until recently, student loan default management at SUNY was handled entirely as individual efforts confined to financial aid offices at our sixty-four institutions. Nearly every campus had some mechanism in place to assist students who had fallen into delinquent status, whether by contracting with a third party to reach out to students about deferral options or using in-house staff, but there was no coordination or management from the system level and little collaboration among constituent schools. This is not unusual and is in fact the standard way in which financial aid and loan default is managed nationally. Beginning in 2010, however, SUNY's central financial aid services office started looking at default management in a way that turned the process on its head, resulting in the creation of an entirely new model—from an after-the-fact, reactive approach to *proactive default prevention* as a means of promoting *student retention.*

Informed by federal data that show that students who complete their degrees are less likely to default, the system leadership formed a system-level Default Prevention Task Force and began to co-venture with campus partners as well as representatives from the US Department of Education to explore interventions and mechanisms aimed at retention and completion. The team moved forward, operating under the theory that if the schools could engage and educate students on college financing *early, consistently,* and *creatively,* more students would be more likely to graduate and repay their loans, and default rates would go down.

When it came to building a default prevention–student retention plat-form, SUNY started from zero. There was, as noted, no system-wide ap-proach in place, no unified, collaborative method to keep borrowing students enrolled or to prevent them from defaulting on their loans. There was also no precedent that we knew of at any other university system that approached student retention and completion from the angle of de-fault prevention. Having a central system administration was absolutely essential to New York's public university system being able to address holistically and preventatively the student debt crisis in the state. That SUNY had a central financial aid office that could look at the system as a whole, connect with campuses, coordinate the key leaders, and collect data created a foundation for effective interventions.

The task force began meeting with campus partners in 2012, having identified six SUNY schools—three two-year schools and three four-year schools—where our team members had already strong alliances that could facilitate the work. We kept the central team small, no more than a half-dozen people. This allowed the group to be nimble—its members could focus on the work at hand, engaging each other and the cam-puses, without getting bogged down in administrative procedures. What emerged were collaborations on multiple levels engaging a broad span of partners, including campus presidents and provosts, faculty, registrar's offices, bursars, financial aid and career counselors, athletic departments, and even campus childcare centers. It also underscored the commonly acknowledged federal student aid motto that default is "not just a finan-cial aid problem," it is an all-campus problem.

During late 2013 and early 2014, all SUNY campuses were brought into the collaboration, and links to new financial literacy resources for students are now available on all SUNY campus websites. SUNY is the first large state system in the country to offer statewide financial literacy services for students at all campuses. Financial literacy modules vary by topic and include budgeting, saving, the use of credit, identity theft, and financing a college education. The modules are regularly refreshed, and new financial-themed modules are under consideration. Remarkably,

What is the most important piece of advice you would offer to a leader developing a higher education partnership this year?

Patience. Cross-sector partnerships do not develop overnight. They require pa-tience and skill to get all key stakeholders speaking the same language and agree-ing on goals and the means to achieve them.

the online Smart Track financial literacy tools are available to anyone in the world who wants to use them; one need not be a SUNY student.[9]

4. Seamless Transfer Mechanisms

The final and perhaps most important purpose of systemness is to facilitate seamless transfer between institutions. It is one of the best challenges to partnership's flexibility and effectiveness. Each year, about 30,000 students transfer from one SUNY institution to another, and SUNY transfer students graduate at nearly the same rate as "native freshmen"—that is, 61 percent and 63 percent, respectively, at six years— far exceeding the national average of 51 percent. Despite this positive statistic, the system historically experienced widespread transfer challenges, and there was clear need for improvement. Overall, the system had few checks and balances on those transfer decisions made by individual faculty and departments. Guidance mechanisms to ensure that transfer students chose the right courses in their major to graduate on time were inconsistent across the system and, at some institutions, in many disciplines, were absent entirely.

SUNY's 2010 strategic plan provided the charge to resolve all lingering transfer challenges. Meeting this charge required a disciplined, productive collaboration among many stakeholders: system and campus leaders, the leadership of SUNY's faculty governance organizations, individual campus faculty governance leaders, transfer advisors, and admission directors. That SUNY is a system—that the university has a central administrative hub that understands the system as a whole body— positioned it to do the intellectual, organizational, and procedural lifting necessary to complete this massive project. Finally, in December 2012, the SUNY Board of Trustees set the new policy to ensure seamless student transfer across the system's sixty-four campuses. The policy, driven by faculty and vetted through the university-wide consultative process, marked a milestone for the system as a whole. The resolution was reflective of the many lessons learned through years of conversations and policies on transfer and mobility at SUNY, yet it still represented a new approach to this work. It utilized a comprehensive research effort coupled with scores of alliances within the institution that moved the system from a conceptual agreement on the importance of seamless transfer to the design and implementation of the systemic infrastructure required for this initiative.

SUNY's seamless transfer policy established transfer of credits within majors and those in general education. The most time-intensive goal was to establish transfer within majors across the system and to engage faculty at the two- and four-year levels in the process. Staff in the system provost's office spent many hours compiling information from campus catalogs to identify course requirements for the first two years of study at all campuses. That information was sent to more than 400 two- and four-year school faculty in various disciplines who developed new, common course descriptions. Campuses ultimately identified 15,000 courses that fit these descriptions, courses *guaranteed* to transfer in the major designated. This information is maintained online at the system level with a review process that allows campuses to continue to add courses over time and challenge courses that do not meet the required learning standards. Importantly, the information is also now a universally available student and advisor resource. Campuses are able to develop semester plans for transfer students outlining course options that, if followed, will result in timely graduation.

At the system level, SUNY invested in customized, Web-based, degree-auditing software, a program called Degree Works, which is being implemented at every campus. As courses are entered into the system, they are identified as general education or transfer-path courses. Through this online tool, students can easily track their progress to degree completion at their home campus or at another SUNY campus, if they are seeking to transfer.

SUNY's work with respect to seamless transfer can serve as a model for the benefits of collaboration and partnership development inside of large systems. With a clear focus on the positive results of seamless transfer—including improved graduation rates, decreased time to graduation, and cost savings for students—the institution moved from a system-level concept to implemented standards, in part because of an open and consultative process as well as alliances and affiliations among faculty, central system staff, and individual campus leaders. Perhaps more than other sectors, education is highly siloed, and colleges within university systems too often operate as islands when they could be sharing best practices and policies, resources, and services. To overcome these challenges and lead education systems that serve our society more effectively requires a shift toward viewing all of these constituents as opportunities for partnership building.

Notes

Special thanks to Jessica Fisher Neidl, senior writer and editor, Office of the Chancellor; Patricia R. Thompson, assistant vice chancellor for student financial aid services; Cynthia Proctor, executive vice chancellor and director of communications and chief of staff, SUNY Office of the Provost; and Paul Marthers, associate vice chancellor for enrollment management and student services, for their contributions to this chapter.

1. For a comprehensive study of SUNY's economic impact, see Nelson A. Rockefeller Institute of Government, *How SUNY Matters*.

2. Clark, Leslie, and O'Brien, *SUNY at 60*.

3. Zimpher and Neidl, "Statewide University Systems," 198.

4. ReadyNation, *Closing the Job Skills Gap with New Yorkers*.

5. As of this writing, SUNY considers the Ohio State University's Division of Enrollment Services to be an excellent model for how to organize a strategic enrollment management operation. Indiana University has a less robust but similarly student-success-focused SEM division.

6. Nelson, "Summoned to the White House."

7. Woo, *Degrees of Debt*, 4; Institute for College Access and Success, *Student Loan Debt and the Class of 2013*; Denhart, "How the $1.2 Trillion College Debt Crisis Is Crippling Students, Parents, and the Economy."

8. For default rates, the US Department of Education does not calculate by system, but rather by individual schools, whether part of a system or not.

9. State University of New York, "Smart Track Empowered Financial Planning," accessed April 9, 2016, https://www.suny.edu/smarttrack/.

CHAPTER FIVE

Presidential Vision and Partnership Development: An Evolving View

Pamela Eibeck

The finances of a traditional education have become unsustainable as costs continue to rise and students are less able to afford the price of their degrees. This chapter is about some of the changes I believe traditional colleges and universities now need to implement to provide most students with an affordable education. These changes will take many forms, and while some will occur within a university, the ones I focus on principally involve multiple ways to consolidate two or more institutions, including partnerships, co-ventures, strategic alliances, and even full mergers.

Partnering with other institutions is not new to California's University of the Pacific. Fifty years ago, the university merged with two independent professional schools: McGeorge School of Law in Sacramento and the College of Physicians and Surgeons, now the Dugoni School of Dentistry, in San Francisco. They joined our other colleges but retained a level of greater independence, largely owing to their geographic distance from the Stockton campus and their well-established brands. While the independence has served them well, duplicative administrative functions, relative autonomy in decision making, and distinctive cultures have contributed to higher overhead costs and branding challenges for the university as a whole.

In 2015, the university engaged in informal discussions with another university about a partnership. The institution was a private university, about one quarter our size, over a hundred years old with a focused mission and strong reputation for the programs in the sciences. A strategic alliance would help the University of the Pacific advance the strategy to expand academic program offerings in an area of strength at both schools and expand our geographic base. Our counterpart would benefit from affiliating with a comprehensive university through interdisciplinary collaborations that would enhance the other institution's programs. In the process, they could expand their geographic footprint, and our marketing and reputation could result in greater visibility for them as well as us. Both institutions would benefit from economies of scale for administrative services and the added financial stability that comes from a common bottom line.

Our discussions thus far have revealed the complexity of issues that arise when considering a partnership. As an immediate example, the other university would like to retain significant autonomy in their operations, as they are a nimble, student-focused organization with relatively low capital costs, no tenure system or unions, and comfortable with change. This has triggered many questions for me as a chief executive officer about how a consolidation might best be structured. If they merged with us, they could become a college within our university, analogous to our law and dental schools with a high level of independence. Yet would this decision then force a cultural and operational adjustment that mandates a highly functioning square peg to fit in the round hole of Pacific's governance systems? Could it also diminish the attributes of our potential partner that are the very characteristics that make them appealing to us? Furthermore, how could we create a flexible system that retains the best of their operations while avoiding competition across some departments and still achieve a common bottom line that reduces administrative costs per student? Regardless of the outcomes of these specific discussions, I have come to appreciate the depth and variety of benefits that can come to institutions that are willing to consolidate and work together to meet the changing needs of student learners. Through partnerships, we can bring together complementary assets, business models, and synergies that ultimately will allow mutual institutional growth and, most important, well-educated, workforce-ready graduates.

My goal in writing this chapter is to encourage conversations among college and university presidents, trustees, and leadership teams about the benefits of institutional partnerships. I begin by highlighting how costs and demographics will pressure such changes in the future and discussing several consolidations that have taken place, and then close with a group of lessons learned for planners considering this option.

Pressures Forcing Change

There are two predominant external pressures that are the drivers forcing traditional colleges and universities to change structures and business models: rising unaffordability and changing student needs.

The Unaffordability Conundrum

The very nature of traditional universities that makes them so useful also makes them prohibitively expensive, whether they are private or public: students dedicating years of their lives in residence and learning intensely in and out of a classroom; talented faculty inspiring students while also conducting scholarship; staff members working to ensure student success; sophisticated technology systems that support teaching and learning, student services, and business operations; and a small city that includes housing, dining, healthcare, public safety, and athletics.

The majority of aspiring college students can no longer afford a college degree from the University of the Pacific or any other traditional university. Over the past thirty years, while inflation-adjusted family incomes have increased by 16 percent, the tuition at private, nonprofit universities has increased by 146 percent while in-state tuition at public universities has increased 225 percent.[1] Meanwhile, there are simply fewer families able to pay tuition. According to the Center on Budget and Policy Priorities, US income inequality is the highest it's been since the 1920s, and family wealth inequality is even greater than income inequality.[2] Overall, 90 percent of the population only earns 53 percent of the total income and only has 25 percent of the total wealth in the nation. These financial constraints facing first-year college students are reflected by the growth in discounting. On average, private colleges' discount rate reached 48 percent for freshmen in 2014, up from 46.4 percent the year before, according to the National Association of College and University Business Officers' 2014 Tuition Discounting Study. Net revenue of institutions is expected to grow just 0.4 percent per student next year, the report states. After adjusting for inflation, tuition revenue has been flat for the last thirteen years.[3]

The story is the same, whether at a public university for which the state is simply unwilling or unable to fill in the budgetary gap, or at a private one that must turn to reserves and donations to balance its annual budget. While some cost cutting is healthy, a strategy relying on cost cutting alone denies the fundamental fact that there are simply not enough students with the wealth to sustain the current number of traditional residential colleges and universities.

Changing Student Needs

The need for learning has never been greater than it is today, but the nature of future learners is changing. According to the US Department of

Education's Projection of Education Statistics to 2022, while the total number of high school graduates increased 27 percent between 1998 and 2010, it is projected to decrease 2 percent between 2010 and 2023.[4] Graduates of private high schools, often the most coveted by private universities, are projected to decrease 29 percent between 2010 and 2023. At the same time, the number of postsecondary students who are 25 to 34 years old is projected to increase 20 percent, and students aged 35 and older will increase 23 percent between 2011 and 2022. In other words, more learners today are adults pursuing their education while fully immersed in the family and work aspects of the adult world. For this growing segment of future students, an effective education is defined as one that is affordable, convenient, and closely aligned with their career goals.

Such an education will continue to be needed and pursued, if available and affordable, but there will be many fewer full-time students on college campuses. As well, the forms of delivery to meet the needs of these learners will be driven less by the process of learning and increasingly by the desired learning outcomes as competency assessment becomes more important than time spent in a class or online. This phenomenon is considered in more depth in chapter 10 in this volume.

Partnerships as a Strategic Response

Unless colleges and universities provide *lower-cost* education that serves the needs of the growing part-time adult students as well as full-time traditionally aged students, they risk lower enrollments and financial strains that can lead to closure. A promising response to these pressures is for colleges to diversify the students they serve and how they serve them. I envision the university of the future offering at least four delivery modes: (1) a traditional college campus option, (2) distributed sites offering evening courses to local students, (3) online options available to widely distributed students, and (4) competency-based paths to their degrees. While the tuition and business model will vary with the different educational modes, students will easily navigate across these learning options as they pursue their various educational goals over time. The college or university—through consolidated administrative support, finances, and assets—can allow financial benefits from one delivery mode to support the others.

Some universities have been able to diversify the students they serve and how they serve them by expanding or creating alternative delivery modes for academic programs, such as online or distance sites, which become strong operations that are parallel to their traditional educational

Four Strategic Partnership Benefits
1. Shared administrative services
2. Multiple, coordinated delivery models
3. Scale-driven cost reductions
4. Broader sources of new capital

offerings. Between 2003 and 2013, for example, Northern Arizona University expanded online enrollments from fewer than 500 students to nearly 4,000 students while the overall university enrollments grew 39 percent.[5] The net revenues from its distance programs, as large as $12 million to $13 million dollars, came back to the general budget of the university, thereby supporting the traditional residential campus in Flagstaff. In addition, NAU built a conference center, hotel, and student housing to expand auxiliary revenues. According to John Haeger, the former NAU president who led this transition, "The university has to maximize its profit centers and reduce its not for profit programs and centers to achieve a balanced budget."[6]

In 2009, Chapman University converted its University College, an entity started in 1958 to deliver adult education to military personnel, into Brandman University, which now serves over 12,000 adult students at more than 25 campuses throughout California and Washington and a virtual campus online.[7] Brandman is a separate, fully accredited university within the Chapman University System, with its own board of regents and consolidated financials with the system.[8] In these two examples, traditional universities expanded existing operations with lower-cost delivery modes in order to better serve adult students and broaden their geographic reach, while assuring the traditional campus and the adult student operations benefit from consolidated financials.

Strategic alliances between two or more institutions can result in an organization that is able to respond to the changing nature of students and develop a stronger financial foundation, especially if the institutions bring different academic programs and yet serve a complementary set of students. In other words, consolidated colleges can reach more and different students, provide a wider set of educational opportunities, be better able to market to a broader geographic region, and share access to capital while benefitting from economies of scale. Four examples in particular stand out as immediate benefits.

1. Shared Administrative Services

The idea of sharing administrative services among colleges is not new. For nearly one hundred years, the Claremont University Consortium has been providing shared services to the Claremont Colleges, a group of closely proximate but independent institutions. The consortium provides a shared library, student health services, campus mail system, financial and human resource offices, telecommunications, risk management, real estate, and physical plant maintenance.[9] With the predominance of online services today, geographic proximity is no longer a constraint for shared administrative services. TCS Educational System, founded in 2009 from the Chicago School of Professional Psychology, has created a network of shared "back-office" resources to colleges and universities that provides expertise in accreditation, marketing, enrollment management, and other shared resources to "ensure sustainability, adaptability, and positive social impact in the rapidly changing environment of education."[10] By 2015, the TCS Education System had grown from one college in one city to five colleges in eleven cities serving nearly 6,500 students.

2. Multiple, Coordinated Delivery Models

National University, founded in 1971, offers a nontraditional university education to serve diverse, lifelong learners at community sites, online, and at residential campus settings. National is now the second-largest private nonprofit institution of higher education in California, educating over 26,000 students, offering 100 undergraduate and graduate degree programs at more than 25 sites as well as 70 degrees offered online. In 2001, the National University System was created to encompass not only National University but also six other affiliated colleges and five related entities, and educates students in California, Florida, Nevada, and Virginia.[11]

3. Scale-Driven Cost Reductions

In 2011, Chancellor Hank M. Huckaby of the University System of Georgia announced an initiative to review the potential for consolidation to "assess if any campus consolidations would further the USG's teaching, research and service missions in a more fiscally prudent way."[12] Thus far, Georgia has merged a dozen institutions into six. One of these mergers is hailed as a higher education success story. According to *Diverse: Issues in Higher Education*, the consolidation of Southern Polytechnic State

University into Kennesaw State University was a success thanks to the visionary leadership of President Daniel S. Papp, who stated, "whatever angst existed, we were able to overcome, and we convinced people that this was right from day one."[13] He engaged people from both universities as part of eighty-one operational working groups to examine everything from the vision and mission statements of the universities, to academic and degree programs, to diversity and inclusion activities.

4. Broader Sources of New Capital

In February 2015, Alliant International University President Geoff Cox announced that the not-for-profit university was converting to a benefit corporation and would become the first university to be part of Arist Educational System, a for-profit system focused on providing health and human sciences education.[14] According to Cox, "Transitioning to a benefit corporation structure enabled the university to attract capital investments to enhance their program offerings, technology, student services and student outcomes. More importantly, by becoming a benefit corporation, Alliant reaffirmed its educational mission and gained access to resources that enable us to achieve it."[15] A similar shift of a not-for-profit to for-profit status occurred in 2004 when Grand Canyon University, founded in 1949 by the Southern Baptist Church and struggling to maintain the scope and quality of its academic experience in the face of reduced financial resources, was acquired by Significant Education LLC. The president at the time the board made that decision, Gil Stafford, said the conversion to for-profit status was "a new, creative and innovative way to . . . ensure the future for the university" that had been put at risk by lack of adequate attention to the university's business.[16] GCU now offers a wide variety of flexible and accelerated programs to serve both working adults who are interested in earning a college degree and traditional programs for students interested in a full campus experience.

What is the greatest challenge for a president now starting to develop a partnership or affiliation?

For presidents, the road ahead is clear: we will need to change the basic structures of higher education, and many of these changes will be difficult for our campus communities to accomplish. But it will be critical to adjust to changing expectations without abandoning the traditional higher education residential model.

Strategies and Results from a Parallel Industry

Colleges and universities are undergoing pressures for change that are similar to those faced by another sector dedicated to serving the needs of people: the healthcare industry. One of the responses to those pressures by the industry was the consolidation of independent hospitals into networks of health providers.

In the last thirty years, costs for healthcare went from an 8 percent share of US gross domestic product to an 18 percent share, while for-profit entities displaced nonprofits as the main providers of the healthcare services.[17] In the view of many college and university presidents, the conditions that made healthcare ripe for disruption are strikingly similar to those that exist in higher education today: the perceived value of healthcare service was declining; costs were growing rapidly, leaving healthcare inaccessible to many; the government, which had considerable healthcare expenditures, was pushing back; and healthcare providers were low on convenience to consumers.

The reaction of hospitals to these pressures has been to partner and consolidate, thereby expanding geographic reach and ability to provide specialized care, and creating a network of feeder systems and benefits from economies of scale—all results that many higher education administrators and trustees are also seeking. According to Mitch Morris, vice chairman and national health care provider lead at Deloitte LLP, that industry went through significant mergers in the 1990s.[18] Now, in light of the Affordable Care Act, the consolidation of hospitals has been accelerating. Hospital executives say they have little choice but to combine given the coming changes in the industry.[19] According to a report published by Dixon Hughes Goodman, in 2010, 60 percent of hospitals were in health systems and 78 percent of independent hospitals were either exploring possible hospital consolidation transactions or were in the midst of a transaction with another organization.[20] Only 13 percent of hospitals had a strategy to maintain complete independence.

In spite of concerns that healthcare costs would not be reduced as a result of hospital mergers in the 1990s, more recent studies have shown that hospital mergers offer benefits to patients, including improved service offerings, cost reduction, and enhanced competitiveness.[21] Through consolidation, hospitals and other industry players not only improve efficiency by streamlining administration, reducing duplicated care, and eliminating excess capacity, but they can also afford the investments in information technology required to achieve compliance and upgrade facilities to attract high-value consumers.

> *What is the most important piece of advice for presidents beginning to develop a partnership?*
>
> Be candid. Partners benefit from a candid assessment of their strengths and weaknesses upon entering the partnership. Whether as the leader of a small college or a large university, be clear from the outset about what you will bring to the agreement and what you expect your partner to bring to the agreement.

The five models described in the Dixon Hughes Goodman study have direct applicability for many college and university strategic planners:

1. *Affiliation.* Affiliations are the most flexible form of consolidation and can be weak or strong. They can help partners increase footprint, gain economy of scale, or supplement successful set of services. These affiliations do not necessarily cause changes in governance models.

2. *Joint venture.* Joint ventures are flexible agreements focused on a specific area of collaboration to create something that would be difficult to accomplish independently. These have shared governance between partners and include some profit- and risk-sharing.

3. *Joint operating agreements.* Joint operating agreements can be thought of as "virtual mergers" in which assets remain separate but services are coordinated. A new board is created, but each entity also keeps its own board. The merged entities may borrow for capital expenses as one entity.

4. *Merger.* Mergers occur when the decision is made mutually to combine each other's assets and debts and move governance and management into one organization.

5. *Acquisition.* Acquisition is the purchase of one entity by a for-profit institution. The purchased entity may continue to function semi-independently or make transformational changes to match the buying institution.

How Partnership Planning Is Transforming My Institution

When I consider the financial pressures confronting both students and institutions, in this case at my own college, it is clear that the basic structures of the higher education model will need to change going forward, and that many of these changes will be difficult to accomplish in our present circumstances. But many of the innovations highlighted in this chapter, in both education and healthcare, leave me optimistic that we can find ways to adjust to changing expectations without abandoning the traditional higher education residential model. I offer these six observations on the positive impact of partnership planning at my own university and at several colleague institutions:

- The likelihood that we will see a *significant growth* in the consolidation of higher education institutions over the next two decades is high, in my view. Universities will consider the opportunities that can result from previously improbable partnerships, such as affiliations and joint ventures, even mergers, between institutions that may serve different students with different missions and different modalities. Through partnerships, we can bring together complementary assets, business models, and synergies that will ultimately produce mutual institutional growth.

- A consolidation will not mean that the faculty and administration of the university will lose sight of its *ongoing mission*. An important lesson from healthcare changes is captured by Steven Wantz, a senior administrator during decades of change and mergers at his hospitals. He states: "Part of what we had to do . . . was to help staff rediscover their purpose in the midst of trying to facilitate change. We still had to pay attention to cost and revenue, but also remind everyone of our mission."[22]

- There are a *wide variety* of partnership models that can benefit both institutions, from full merger to a much more focused affiliation in which both colleges or universities retain their mission, values, and long-range aspirations while strengthening themselves through an alliance.

- Partners benefit from a *candid assessment* of their present strengths and weaknesses. Even a small college that is preparing to merge with a larger university can shape a more effective agreement if it is clear what the smaller institution brings to the partnership in terms of both academic program strengths and financial assets.

- A partnership should allow the whole to be greater than the sum of the parts. Put differently, the affiliated institutions need to bring *enhanced value* to their students. Are there now lower-cost options for a degree? Can the university serve students from other regions?

Eight Action Steps

1. Be candid
2. Engage the board
3. Allocate time to succeed
4. Create a common vision
5. Find and preserve a cultural fit
6. Perform thorough due diligence
7. Use consultants when and where needed
8. Develop a presidential bond of trust

Future students moving through the affiliated system need easy access to alternative majors and learning modes, interdisciplinary majors, and combined networks for jobs.

- An affiliation can, and should, allow the partners to *reduce costs*. The criticisms of consolidated healthcare systems in the 1990s for not controlling costs should be a lesson to higher education. If a consolidation does not reduce costs through sharing administrative services and economies of scale, then little has been gained for either financially strengthening the participating institutions or for reducing the costs facing students they serve. Cost reductions should remain one of the foremost objectives within partnership agreements.

Conclusion: Eight Action Steps for Presidents and Other Planners

These action steps summarize the key decisions necessary to achieve an affiliation that is both durable and flexible.

1. Be Candid

Understand the business realities at your college or university. Is it sustainable given rising financial pressures? Will the status quo attract and serve future students? It is likely that most presidents already know that their institutions will need to go through significant change in order to be financially sound in an era when the cost of a college degree must be lower.

2. Engage the Board

Develop a strategy with your board that can be enhanced by strategic partnerships. As you chart this future, hold on to the mission and values of your institution, but also recognize that your college or university can achieve its mission in many different ways, without letting go of its values. Help the people in your organization see that, even within a time of change, even with a full merger, you will retain institutional values and purpose.

3. Allocate Time to Succeed

Do not underestimate the hard work, time, and expense required to conceptualize, design, and implement partnership agreement. Many faculty and staff will need to buy in and become engaged. Investing in experienced lawyers, consultants, and project managers, as necessary, is wise.

4. Create a Common Vision

The primary factor for success is making sure leadership from both organizations have common vision followed by adequate buy-in. Key leaders need to believe that the terms of the deal are in the mutual interest for each organization as well as reflect a common vision.

5. Find and Preserve a Cultural Fit

According to Dixon Hughes Goodman, just under half of all terminated potential partnerships of hospitals cited lack of culture fit as the primary reason. Do the potential partners share the same values even if they have different speeds of making decisions or different faculty contractual arrangements? Can colleges and universities with different faculty employment conditions and shared governance systems work together? Can for-profit and nonprofit higher educational institutions partner or combine—do they share a purpose and mission even if they have achieved those ends under different business models?

6. Perform Thorough Due Diligence

Due diligence is critically important at the front end, especially for a merger. There is no recourse after a merger of nonprofit entities, even if the result is buyer's remorse. Once you merge, you have accepted all of the liabilities of the combined institutions, regardless of whether you realized the extent of those liabilities in advance. A thorough due diligence includes reviewing the institution's legal policy and governance framework, personnel, insurance, academic programs, faculty and staff, licensure and accreditation, fiscal profile, contracts, student financial aid, federal and state regulatory compliance, pending litigation and claims, intellectual property, information technology systems and networks, and data security.[23]

7. Use Consultants When and Where Needed

You will need a wise team of internal experts as well as external consultants. In addition to needing the expertise to assess due diligence materials, you will need people with strong organizational skills to coordinate large amounts of data and to keep the institutional community on task. You may also want an external public relations firm to assist with both internal and external communications.

8. Develop a Presidential Bond of Trust

Finally, it will be the two presidents that make the deal happen, or stop it cold. It is open discussions, leader to leader, that will answer key questions: Are we a match? Does this make sense? Do we share a common vision? Effective presidents will also grasp that the best outcome for their own institutions may involve a leadership transition. In these cases, the agreement and its long-term benefits should drive this decision.

Consolidations will be an important part of the spectrum of change and innovation that American higher education will adopt as it responds to changing student needs and expectations. There are many potential partners and forms of strategic alliance, and the best choices will be those that help your institution better serve tomorrow's students while building the financial robustness to support your mission. Most important, even in the midst of the change and financial pressures now challenging us, remain focused on the core purposes that we share whatever the partnership model: to transform the lives of our students and enhance the future of our society.

Notes
1. Stone et al., *Guide to Statistics on Historical Trends in Income Inequality.*
2. Ibid.
3. Woodhouse, "Discounting Grows Again."

4. Hussar and Bailey, *Projections of Education Statistics to 2022.*

5. Northern Arizona University, "Planning and Institutional Research: Enrollment Data," accessed April 9, 2016, https://nau.edu/pair/enrollment-data/.

6. John Haeger, e-mail to author, September 16, 2015.

7. Brandman University, "About," accessed April 9, 2016, https://www.brandman.edu/about.

8. President Jim Doti, discussion with author, April 13, 2015.

9. Claremont Colleges website, accessed April 9, 2016, http://www.claremont.edu/.

10. "Expertise," TCS Education System, accessed April 9, 2016, http://www.tcsedsystem.edu/expertise/.

11. "About National University," National University, accessed April 9, 2016, http://www.nu.edu/OurUniversity/TheUniversity.html.

12. "Serving Our Students, Serving the State," University System of Georgia, modified December 8, 2015, http://www.usg.edu/consolidation.

13. Watson, "Merger Creates Higher Education Success Story."

14. "The History of Alliant International University," Alliant International University, accessed April 9, 2016, http://www.alliant.edu/about-alliant/history.php.

15. Geoff Cox, personal discussion with author, September 16, 2015.

16. Lebetter, "Grand Canyon Univ. Sold."

17. Sussman and Kim, "6 Signs of Disruption."

18. Don McCanne, "Deloitte's Take on Hospital Mergers and Acquisitions," *Physicians for a National Health Program* (blog), November 12, 2013, http://pnhp.org/blog/2013/11/12/deloittes-take-on-hospital-mergers-and-acquisitions/.

19. Creswell and Abelson, "New Laws and Rising Costs Create a Surge of Supersizing Hospitals."

20. Yanci, Wolford, and Young, *What Hospital Executives Should Be Considering in Hospital Mergers and Acquisitions.*

21. Guerin-Calvert and Maki, *Hospital Realignment.*

22. Eckel and Hignite, *Finding the Right Prescription for Higher Education's Ills.*

23. Samels, "Higher Education Mergers, Consolidations, Consortia, and Affiliations."

CHAPTER SIX

"We Never Thought This Way Ten Years Ago":
How Partnerships Are Reshaping Academic
Leadership Expectations

Vita Rabinowitz and James Stellar

Gone forever are the days when colleges and universities could simply—
and effectively—rely on their own work, execute their own missions,
teach their own students, and form strategic alliances only where they
served their own strong core. Today, with relentless demands on institutions to be more cost effective, relevant to workforce needs, and on the
leading edge of research and pedagogy, we need partners.

This chapter is written from the perspective of two senior administrators, one the university systems provost at the City University of New
York (CUNY), and the other the provost at the University at Albany in
the State University of New York (SUNY) system. In our view, student
success and, increasingly, faculty productivity are defined not just by evidence of learning but also by on-time graduation and productive employment or entrance into graduate schools, and these pressures are steadily
converging on academic leaders to build the partnerships, co-ventures,
and strategic alliances for which this chapter is titled.

Traditional Academic Partnerships: How We Used to Do It

Higher education collaboration can come in many forms. On the explicit end of the spectrum are direct contractual arrangements. Colleges
and universities may enter into such formal relationships to offer academic programs that they cannot easily offer on the home campus.
Institutions may also work with outside organizations to develop agreements to support student internship programs. Some institutions have
maintained long-term relationships with companies to provide full-time
paid internships within their cooperative education divisions. Drexel

University, as one example, stated in a recent report that of the 200 engineers graduating in 2013, 58 percent got jobs directly with their co-op employer, and 94 percent said their co-op experience was important to their current job even if it was not with a co-op employer. Statistics for the entire Drexel campus are comparable.[1] International organizations like the World Association of Cooperative Education broker academic-industry partnerships in cooperative education as well as in experiential education more broadly.[2] Our own State of New York mandated in 2014 that all graduates of New York public institutions of higher learning incorporate meaningful experiential learning in their students' undergraduate studies.[3]

Foundations and other agencies may partner with specific universities to produce focused analyses of the educational process. Recent examples include the recent Gallup-Purdue poll on the role of engagement in work and the role of higher education in producing that engagement in college, and the Mellon Foundation grant supporting a public-private digital humanities collaboration between Grinnell College and the University of Iowa.[4] Similarly, national organizations like the Association of American Colleges and Universities (AACU) partner with higher education institutions to promote programs such as High Impact Practice and LEAP (Liberal Education and America's Promise), along with the American Council on Education (ACE), which maintains a successful program of exchanging ACE fellows between universities for one year, often leading to provost and president positions later in careers.

Wherever partnerships develop and regardless of how formal or explicit they are, the pace of their formation has noticeably quickened in recent years, with greater e-interconnectedness, social media, links, and strategic data accessibility. Along with speed of partnership formation, there is also a new depth of engagement from the high-tech start-up sector in data analytics that assess campus activities using apps to promote campus security or track student registration and persistence. Today's higher education institutions have high hopes for technology-based instruction deliveries, from fully online programs to hybrid courses that potentially allow students to lower their costs and shorten their times to degrees. All of these innovations and technological enhancements have helped to create an infrastructure for partnership design generally, and comfortably, within the leadership capabilities of most provosts and deans.

Although we live in a thoroughly interconnected environment, we still do not typically view the internal division of universities into academic departments and divisions as a collection of partnerships, even though many of them work together as partners on many campuses to produce

What is the greatest challenge for the institution's chief academic officer in developing a partnership or strategic alliance?

As new technologies evolve—and the external, financial climate shifts rapidly—chief academic officers need to make among their highest partnership priorities agreements that can potentially cut costs and uncover new revenue streams.

interdisciplinary programs and joint degrees. One of our SUNY institutions, the University at Albany, is pursuing a relationship just short of a merger with Albany Law School that is being described as a *deep affiliation*. In this case, the two institutions are engaging each other to address obvious needs, such as involving Albany Law faculty in the teaching of classes in the prelaw curriculum at the University at Albany and the other way around, in which international recruiters at the University at Albany will help in promoting the Albany Law School's current master of laws program for international students. Beyond these beginnings, the relationship is likely to develop further with the creation of new programs of mutual interest in education and research, starting with an initial area of shared faculty strengths in homeland security.

Partnerships within Our Institutions: How We Do It Now

Moving beyond the more typical forms of partnership discussed above, we now examine the potential in new ways to co-venture within our own institutions and the opportunities and challenges these offer to chief academic officers (CAOs).

CAO to CAO: The CUNY Provosts Council

Once a month during the academic year, the provosts of CUNY's twenty-four institutions gather at the central office for a standard administrative agenda. The CUNY executive vice chancellor and university provost convene the meeting, which includes provosts from across the system's community colleges, comprehensive colleges, and graduate and professional schools. The fifty-member group discusses academic issues of national and more local CUNY interest; however, the specific topics are not the key issues here. Rather, what is important is that this steady contact among provosts leads to numerous productive professional partnerships. We are not aware of another higher education system that features the number and diversity of schools or size of a student body (270,000 degree seekers) that still offers the physical travel capacity to assemble monthly as a whole as well as to meet much more often in smaller groups and clusters.

These relationships among members of the CUNY Academic Council are also programmatically enhanced by an official "buddy system" through which a new provost is assigned a more experienced colleague to guide him or her through the first year.[5] It is further complemented by a less formal system of meetings outside the central office among provosts of similar institutions where best practices, the role of constituent colleges within the larger system, and the challenges and opportunities inherent in the role of provosts can be discussed. For all of the CAOs involved, the buddy system and its associated gatherings stand out as low-cost, highly valued opportunities to begin personal conversations that eventually lead to professional partnerships. CUNY's first reverse transfer initiative was born among provosts from Bronx-area colleges working together to award en route associate degrees to community college students transferring to Lehman College, an initiative that was then instituted in Queens College. In systems that are more geographically distant, the invitation to exchange ideas for collaboration with other provosts may only occur at annual meetings of professional associations or between academic officers of neighboring institutions. Crossing geographic boundaries in our curricula, pedagogy, scholarship, and practice is an imperative for all CAOs, and the CUNY Provosts Council continues to play a critical role in stimulating sustainable partnerships in the state of New York.

The CUNY Service Corps: A National Model for Local Circumstances

The CUNY Service Corps began as a vision of the chancellor after the devastation by Hurricane Sandy in 2012. It was generated on the basis of reports of high student volunteerism to help the hurricane's victims. With the stated purpose to serve New York City, the program also represents a powerful partnership between the university and multiple city service providers. In its first year, 2013–14, some 750 undergraduate students across 8 participating CUNY Colleges worked with more than 90 New York City–area service organizations 12 to 15 hours a week over 2 semesters. Currently, more than 900 students are participating in Service Corps.[6]

From our perspective and the perspectives of various higher education researchers, service-learning programs are viewed as a partnership in the education of students.[7] In a year-end Service Corps conference at which the students presented their experiences, it was clear the program had an impact beyond the volunteer activities, as students had bonded with each other and with their institution. In most cases, this commitment led to clarification of students' academic aspirations and career goals. CUNY is currently studying the impact of participation in the Service Corps on employment after graduation for seniors and on the persistence of returning students. These are success indicators that the university could not have delivered without the partnership with the service providers. Of course, these service providers also benefited, and that is why an overwhelming number of them signed up again for the second year of the program.

Facilities and Real Estate: Partnerships about the Bottom Line

Informal collaborations among researchers at Hunter College and Weill Cornell Medical College led to a series of progressively more formal partnerships that culminated in an eventual joint real estate transaction that co-located scientists from Hunter and WCMC in a purpose-built research facility.[8] Collaborations among individual scientists from the two institutions had regularly occurred, but the relationship was set on a new course when WCMC invited Hunter to join its application to become a clinical translational science center sponsored by the National Institutes of Health (NIH).[9] The translational science center initiative launched by the NIH in the mid-2000s required multi-institutional collaborations and explicitly encouraged public-private partnerships. WCMC, without its own nursing school, was particularly interested in partnering with Hunter's School of Nursing at the same time Hunter was seeking new professional development opportunities for its nursing faculty and also its biologists, chemists, physicists, and faculty in various health professions. The WCMC-led consortium, which also included Memorial Sloan Kettering Cancer Center and the Hospital for Special Surgery, was funded by the NIH for $47 million, and created the conditions for new and deeper research and programmatic opportunities for scientists and practitioners.[10] The partnership intensified on all levels, bringing Hunter's president and WCMC's dean in close collaboration on matters extending from research to curricula to community service and, ultimately, to an innovative real estate agreement through which Hunter purchased a floor of WCMC's new facility, the Belfer Research Building. WCMC's dean at that time, Anthony Gatto, called the Hunter-WCMC deal "more than a real estate transaction—a real partnership."[11] As of 2015, twelve Hunter scientists are conducting research alongside their

WCMC colleagues in a co-venture that leverages the strengths of both institutions.

CUNY's ASAP: New Degree Pathways for Timely Graduation

In 2007, the New York City Office of the Mayor in New York City invited proposals to improve the economic prospects of low-income New Yorkers. CUNY responded by developing a structured degree pathway, ASAP,[12] aimed at increasing the timely graduation rate of its community college students. Seven of CUNY's community colleges partnered in the ASAP initiative to provide comprehensive, coordinated services, including academic advising, financial resources, and block scheduling to facilitate full-time attendance and enhanced student engagement. CUNY also worked with the Robin Hood Foundation and the Stella and Charles Guttman Foundation, among others, to start this program.

ASAP incorporates multiple high-impact practices into a structured student experience with the key elements of full-time attendance, waiving of tuition and fees, complimentary New York Transit MetroCards, free use of textbooks, and opportunities for no-cost winter and summer courses. All incoming students attend a summer institute and sign a contract acknowledging their understanding of the program's requirements and expectations. During their first year, students participate in the ASAP Seminar, a two-semester, noncredit group advisement experience that addresses time management, communication, and other student success skills. Building on the intensive advising at the core of ASAP, each student is assigned a mentor who offers close guidance from date of entry to graduation. All ASAP students also receive support from a career and employment specialist who addresses immediate employment needs and helps students develop their long-term career goals.

Randomized studies have shown dramatic improvement in retention and graduation rates. ASAP students' three-year graduation rates are about three times as high as the national average of 16 percent for similar students. In the spring of 2015, the mayor of New York vowed to increase ASAP program from its enrollment of 4,000 CUNY students to 25,000 students over a three-year period. The mayor then allocated $77 million to finance this expansion. These results have also attracted the attention of educators and policy makers in the administration of Barack Obama, who mentioned ASAP in one of his State of the Union addresses. New partners have joined ASAP, including the Leona M. and Harry B. Helmsley Charitable Trust, the Jewish Foundation for the Education of Women, and the Sidney and Laura Gilbert Scholarship Fund, and CUNY

Seven Things We Wish We Had Known

1. Build and base things on trust
2. Define and agree on shared returns on investment
3. Partner only for as long as it is useful
4. Use existing resources as much as possible
5. Think ahead about funding
6. Build broadly to accommodate leadership change
7. Assess regularly and candidly

leaders are seeing the ASAP model and structure being considered for implementation in several other states.

Partnership Advice for Provosts: Seven Things We Wish We Had Known Ten Years Ago
1. Build and Base Things on Trust

The first principle is the development of trust that depends not only on shared mission and the perception of mutually beneficial outcomes but also on taking the time to pick partners strategically and getting to know them well enough that trust can develop. A common mistake in new partnerships is to let a shared initial enthusiasm obscure the need for partners to carefully define their interests, identify potential differences, propose responses, and, in this process, to become familiar with the new partner's work culture and ways of achieving goals. That way, when conflicts arise, as they inevitably will, members are invested enough in the work and are trusting enough to challenge and engage each other.[13] Well-established findings in the field of group dynamics point to the particular importance of positive nonverbal communication between members of the partner groups. It is therefore important to take time and let the parties develop a sense of team before rushing forward.

2. Define and Agree on Shared Returns on Investment

Partnerships endure only when there is a clearly defined common mission and clearly defined returns on investment (ROIs) for both parties. Over the course of the partnership, more opportunities may be uncovered to do additional joint projects or to do what was formerly planned in a better way. This form of "mission creep" is good so long as it does not divert resources from the original mission or delay its ongoing outcomes.

3. Partner Only for as Long as It Is Useful

Some partnerships, particularly those that involve property and elements of a contractual merger, may last virtually forever. Others may dissipate as national or local conditions change and factors that supported the original plan, such as leadership changes or funding allocations, shift. This is natural, and holding on to partnerships too long can be unwise in a rapidly changing market place.

4. Use Existing Resources as Much as Possible

It is hard to attract quality partners or form a successful partnership when you do not have the credibility, experience, or resources to deliver for the partnership. Successful partnerships combine complementary assets with their ambitions tailored to the resources they bring to bear. Louis Soares recounts how Columbia Gorge Community College partnered with representatives from several local and national companies and the US Army Corps of Engineers, building on its existing curriculum and data systems, to create new interdisciplinary programs for a number of energy-generation fields, thus making its graduates more employable across the region's workforce.[14]

5. Think Ahead about Funding

The partnership must soon, if not immediately, generate a revenue stream or save on an expense so that a potentially charismatic beginning can be later supported through multiple budget cycles. In our experience, the ending of grant periods or original budget commitments is a common cause of partnership failure.

6. Build Broadly to Accommodate Leadership Change

Often a partnership is born from the passion of two people with a galvanizing idea and the authority to mobilize resources, and without building a larger base of adopters. Such partnerships may falter or fail when leadership teams change. To avoid failure, a number of key decision makers will need to understand the mutual ROI, be actively involved in its implementation, and come to own the core ideas involved. Nancy Thomas's study of transformational partnerships suggests that partnerships

*What is the most important piece of advice you would offer
a chief academic officer now developing a partnership?*

Look inward. Do not hesitate to move beyond typical forms of partnership, even those discussed in this chapter, or to consider the potential in new ways to co-venture within your own institution. Crossing geographic boundaries can be useful, but sometimes the most sustainable partnerships are built among colleagues on your own campus.

that achieve true change must last at least seven to ten years.[15] Institutionalizing the affiliation at multiple levels, celebrating it publicly and on a regular basis, and distributing the credit for its accomplishments make it less likely that the partnership will fail when its leaders change.

7. Assess Regularly and Candidly

Regular assessment of institutional effectiveness and student outcomes is now part of the fabric of higher education, and both formative and summative assessment activities are especially important in partnerships. We have learned that it is incorrect to assume that a detailed, ongoing assessment plan has been built into the ROI calculation so that both sides can see whether the partnership is on target to meet its goals, but too often it is not. Having clear formative and summative assessment plans not only makes it more likely that the partnership will continue to accomplish its goals, but it also compels regular communication among partnership planners that can focus directly on improvements.

Conclusion: Partner or Perish

Presidents and provosts learn quickly, sometimes harshly, that as technology evolves and financial climates shift, the world of higher education is changing dramatically. Tuition and fees are rising and public funding for higher education is decreasing, as academic leaders search for ways to cut costs and uncover new revenue streams. A recent report by the Economist Intelligence Unit, on behalf of Academic Partnerships, presents the results of a survey of more than 300 higher education practitioners from around the world to identify the strategies that institutions are taking to remain viable and relevant in this new climate.[16] Partnerships with industry, governments, foundations, philanthropists, and other institutions of higher education were are at the heart of the four main strategies that respondents believed to be vital to their futures: crossing geographical boundaries and achieving global visibility, cutting costs and finding new sources of revenue, delivering technology-based instruction, and increasing professional and technical preparation.

Achieving these ambitious and challenging goals will require new ways of operating and an openness to partnering within and beyond professional and geographic borders. Many chief executive and chief academic officers are coming to realize that their natural tendencies to compete with counterparts at other institutions need to be redirected. CUNY's College of Staten Island, for example, recently formed a historic partnership with two other colleges on Staten Island to raise comparatively low college completion rates throughout that borough.[17] Our real competition is not the sister school in our system but perhaps a for-profit institution that offers alternative models to earn degrees and credentials.

Public university systems have particular opportunities to collaborate with each other and, in the process, become larger than the sum of their parts. Provosts and deans need to encourage and incentivize such partnerships, and to communicate that any perceived costs associated with "giving something up" are far outweighed by the long-term advantages of co-venturing. Beyond our campuses, partnering with industry carries particular challenges because of the fundamental differences in mission, goals, and modes of operation. Forming partnerships with private companies may impinge on cherished values such as academic freedom and shared governance, yet partnerships are often formed for two reasons—mutual benefit and need—and the most effective, long-lasting ones address and overcome this type of concern while fostering interdependence and mutual respect.

In closing, it is our view that presidents and provosts will be known by their partners. Thus it is vital to choose those partners for their quality, integrity, and commitment. We would cite the close relationships among President Jennifer Raab of Hunter College and Deans Anthony Gotto and Dean Laurie Glimcher of WCMC, intentionally cultivated and expanded over many years, as critical to the enduring, transformative agreements between those institutions. A review of the literature on partnerships suggests that the most successful ones are among institutions that have a demonstrated history of collaboration internally and externally as well as an infrastructure led by a committed leader who can appreciate differences in institutional cultures while maintaining strong relationships.[18] These are the partners one should actively cultivate.

We end this chapter with a call for a more robust literature on best practices in academic partnerships, such as that provided in this volume.

It is needed and overdue. Academic leaders are entering an era that will spur even more expansive and creative affiliations and co-ventures. As we adapt to stay vital moving forward, we need to know what works well, how, and why, and nowhere is this thinking more important than in the design and support of academic partnerships.[19]

Notes

1. Office of Institutional Research, Assessment and Effectiveness, *2014–2015 Drexel Factbook.*

2. "About," WACE: Advancing Cooperative & Work-Integrated Education, accessed March 26, 2016, http://www.waceinc.org.

3. Article VII, "Education, Labor and Family Assistance Memorandum in Support," New York State Executive Budget, 2015–16, accessed May 4, 2016, https://www.budget.ny.gov/pubs/archive/fy0405archive/fy0405articleVIIbills/elfa _memo.html.

4. Ray and Kafka, "Life in College Matters for Life after College"; Straumsheim, "Grinnell College and the University of Iowa Announce a Digital Humanities Partnership."

5. The two authors of this chapter met at Provost's Council when J.S. arrived at CUNY in 2009 and V.R. was already a longtime member and was assigned to be his "buddy."

6. "CUNY Service Corps," City University of New York, accessed March 26, 2016, http://www1.cuny.edu/sites/servicecorps/.

7. Birge, Beaird, and Torres, "Partnerships among Colleges and Universities for Service Learning."

8. "Hunter College and Weill Cornell Medical College Join Forces" to Advance Bench-to-Bedside Medical Discoveries," Weill Cornell Medical College, October 24, 2013, http://weill.cornell.edu/news/pr/2013/10/hunter-college-and-weill-cornell -medical-college-join-forces-to-advance-bench-to-bedside-medical-dis.html.

9. The invitation from Weill Cornell Medical College to Hunter College was extended in 2006.

10. "Weill Cornell Received $49.6 Million NIH Renewal Grant Award for Its Clinical and Translational Science Center," Weill Cornell Medical College, August 1, 2012, http://weill.cornell.edu/news/pr/2012/08/weill-cornell-receives-496-million -nih-renewal-grant-award-for-its-clinical-and-translational-scienc.html.

11. President Raab and Provost Rabinowitz, "Invitation to a Breakfast Meeting at the WCMC's Belfer Research Building," e-mail to WCMC faculty, January 31, 2014, https://mailcaster.hunter.cuny.edu/archive/communications/special -distribution-messages/2014-0131-152606.159.

12. ASAP: Accelerated Study in Associate Programs website, accessed March 26, 2016, http://www1.cuny.edu/sites/asap/.

13. Cauley, "Principle 1," 13–17.

14. Soares, *Community College and Industry Partnerships.*

15. Thomas, *An Examination of Multi-Institutional Networks.*

16. Economist Intelligence Unit, *Higher Education in the 21st Century.*

17. Regan, "Program Aims to Boost the Borough's Brain Power."

18. Birge, Beaird, and Torres, "Partnerships among Colleges and Universities for Service Learning."

19. We acknowledge the enormous pressure that all of higher education faces currently from society and government to deliver student success at an affordable price as reflected in a series of recent books. See, for example, Crow and Dabars, *Designing the American University*, and Cary, *End of College*.

CHAPTER SEVEN

Why, and How, Elite Colleges and Universities Are Joining Forces

J. Matthew Hartley and Alan Ruby

The University of Pennsylvania is the oldest institution in America to hold the designation of university in the United States, and the pragmatism and civic mindedness of its founder, Benjamin Franklin, are woven into its organizational DNA. While highly selective, it remains an institution dedicated to pragmatically partnering with others to address pressing social, economic, and educational issues. Penn faculty and students engage in these activities not simply because they are meritorious, but because they are the best means to achieve action and progressive change. In this sense, co-ventures and strategic alliances are integral to Penn's ability to fulfill its promise as a research university.

This chapter provides several examples of Penn as a partner in fulfilling its core work as a university. These alliances involved the development of joint academic programs to leverage the strengths of each participant and also outreaches to the city of Philadelphia and community partners in the development of collaborative research projects that would not have been possible otherwise.

Leveraging Strengths through Curricular Joint Ventures

One of the most common forms of partnership at universities are curricular joint ventures (CJVs) in which two or more institutions collaborate to develop an academic venture neither partner could launch on its own.[1] As one recent example, the Wharton School of Business and the Johns Hopkins School of Advanced International Studies (SAIS) have created a dual-degree program that prepares students interested in international business or in careers involving international trade and foreign policy. Applicants spend their first year at Wharton, second year

90

Elite Liberal Arts Colleges and Native American Engagement: Building Bridges to Communities—Wabanaki, Bates, Bowdoin, and Colby

JANICE ARMO KASSMAN

In 2007, the presidents of Bates, Bowdoin, and Colby Colleges in Maine met with four Native American chiefs from the Wabanaki tribes in Maine—Maliseet, Micmac, Passamaquoddy, and Penobscot—to forge a union among the colleges and the tribes.

Principal Goals

The goals of this union were to link both cohorts by encouraging more Native American youth to consider higher education at the premier liberal arts colleges in the state, and for the campus communities to become more aware of the long history and rich tradition of the Wabanaki people.

Initial Projects

- *Early college awareness.* Visits to middle school students in northern and eastern Maine promoted college awareness among Wabanaki youth during the spring breaks of the Bates, Bowdoin, and Colby students. These visits were designed by the college students and featured interactive games, photos of campus life, and a sampling of academic programs. One college team highlighted the experiences of studying abroad in countries from South Africa to Australia; another group showcased the ways one can view and appreciate works of art, featured in the college museum; and another engaged the native youth through interactive scientific experiments.
- *Summer aspirations program.* In this program, Maine Indian high school students and their counselors made visits to the three college campuses. These visits featured an overnight stay, a day of campus tours, and work-shops on the application process, academic offerings, campus activities, and college life. Staff from each college in admissions and student affairs, along with faculty from various academic departments, were key constituents in delivering these programs.
- *Academic and campus climate enhancement.* Enhancement efforts on each campus sought to improve the campus climate to support native cultural and academic activities and increase awareness and understanding of Wabanaki history and contemporary issues in the college communities. The colleges joined forces and received a Mellon Foundation grant to support programs

(*continued*)

on sovereignty with regard to environmental issues and water rights, Wabanaki voices in history, and the role of basket making in Wabanaki culture.

Janice Armo Kassman worked at Colby as dean of students for twenty-five
years and was named the college's first vice president of student affairs. She also
served as special assistant to the president for external affairs, and it was in this
capacity that she led this program for Colby. She is currently the principal of
Kassman Consulting.

at SAIS, and a semester in their third year at each institution. Wharton
has a similar dual-degree program with Harvard's Kennedy School of
Government that serves students interested in the intersections of business and public policy. These programs benefit students by exposing
them to a larger body of faculty scholars from both institutions and by
providing a wider array of courses and internships than would be available if they were enrolled at a single institution.[2]

Thinking Globally: Penn and Nazarbayev University, Kazakhstan

Another example of partnership design at Penn involves an international collaboration among faculty members from the Alliance for
Higher Education and Democracy (AHEAD) at Penn's Graduate School
of Education (GSE). AHEAD is a center whose efforts focus on advancing the public purposes of higher education. In 2009, a group of curriculum planners began working with higher education colleagues in
Kazakhstan tasked with establishing that nation's first research university. Land locked but resource rich, Kazakhstan (along with Siberia)
served as a place of internal exile during the Soviet period. Its system of
higher education during that period and after the nation declared its
independence in 1991 has remained highly centralized, with a ministry
dictating not only broad policies but also curricular and personnel decisions. Recent governmental reforms have been pushing for greater institutional autonomy. The new university, named Nazarbayev University
(NU) after the nation's first president, is intended to serve as a model
for institutional autonomy, shared governance, and academic freedom.

The initial partnership, coordinated by the authors of this chapter and
one other colleague, focused on capacity building and providing advice
on structuring the university based on models of shared governance and
institutional autonomy in other countries. The positive response to this

early work led our partners to seek a broader engagement. Initially, this came in the form of a request for us to create and run a school of education for the new university. Believing the approach was not likely to produce long-term success, we proposed the establishment of an education policy center that would support a core group of researchers examining educational policies and processes, and serve as a nucleus for a graduate school of education.

Before becoming involved in a region where Penn GSE had little experience, we completed a due diligence process that allowed us to assess the demand for education policy services, the extent and quality of existing services, the shape and direction of the nation's higher education system, and the enabling environment. We visited public and private universities in several cities and met with representatives of the United Nations Children's Emergency Fund (UNICEF) and the World Bank as well as bilateral agencies like the British Council. Representatives of major employers and industries and advocacy groups like the Open Society Institute also offered useful perspectives on the current and future priorities for education and training in Kazakhstan. As well, Penn's Office of Global Affairs provided valuable insights regarding health and safety concerns for expatriate employees, the stability of the currency and communication systems, transport infrastructure sophistication, and the strength of the "rule of law." It also made an assessment of the reputational and operational risks involved in developing a closer relationship with the emerging university.

Another partnership factor was to establish a set of principles for engagement so that our partners understood Penn's framing perspectives. First, it was key to build local capacity. Although all partners are important, our colleagues at NU are the principal partners when it comes to the future of their institution. Our aim was to increase the knowledge, skills, and analytical capabilities of the professionals in Kazakhstan. Second, Penn's work in the region should be of mutual benefit. Just as we hoped Kazakhstan would benefit from increased capacity and effectiveness, we also were involved because we wanted Penn to enhance its understanding and grasp of institutional reform and human development in new nations. Third, we believe that, in addition to teaching and service, a partnership involving faculty from a research university like Penn must be actively engaged in rigorous research and systematic inquiry into the fundamental issues in the field. The research should be developed, designed, and conducted collaboratively, engaging emerging scholars in research agendas, resource allocation, project design and analysis, standard setting, peer review, and eventual dissemination and publication. Finally, the researchers involved must adhere to the highest ethical standards, such as those of the British and American Education

> ## What is the greatest challenge to developing a successful partnership between higher education institutions?
>
> Periodically take stock of the original agreement. Effective alliances and partnerships grow, evolve, and change, so it is key to assess their effectiveness on a regular schedule and make changes when and where necessary.

Research Associations, and share the knowledge that is generated publicly through peer-reviewed journals.

This early work led to the signing in September 2010 of a formal contract between Penn and NU's Centre for Educational Policy, a private not-for-profit entity established under the laws of Kazakhstan and housed and operating within the now-open university. The center became operational relatively quickly. Shortly thereafter arose a renewed interest from the national government to create the previously mentioned Graduate School of Education at Nazarbayev University. The leadership at NU thus established a three-way partnership among NU, the University of Cambridge, and Penn GSE's Higher Education Division. The partners developed a master's curriculum that could be launched within a year. The values statement previously originated by Penn became an important touchstone for the later, broader strategic alliance. The partners framed a statement of principle informing the work of Cambridge and Penn faculty members as they worked together to establish Nazarbayev University's Graduate School of Education:

> The Graduate Schools of Education at Cambridge University and the University of Pennsylvania will support Nazarbayev University to establish a Graduate School of Education that prepares graduates for careers in the nation, the region and globally as researchers, scholars, policy advisors and educational leaders. Our shared aim is to have a first class school operating at full capacity and internationally recognized by 2020 and to support the school through an ongoing partnership that promotes high quality research, fosters excellent teaching and learning and maintains the integrity of student assessment and personnel practices.[3]

A partnership contract specifying the roles of the various parties was signed in 2012. Initial activities concentrated on recruiting a dean and faculty, and designing the first master's degree programs. Over time, attention has turned to providing an independent check on admissions standards in the master's programs conducting joint quality-assurance visits by faculty

RECIPROCITY & MUTUAL BENEFIT

COLLEGIALITY & COMPLEMENTARY SCHOLARSHIP

FORMAL AGREEMENT & BRANDING OPPORTUNITIES

STRATEGIC & TRANSACTIONAL OBJECTIVES

SHARED SERVICE & MISSION

Stages of successful partnership development.

from both universities. The relationship has changed in intensity as the size of the faculty has increased and the programs and policies of the new school and the wider university have developed and stabilized. Penn still participates in faculty selection processes and in moderating assessments and monitoring the admissions processes, however.

While there have been successes, the relationship has not always been smooth. For example, learning that all "deliverables" need to be formally documented seems trivial but reflects a major cultural shift. More significant have been the challenges in accommodating a fundamentally different budget process and time line that is not governed by either a US or a UK academic calendar and is driven by oil and commodity prices. Still, what have defined this partnership are the ongoing opportunities for mutual learning and growth. Working with experienced professionals from different national and cultural contexts has enabled the Penn partnership team to answer questions about international higher education systems, including:

- What is the proper balance between central oversight and control and institutional autonomy and innovation?

- How does the institution create appropriate systems of oversight, such as the establishment of boards of trustees, for institutions not used to deliberative governance processes?

- How does the institution create environments that invite faculty creativity and innovation?

- What constitutes an effective and appropriate relationship between universities and companies who employ their graduates?

- What are the characteristics of a graduate school of education that prepares students for the jobs of today and leadership in the future?

Partnering Elite Institutions: An Interview with Kristine Dillon, President of the Consortium on Financing Higher Education

Founded in the mid-1970s, the Consortium on Financing Higher Education (COFHE) is an "unincorporated, voluntary, institutionally-supported group of 35 highly selective, private liberal arts colleges and universities, all of which are committed to meeting the demonstrated financial need of admitted students." With members including Amherst, Harvard, Johns Hopkins, Pomona, Princeton, and Stanford, COFHE epitomizes the reasons why it is wise for even elite institutions to form alliances and partnerships in the current marketplace. COFHE publishes reports on undergraduate admissions and financial aid, and its staff members collect and disseminate data useful to members on issues such as access, affordability, and assessment.[1]

Beyond annual data collection, however, over the past thirty years the consortium has also, in its own words, "crafted a suite of surveys that allows for a systematic and robust examination of the undergraduate experience."[2] Housed on the campus of the Massachusetts Institute of Technology in Cambridge and led for more than a decade by Kristine Dillon, COFHE represents a stylish model of leveraging collective strengths and brands that its leader believes can be utilized by many colleague institutions. In Dillon's words, "Working collaboratively as a group of schools—whether the group shares geographic or economic or philosophical proximities—can yield significant benefits. Such clusters of schools often find that the challenge of identifying common definitions leads in itself to better internal understanding of topics but the comparative results gained from the collaboration greatly enhance management information. For even well-resourced, selective institutions, being distinctive educationally does not mean that cost savings, best practices in delivery of services, and strengthening academic programs lack value. For such schools, a focus on improvement is part of the excellent reputations they seek to maintain."[3]

In her view, the most important piece of advice she would share with leaders of institutions now considering a partnership is to "set reasonable priorities for what the collaboration can achieve in the short-term. All participants will need to see some value in the results of collaboration in order to bring enthusiasm to future projects. Endorsement and involvement by the senior leadership team and periodic reinforcement of the value of the collaborative project will be critical."[4]

Dillon also cautions that the road to durable, trusting partnerships is sometimes an uphill climb. When asked about the largest challenge leaders will face, Dillon responded simply, "Sharing sensitive information is difficult in a world that has complex legal realities and constant media attention. Finding trustworthy partners for collaborative ventures is easier than overcoming the natural worries about confidentiality breaches. The results of collaboration are very worthwhile but the reluctance to begin the collaboration due to the many perceived obstacles and effort involved is natural and must be acknowledged if the effort is to be successful."[5]

1. "About COFHE," Consortium on Financing Higher Education, http://web.mit.edu/cofhe/assessment/statement/index_files/Page353.htm.
2. "What Is COFHE," Consortium on Financing Higher Education document sent to James Martin by Kristine Dillon, November 2015.
3. Kristine Dillon, e-mail to James Martin, December 12, 2015.
4. Ibid.
5. Ibid.

The partnership has not been a technocratic exercise of bringing the expertise of faculty from the West to aid Kazakhstan. Rather, it has been a continuing, reciprocal collaboration. A notable outcome has been realized in scholarly production. Numerous journal articles have come from joint work between Penn and NU researchers, and more are in development or under review as the presence of the graduate school in international forums has escalated.[4]

For Penn faculty, the most striking benefit has been the intellectual stimulus of engaging recurring issues like affordability of higher education and institutional governance in a fundamentally different context. The contours and norms of a post-Soviet state that is grappling with market principles and defining a national identity demand a fresh interpretation of topics and themes that seemed fully explored in a Western democracy. There is also the benefit of demonstrating governance practices that we have long taken for granted, such as voluntary boards of trustees for a new local environment. Equally stimulating are the opportunities to observe and reflect on institutional practices that were shaped by a very different political, social, and economic history. These differences have sparked questions about why things were done in particular ways and what benefits and costs were realized and incurred, in turn encouraging cross-national comparisons as well as new lines of inquiry and research.

Thinking Locally: Penn and Its West Philadelphia Community

Two decades ago, Penn's relationship with West Philadelphia was troubled. During an urban revitalization effort in the 1950s and 1960s, the university purchased surrounding residential areas by eminent domain. The action displaced hundreds of families and provided a focal point for lingering community resentment toward the university.[5] Philadelphia, like many other cities, experienced significant economic decline during the 1960s and 1970s.

In an effort to build closer ties with West Philadelphia, in 1992 President Sheldon Hackney founded the Center for Community Partnerships. CCP was designed as the university-wide structure for engaging and coordinating students and faculty, as well as other institutional resources, with West Philadelphia. Having the term "partnerships" in the center's name conveyed Penn's recognition of its interdependence as one institutional citizen among many working to improve civic life in West Philadelphia. CCP established a community advisory board, which has proved a key mechanism for building collaborative partnership work. A center wholly dedicated to community partnerships and co-ventures reflected a presidential commitment to working more closely with its neighbors. CCP was a public affirmation that Penn's future and the future of West Philadelphia—and the city at large—were intertwined. At the same time, the effort was born out of a sense of enlightened self-interest and a recognition by the university that engaging in real-world problem solving is one of the best means for Penn to fulfill its overall mission of advancing and transmitting knowledge.

Since renamed the Netter Center for Community Partnerships, CCP plays an active role in promoting community development. The centerpiece of this work has been Academically Based Community Service. ABCS is a service rooted in and intrinsically connected to teaching, research, and learning. It was important to Penn's leadership to encompass both service-learning and problem-based research in light of Penn's role as a research university. ABCS courses focus on action-oriented community problem solving and the integration of research, teaching, learning, and service related to issues of poverty, racism, and crime. The organization's four objectives are as follows:

1. Improve the quality of life in the community and the quality of learning and scholarship in the university through collaborative problem solving in K–20 education.

What is the most important piece of advice you would offer to a leader developing a higher education partnership this year?

Always be clear about the larger purpose your institution is planning to accomplish by joining forces.

2. Foster structural community improvement (e.g., effective public schools, neighborhood economic development).

3. Emphasize student and faculty reflection on the service experience.

4. Help students to become active, creative, contributing citizens of a democratic society.[6]

To date, over 200 such courses that work with schools and community organizations to solve strategic community problems have been developed at Penn. In the 2014–15 academic year, 63 ABCS courses—across 8 schools and 26 departments involving 1,600 Penn undergraduate and graduate students—were offered. All of these courses challenge the university's students to become active learners, creative real-world problem solvers, and producers, rather than passive consumers, of knowledge.

A good example of the benefits of deep partnering include the work of Francis Johnston, a renowned expert on nutritional anthropology who served for many years as Penn's chair of the Anthropology Department. In 1992, Professor Johnston decided to redesign a course, Anthropology 210, to address the local, community-identified problem of poor nutrition, in collaboration with the leaders at Turner Middle School. This course became the prototype for ABCS courses. Over the next few years, a widening circle of Penn faculty and students worked with Johnston in collaboration with local middle school teachers and students to understand nutritional practices in the community. The course addressed this problem through a series of projects aimed at encouraging better nutrition, including a school-based garden, an in-school market offering healthy snacks, and a nutritional outreach program for community members. Anthropology 210's success not only influenced the Anthropology Department, which went on to develop an academic track on public interest anthropology, but it also inspired other Penn departments and schools to become involved in the community.[7] Furthermore, it led to the development of the Agatston Urban Nutrition Initiative, which engages and empowers youth, university students, and community members to promote healthy lifestyles and build a just and sustainable food system. Today, the Agatston Urban Nutrition Initiative works with twenty Philadelphia public schools and serves more than ten thousand students monthly.[8]

When colleges and universities give a high priority to co-venturing with their local communities, a much greater likelihood exists that they will significantly advance research, teaching, learning, service, and interdisciplinary collaboration, and simultaneously reduce what Benjamin Franklin in 1789 called the "ancient Customs and Habitudes" of the academy that

A Catholic-Corporate Connection: Emmanuel College and Merck Research Laboratories—an Interview with Sister Anne Donovan, Emmanuel Vice President of Finance and Treasurer

Emmanuel is a relatively small Catholic liberal arts college in downtown Boston. As the *New York Times* reported at the time of the agreement in 2003, the college was "cash-poor but land-rich," with seventeen prime acres located not much more than a long foul ball from home plate in Fenway Park. Like many other small, tuition-dependent, religiously affiliated institutions in the Northeast, however, Emmanuel was suffering in the competitive recruitment game each fall, so it decided to develop an innovative partnership with a major corporation and thereby use some of its land as an endowment growth strategy.

In fact, as Sister Anne Donovan, Emmanuel's chief financial officer then and now, explains, although Merck Research Laboratories, the college's eventual partner, sought ten acres, Emmanuel leased them between three and four acres from what it called its "endowment campus." Fearing that any agreement might lead to research activities right next door that would be antithetical to the tenets of the Catholic Church, the final agreement had to include what Sister Anne described as "a Catholic clause," by which Merck would be barred from conducting research using stem cells from "electively aborted fetuses."

The partnership agreement took 2 years to negotiate and, as a result, Merck received a lease for 75 years and constructed a 12-story building with 300,000 square feet of space, and Emmanuel received an increase in its endowment from $7 million to $49 million. At the time of implementation, Emmanuel's president, Sister Janet Eisner, assessed the college's situation as "We're still poor, but we're not quite as poor."

Interviewed by James Martin in December 2015, and asked what leadership lessons might be drawn from their partnership with an international, for-profit, research corporation, Sister Anne offered two that were present initially and have characterized the alliance for over a decade: "Develop and work from mutual respect," and "be honest as the day is long."

During the span of the partnership, Merck has changed leadership teams at least three times, and Sister Anne said that the agreement between the "pharmaceutical giant and a small Catholic women's college" has proceeded "without a flaw." Emmanuel, now a co-ed institution, receives internship and employment opportunities for its students and equipment and research expertise from Merck, and the corporation receives college library and gymnasium access along with critical acreage only a few feet away from several of the nation's most famous teaching hospitals. The city of Boston, for its part, was convinced by Merck's pledge to provide several hundred high-paying jobs.

As the chairman of the development company that brought Emmanuel to the table in the first place summed it up, "They were very nice but very shrewd. They made sure that Emmanuel got the best deal."

Resources consulted include: Sister Anne Donovan, telephone interview with James Martin, December 3, 2015; Pristin, "Drug Company Lease Gives Security to a College."

assume it to be a place apart harboring esoteric knowledge, rather than an actor for positive change based on mutually beneficial partnerships.[9]

Conclusion: Six Lessons for Partnership Developers

While Penn's partnership experiences are distinctive, they also offer at least six general lessons for planners:

1. *Know why you are in a partnership.* Effective partnerships endure because they are mutually beneficial, and a core of mutual satisfaction comes from having a clear sense of purpose. What are the expectations of the partners? What shared values or goals draw them together? It is also important to be clear whether one is, at the end of the day, selling services or "spreading the light." Focusing on short-term gain is unlikely to produce an enduring partnership. There must be some larger purpose built on a shared set of ideas and ideals and focused intently on building long-term relationships built on mutual trust.

2. *Due diligence pays off.* Undervalued in the pursuit of a partnership or alliance and in the initial evaluation of its opportunities, due diligence is the systematic inquiry and discovery that evaluates the legal and financial operating environment and the presence or absence of competition. It also identifies risks, especially those that are large and probable. In higher education, due diligence might include determining whether there are political and cultural barriers to a partnership, including regulatory requirements or financial guarantees. It takes time and effort and has a real cost, but it inserts a strong dose of reality into the decision-making process.

3. *Mutuality and interdependence are at the heart of an effective partnership.* There is a prevailing view in higher education that assumes that expertise is found inside universities, yet effective partnerships are built on actively recognizing the essential strengths of

other partners. Sometimes this strength comes in the form of "cultural intuition," that is, a useful understanding of a particular context that enhances understanding. Penn's experience has confirmed that the involvement of partners is often a key to legitimacy. When discussing an issue at another university, in another country, or in the community, the Kazakh proverb rings true: "A crow from your land is better than a hawk from a foreign land." Insiders are often key to communicating important information and findings as well as securing the support of people who are needed to enable the partnership to succeed and endure.

4. *Know what you are expected to deliver and what it should look like.* Different partners may have different ideas or priorities about what the partnership should yield. We have also learned that deliverables are culturally and contextually defined. Knowing in advance how accountability requirements are judged and monitored will avoid later difficulties and potential ill will.

5. *Set out your core values and operating principles and share them with all parties.* Being transparent about what values matter to your college or university and about expectations of how business will be conducted establishes a good basis for an enduring collaboration. We have approached our colleagues at Nazarbayev and Cambridge in this manner. Clearly, belonging to the same broad discipline or industry has helped, but being explicit about our desire to seek mutual benefit through mutual respect and shared endeavor has been the driver.

6. *Know when to say, "We are not good at that."* Mission creep is easy at home; it is even easier ten time zones away, where the strength of institutional oversight is diminished and the desire to be helpful and responsive is high. In Penn's strategic partnerships, we have benefited significantly by saying "No, we are not the right people to do what you are asking." Trying to deliver services or programs that are not core values of your college or university is unwise and prone to either failure or degraded quality.

The discussions outlined in this chapter underscore the significant benefits of partnering for an elite institution. Yet, regardless of their human and financial resources, those resources are finite, and each college or university still has areas of relative strength and weakness. Partnerships and strategic alliances enable others whose missions, capacities, and expertise complement their own and help to achieve goals that would otherwise be impossible. These collaborations are pragmatic ways to fulfill the primary purpose of expanding the bounds of human knowledge through research and by engaging students in work that requires them to apply what they have learned to accomplish societal change.

Notes

1. Eckel and Hartley, "Developing Academic Strategic Alliances"; Dussauge and Garrette, *Cooperative Strategy*; Hamel, "Strategy as Revolution"; Porter, "What Is Strategy?"

2. The benefits of joint collaborations are well documented in the organizational literature. Companies seek out partnerships because individual partners cannot accomplish what they want on their own. Partnerships open new markets by producing new combinations of products, services, and expertise. Partnerships have been shown to facilitate the development of new ideas and products and allow participating organizations to "leapfrog" into new areas. Partners often learn from one another, which is an advantage because buying knowledge expertise by employing individuals can be prohibitively expensive. Together, organizations may find it easier to monitor the changing environment and better understand emerging opportunities or risks. Finally, an organization may join an alliance to gain legitimacy through association with others, particularly larger, visible, reputable, and prestigious firms. Colleges and universities also have a long and rich history of collaboration. See Barringer and Harrison, "Walking a Tightrope"; Bailey and Koney, *Strategic Alliances among Health and Human Services Organizations*; Gulati and Singh, "Architecture of Cooperation"; Hagedoorn, "Understanding the Rationale of Strategic Technology Partnering"; Oliver, "Determinants of Interorganizational Relationships"; Doz, "Evolution of Cooperation in Strategic Alliances"; Johnson and Noftsinger, "Getting a Grip on Strategic Alliances"; Harkavy and Hartley, "Pursuing Franklin's Dream"; Harkavy and Puckett, "Mediating Structures in University and Community Revitalization"; Franklin, "Proposals Relating to the Education of Youth in Pennsilvania [*sic*]."

3. Memo e-mailed to Mike Younger, May 6, 2015.

4. Perna, Orosz, and Jumakulov, "Understanding the Human Capital Benefits of a Government-Funded International Scholarship Program"; Hartley et al., "Learning Autonomy."

5. Harkavy and Puckett, "Mediating Structures in University and Community Revitalization"; Harkavy and Hartley, "Pursuing Franklin's Dream."

6. "About ABCS," Barbara and Edward Netter Center for Community Partnerships, University of Pennsylvania, accessed March 27, 2016, https://www.nettercenter.upenn.edu/abcs-about.

7. Johnston and Harkavy, *Obesity Culture*; Benson, Harkavy, and Puckett, *Dewey's Dream*.

8. "Agatston Urban Nutrition Initiative," Netter Center for Community Partnerships, accessed March 27, 2016, https://www.nettercenter.upenn.edu/programs/agatston-urban-nutrition-initiative.

9. Hartley, Harkavy, and Benson, "Looking Ahead."

CHAPTER EIGHT

The Community College Option:
How Co-ventures Can Leverage Student
and Academic Resources

Kenneth Ender and Charles Middleton

Successful challenges to the supremacy of the higher education system in the United States have become apparent over the past twenty years as more universities outside our borders have outranked US institutions in various global top one hundred lists. This loss of supremacy was one reason why President Obama called for a national initiative to ensure by the year 2025 that the United States would have a citizenry in which 60 percent of working adults would hold at least one postsecondary credential.[1] But the president's call was met by multiple challenges, chief among them the rising cost of attaining a postsecondary credential and the accompanying realization, at least in the recent past, that an increase in the pure number of college-educated individuals did not necessarily correlate to higher learning achievements among those who graduated, an issue that underlies all discussions about affordability and access but receives less attention in the press.

Many critics still overlook the role that declining levels of public financial support for higher education plays in driving up the student's share of the cost. Public higher education cost has increased by 257 percent over the past thirty years, while household income has risen by only 16 percent.[2] Private, nonprofit institutions may be comparatively more affordable because their average increase over that same period of time has been 167 percent, but this is, as they say, a distinction without a difference in the larger issues at play.[3] Second, rising expenses associated with enhanced learning initiatives, broader student support services, and updating and replacing aging facilities have contributed to this shift in who pays for the benefits of postsecondary education, which are considerable, from the public to the individual. Additionally, assessing these ineluctable rising costs, higher education leaders often ignore another factor: the drive to

> *What is the greatest challenge to developing a successful partnership between a university and a community college this year?*
>
> The greatest challenge in developing a successful community college–university partnership currently is ensuring that the president of each institution is fully supportive of the initiative and personally engaged in the necessary ways to develop it expeditiously.

enhance institutional status and place in the marketplace by building stylish new residence halls, expanding student support programs, and providing consumer-driven amenities, which all increase expenses.

The Shape of a Partnership

It was against these environmental factors that we joined forces to consider how Harper College, a large, well-established community college in the northwestern suburbs of Chicago, and Roosevelt University, the only full-service private university located within one mile of the Harper campus, could better service the surrounding communities by creating new pathways of opportunity for local citizens that leveraged the missions, resources, and potential of both institutions. We determined that the best way to frame our discussions was to structure a partnership that addressed and supported the ways students actually live their academic lives and to design any joint programs from the perspective of student learners as they progress through levels of increasingly greater academic challenge, often changing venues at predictable points as their "grade level" progresses. Thinking this way opened up several new perspectives on the current higher education experience for many, often nontraditional, students and their complex needs from institutional providers, whether partnered or not.

Our second consideration focused on the fact that our institutions share a commitment to enhance the economic and civic life of the region in which we are located by serving as two of the key sources of educational opportunity for local citizens. As a result, our relationships with regional business and political leaders have consistently helped to create sustainable jobs requiring postsecondary credentials. Designing our respective strategic plans, it was easy to see that we could accomplish more as partners than as competitors and especially in several specific disciplines that

---

First Seven Action Steps

1. Focus locally
2. Determine workforce needs
3. Create a high-value proposition
4. Design multiple credentials and degrees along the path
5. Encourage faculty collaboration
6. Leverage both institutional brands
7. Start modestly

---

could boost the local economy. For instance, our communities include high concentrations of technology and biomedical corporations, some with their national or international headquarters established locally. We also benefit from proximity to O'Hare International Airport and the rail and road systems of the Midwest, and, finally, Harper was already the largest suburban two-year provider of Roosevelt transfer students. The goal thus became how to implement a large, flexible, distinctive strategic alliance.

The First Seven Action Steps

In our conversations about how best to act on this willingness to collaborate, we clarified the concept of a *strategically planned educational pathway*. Seven action steps drive this concept:

1. *Focus locally* so that prospective students will stay in the area and enhance the regional quality of life.

2. *Determine workforce needs* of local businesses to ensure competitiveness.

3. *Create a high-value proposition* in the cost of attaining credentials spread over the program of study.

4. *Design multiple credentials and degrees along the path* to encourage lifelong learning for those who need to pause for whatever reasons.

5. *Encourage faculty collaboration* to ensure integrated course content and smooth transitions from level to level.

6. *Leverage both institutional brands* in ways that create a program-by-program "super brand," incorporating the best of both institutions into a single product.

7. *Start modestly* so that successes can be replicated as business and educational environments change over time.

We have observed that more institutions across the country are now considering merger as a way to attain these and similar goals. For us, this was not a possibility for two reasons: institutional control—that is, public versus private—and accreditation based on differing levels of degrees offered. Early on, however, we became determined not to let these matters constrain our thinking. In looking at the advantages of mergers, one stood out. Skillfully merged institutions were often more successful in leveraging their resources to attain stronger outcomes, in and out of their classrooms, than either had managed independently. In other words, mergers enabled some institutions not just to survive but also to prosper by making the whole greater than the sum of its parts. This observation became a cornerstone of our collaboration.

The Harper-Roosevelt Communiversity Partnership

For about a year prior to starting our conversation about collaboration, Harper College was leading a robust conversation with the local school superintendents of the feeder high schools of freshman enrollment. What Harper officials came to understand very quickly was that the increasing accountability demands of the K–12 system as well as the variation in expectations of college readiness from high school had caused a misalignment between the high schools and the Harper College curriculum. They quickly sought to develop a collaboration between and among their respective institutions through sharing the time and talent of their staffs and focusing financial investment on joint projects. As these leaders discussed their intentions, they envisioned building a college/school consortium that would be guided by a common vision that every high school student should graduate both career and college ready.

Thus was born the Northwest Educational Council for Student Success (NECSS). The vision would be supported by a revised joint mission statement: "The partnership members will develop programs, share talent, and data, and leverage joint resources to ensure that every elementary, high school and college graduate will have the opportunity to be prepared for a global society, 21st century careers, and post-secondary readiness/success."[4] This formal collaboration between Illinois high school districts 211, 214, 220, and the Illinois community college district 512 (William Rainey Harper College) sought to accomplish four major goals:

1. Increase the college readiness of high school graduates.

2. Reduce the need for incoming college students to take developmental education courses.

3. Expand opportunities for high school students to earn early college credit.

4. Build professional consortia of secondary and postsecondary colleagues to align curriculum pathways across institutional boundaries.

All of these goals were codified and authorized through an intergovernmental agreement signed by each board chairperson and the CEO of the four districts.

The results in this collaboration to date have been noticeable across a broad array of disciplines, and they have been impressive in terms of both student success and access. College readiness has improved across core subject areas: reading, math, and English. This success included a 27 percent increase in recent high school graduates beginning in college-level math over four years. Career Pathways, with early college credit in high school, are established in all the college's career and technical programs. The partnership is also developing a program that will result in high school students earning fifteen college credits prior to graduation, known as the "Power of 15." College access issues are being addressed by the Harper Promise Scholarship Program. This program was jointly developed by regional businesses, the college, and the high school districts, and it allows high school students to earn a free college degree if they meet four criteria. The criteria include attendance, rigor (GPA based and remediation-free at college entry), persistence (advancement and on-time graduation), and community service. The US secretary of education praised this program in September of 2015 as a model for promise access programs nationwide.[5]

As a result, we have begun a discussion about a new partnership for the delivery of education and labor-valued credentials that we call a "communiversity." In it, we imagine a system that networks institutions of higher education through programmatic continuity across multiple levels by leveraging resources that, in particular, incorporate the potential in K–12 systems. In many ways, contemporary community colleges are best positioned to take advantage of the capacities of K–12 systems and their communities. The resulting collaboration can develop and deliver education and career pathways that integrate secondary and postsecondary education through a new delivery paradigm. Combining the

> *What is the most important piece of advice you would offer to a leader now beginning to develop a partnership between a community college and a university?*
>
> Take the time to get to know your counterpart at the other institution, not just in the context of a specific affiliation but also more broadly in how that leader views the enterprise of higher education, student learning, and faculty development.

geographical proximity of community colleges with local K–12 partnerships and anchoring them to select programs offered by a regional university could produce educational and career pathways that are far less costly than typically autonomous, sequential, and distributed higher education systems. We thus decided to build a regional Illinois Communiversity Collaborative that effectively links resources along a continuum to deliver high-quality, high-value, low-cost certificates as well as associate, baccalaureate, and master's degrees virtually and face to face. Further, these educational credentials are delivered locally and are tightly aligned with regional economic development and workforce needs, yet flexible and open to change as our economy and communities change.

As leaders of this partnership, we came to view the core of the communiversity concept as a focus less on our institutions per se, and more on our students *as they achieved their educational goals*. We began to structure our planning discussions more intentionally to reflect the student experience. Instead of viewing students as "going away" to college, we worked to design a model that would keep them productively and comfortably within a single continuum or pipeline from a partnered K–12 system through graduate school. Why not, we wondered, create an institutional structure as a pathway that takes advantage of the natural cohesiveness of a subject matter across various levels of organizational types?

Conclusion: Achieving Results

Most importantly, we needed to integrate the programs so that they were networked through an intellectual connectivity programmatically. At first glance, this seemed to be a daunting task, but as we considered the new model, it became apparent that we had much experience in accomplishing these goals in related projects. We call the new structures "colleges" (of the arts and sciences, business, and engineering), and while there is no single way that we do such organizing of structures inside our institutions, all of these colleges are partnership-driven curricular enterprises. From this platform, we moved ahead to create an interinstitutional curricular pathway with integrated disciplinary tracks. These tracks would be built through faculty alliances among members from all three partners, that is, school district, community college, university. By design, our focus was less on where students took the classes and more on ensuring that the partners delivered. Coursework was sequential, collaborative, and increasingly challenging as it prepared a new workforce.

We capitalized on the advantage of already having developed a joint Harper-Roosevelt program that accepted ten qualified students who had completed their pharmacy program prerequisites at Harper into the doctor of pharmacy program at Roosevelt. From this foundation, the Power of 15 program, mentioned above, was utilized to accelerate the creation of an expanded workforce in science and technology that could be tapped by local corporations in pharmacology and the life sciences more generally.[6] The challenge, however, was in replicating this model in biology especially. High school teachers had to be prepared to teach courses in partnership with a university and using that university's standards if the students in these fields were to be effectively prepared and then competitive. Too many teachers were not able to do so because they generally lacked sustained graduate-level work in biology, and so one more partnership was successfully launched.

Thus was born the Harper-Roosevelt Collaborative for high school teachers who desired to teach dual-credit courses in biology and to be certified by Roosevelt University faculty. Once this initiative was completed, student progress through these pathways was accelerated, as their teachers were providing courses that would earn Harper credit that was transferrable to Roosevelt. In the process, these teachers were also earning credits toward master's degrees in biology. Started in the summer of 2015, these dual programs have quickly proven to be, for both high school students and their teachers, opportunities to earn credits and advance their educations in areas of specific need in the regional economy. From a leadership perspective, this is what we have called co-venturing on a grand scale, enhancing the inherent strengths of each partner and opening our thinking to the benefits of further alliances.

We arrived at these conclusions after observing as presidents that the current industry model of education was designed to serve the nation principally through an autonomous, distributed system of schools, colleges, and universities that was most effective in an era when its main task was to educate the elite. Today and going forward, however, the goal is to provide a majority of Americans with a postsecondary credential.

The co-venture outlined above leverages geography, price point, and connectivity of community colleges both to local school systems and a university partner and distributes postsecondary credentials across several regions in a flexible, inclusive process. Finally, by leveraging the differing cost structures of the participants, a blended tuition model can be implemented that makes the credentials earned more affordable than would be possible in the traditional, stacked model, thus addressing the affordability and accessibility concerns that face all of higher education.

Notes
1. Russell, *Guide to Major U.S. College Completion Initiatives.*
2. Baum and Ma, *Trends in College Pricing.*
3. Ibid.
4. Northwest Educational Council for Student Success, *Guiding Document for NECSS.*
5. Cullotta, "Arne Duncan Visits Harper College."
6. "The Power of 15," D214 High School District, accessed April 10, 2016, http://www.d214.org/assets/1/6/Power_of_15_One_Pager_Final1.pdf.

CHAPTER NINE

Technology as a Driver of Strategic Alliances

Philip Regier and Lynsi Freitag

Higher education has been behind the curve on many trends, but when it comes to technology, colleges and universities are catching up quickly. Globally, investment in educational technology companies during the first half of 2015 totaled more than $3 billion, already surpassing total investment for all of 2014, itself an industry record of $2.42 billion.[1] What's behind this surge in ed-tech adoption? To start, there is an immense need for a more educated workforce that cannot possibly be achieved solely through face-to-face instruction. Additionally, technological advancements are an increasing boon to the student learning experience, enhancing assessment outcomes in ways that are permanently changing the higher education landscape. This chapter offers four examples that detail how technology is creating strategic institutional partnerships that are raising college graduation levels while enhancing individual student learning outcomes within that trend.

The Starbucks College Achievement Plan

In 2013, Arizona State University President Michael Crow and Starbucks CEO Howard Schultz partnered in a shared mission to equalize access to higher education. Together, ASU and Starbucks have developed a first-of-its-kind strategic alliance that tangibly increases the role a public company can play in supporting its employees' goals. The Starbucks College Achievement Plan (SCAP) enables employees (termed "partners") who work as few as twenty hours per week the opportunity to earn a bachelor's degree with full tuition reimbursement through one of ASU's online degree programs. For customers, the face of Starbucks is not Howard Schultz; rather, it is the barista who makes lattes at their local store.

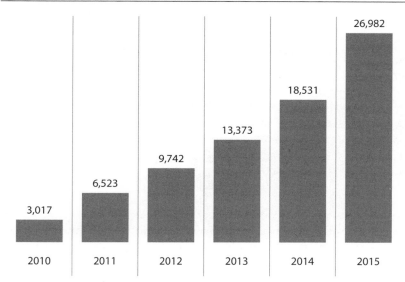

ASU Online student headcount.

Thus Starbucks must hire people who are bright, warm, and able to make an emotional connection; in fact, their business depends on it. They also must look after their partners, because their customers know and care about them. Starbucks research surprisingly discovered that the baristas' well-being matters more to their customers than the traditional corporate social responsibility activities they engage in as a company.

In 1987, Starbucks was among the first retail corporations to offer healthcare to part-time workers. It was a radical move then, and over time, many corporations realized the business sense it made and followed their lead. In 2013, Starbucks employed more than 135,000 people in the United States, and they wanted to do something equally ambitious for the next generation. Corporate leaders researched what their partners really wanted and discovered that their highest priority was the opportunity to advance and make a better life for themselves and their families. Seventy percent of Starbucks' US employees are students or aspiring students, a fact that suggested that free tuition for a bachelor's degree would be highly compelling to more than a third of them. The company's partnership with ASU not only provided this opportunity to its partners but also elevated its brand with consumers. Ultimately, Howard Schultz's objective for SCAP was to create not just an employee benefit, but "a culture transformation and a new operating model."[2]

Under President Crow, Arizona State University has come to measure its success by its degree of inclusion in educational programming. As well,

> *What is the most important piece of advice you would offer to a president or vice president now beginning to develop a college or university partnership?*
>
> Do not overthink revenue splits in the beginning. The overall objective is to develop new sources of revenue, and there will be little monetary reason to bicker over 55 percent, 50 percent, or 45 percent, especially when the amount of revenue in the partnership's early years could be small.

the university remains concerned that students from lower-income families who enroll at a university graduate at a much lower rate than their higher-income peers.[3] As a result, ASU has sharpened its focus on providing different types of support to ensure student success, and the university's leadership team has come to believe that online learning and its new forms of instructional technology are essential to partnership success. When entering partnership planning with Starbucks in 2014, ASU was able to offer support for more than forty online undergraduate degrees to its new partners. As planning got underway, it also became clear that Starbucks' workforce turnover was a key economic motivator for the partnership. Although the company's turnover rate is the envy of some competitors, they still lose 30 percent of their retail staff annually, with an average barista tenure of 1.8 years. It costs approximately $2,700 to replace a barista, and based on this turnover figure, Starbucks is hiring 50,000 people each year in the United States alone. Preliminary data on the return on investment for the Starbucks College Achievement Plan indicate that Starbucks baristas who enroll in SCAP are retained at a rate that is 12 percent higher than partners who do not enroll in the program.

The Mayo Clinic: New Models to Partner Medicine and Technology

The United States is experiencing a major shift in the healthcare landscape with its efforts to lower costs and improve health outcomes by focusing on preventative medicine and care coordination. And new technologies and academic partnerships are foundational to accomplishing these objectives. More than a decade ago, ASU President Michael Crow and then-CEO of the Mayo Clinic in Arizona, Victor Trastek, were at the forefront of this change in thinking, and the resulting partnership has the opportunity to be transformative.[4] In 2002, the two leaders met to discuss forming a focused strategic alliance, and fourteen years later this idea of partnering has expanded far beyond their initial shared vision to include joint research and academic programs not only in healthcare but also in basic science, technology, business, law, and even some areas of the arts and humanities. ASU is a university with a significant interest in health-related care and policy, but it does not have a medical center; the Mayo Clinic is continually innovating and improving care levels, yet it still stands to benefit from the academic expertise a major university can provide.

The benefits of this collaborative relationship can readily be seen in technologies supporting medical education, where the Mayo Medical School is one of eleven medical schools to be awarded an American Medical Association "Accelerating Change in Medical Education" grant. Integration of outstanding ASU faculty and the nationally recognized ASU Online Program into their initiative has facilitated the development of a national model for medical school curricula. The nature of the ASU–Mayo Clinic collaboration can be illustrated in three interrelated areas of work. The first is in the development of new curricula in the Science of Health Care Delivery, a program jointly designed by faculty of the Kern Center for the Science of Health Care Delivery at the Mayo Clinic and the School of Science of Health Care Delivery at ASU. The program is composed of online modules, case-based studies, and clinical experiential learning in seven science of healthcare delivery domains: person-centered care, population-centered care, high-value care, team-based care, health economics, policy and technology, and leadership. Each domain is designed to enhance professional skills in leadership and ensure that students and healthcare professionals develop the ability to advocate for and support successful patient outcomes within complex systems. The curricula will be delivered in three models: infused into the Mayo Medical School curriculum; cobranded through a stand-alone certificate that anyone in the healthcare professions may take; and offered as an open-access primer course available to anyone in the world.

What is the greatest challenge for a leader now developing a higher education partnership?

The greatest challenge in partnering a higher education institution and a for-profit corporation is the imbalance of information regarding what works and what does not. Often, a corporation will have little incentive to reveal to a partner comprehensive information about its products or services.

The second area of the academic partnership involves the transformation of the instructional model for the Mayo Medical School. The medical school was able to take advantage of new technologies, online and blended learning modalities, and instructional design practices from ASU Online to enable it to expand its prior offerings while simultaneously making both current and prior offerings more efficient in terms of learning outcomes. Building on these early results and the shared strategic vision embedded in the partnership, the Mayo Clinic has decided to open a new medical school in Phoenix in 2017.

The collaboration between ASU Online and the Mayo Clinic extends beyond medical school education to the Mayo School of Continuous Professional Development, which provides training for physicians, nurses, and allied health professionals. ASU is working to update many of Mayo's didactic learning modules into a blended learning application that includes interactive videos, quizzes, and exercises utilizing animation and simulations. This will allow the same high-caliber learning experience to be effectively offered across the Mayo Clinic Health System. Whereas healthcare workers were historically required to travel to Rochester, Minnesota, and sit in a classroom or lab to continue their education, the new blended programs enable them to enroll in continuing education courses from their homes and offices. Rather than taking time away from work, they can learn the material online and perform their lab work at a local clinic. The core of the partnership between ASU and Mayo Clinic is partnering to respond more efficiently to the changing needs of their communities. By sharing expertise and utilizing new technologies

Massive Open Online Courses 1.0: What Were We *Thinking*?

JOEL GARREAU

Today's massive open online courses—MOOCs—are yesterday's "educational television." Another beautiful theory murdered by a gang of brutal facts.

I have faculty colleagues working their tails off on their MOOCs, getting up at oh-dark hundred to film their presentations at sunrise in the desert—anything to try and make this technology come alive. But most free MOOCs today are still basically lectures shoveled from existing courses at a novel scale. They are hardly "the revolution that has higher education gasping," embodying "the shimmery hope . . . that free courses can bring the best education in the world to the most remote corners of the planet," as they were touted when millions first enrolled and the *New York Times* proclaimed 2012 to be "The Year of the MOOC."[1]

More recent numbers, unfortunately, are by now equally familiar: dropout rates on MOOCs are as high as 95 percent, with many of those who actually complete already sporting degrees.[2]

To be sure, MOOCs are literally better than nothing. In India and China, the MOOC completion rate is higher than in the United States, but distance learning, especially for skills training, has been around since the state of the art was post offices and correspondence courses for learners. That's why Stanford President John Hennessy in a 2015 interview with *MIT Technology Review* questioned whether today's MOOCs can match traditional instruction in motivating students. Hennessy, a professor of electrical engineering who founded his own computer company and serves as a Google director, said, "The truth is, looking at a talking video for an hour is absolutely no more motivating—perhaps even less motivating—than sitting in a large lecture hall for an hour."[3]

This is not to say that innovative professors are wasting their time messing around with MOOCs. Trying and failing are major components of learning in this context, too. Technology will doubtless play an increasing role in education, as some team of thinkers and users breaks the code on making MOOCs more useful. A lot of work is now focused on incorporating other teaching designs and methods, including face-to-face along with individualized feedback and measurement algorithms, and it is certainly preferable to be in the lead of change, battling to shape it, than to be dragged along behind it. As the computer scientist Alan Kay famously put it, "The best way to predict the future is to invent it."

In fact, there are plenty of disruptive technologies that may soon eclipse today's MOOCs as transformative educational agents: serious games, immersive virtual reality, and cognitive enhancement, to name three. "Technology" has been described as the word we have invented for whatever does not really work yet. That is why my hunch is that today's MOOCs will soon seem quaint, a brief evolutionary step on the way to something that fully succeeds at accelerating and broadening knowledge creation and learning, the need for which is great.[4]

Joel Garreau is author of *Radical Evolution: The Promise and Peril of Enhancing Our Minds, Our Bodies—and What It Means to Be Human* and is a professor of law, culture, and values at the Sandra Day O'Connor College of Law at Arizona State University.

1. Pappano, "Year of the MOOC."
2. Konnikova, "Will MOOCs Be Flukes?"; Watters, "6.003z."
3. Anders, "The Skeptic."
4. Other works consulted include Lapowsky, "Why Free Online Classes Are Still the Future of Education"; Kingkade, "MOOC Skepticism Persists among University Presidents"; Jaschik, "Not a Tsunami."

to develop solutions to individual challenges in healthcare systems and instruction, we are better able to train our workforces collectively to achieve leadership in their professions.

The University Innovation Alliance and "Next Generation" Institutions

In May 2013, a Lumina-funded report by the New America Foundation, titled *The Next Generation University*, highlighted six institutions—Arizona State University; Georgia State University; the University of Buffalo; the University of California, Riverside; the University of Central Florida; and the University of Texas at Arlington—that "have expanded enrollment and achieved higher graduation rates in a cost-effective manner even as their revenues per student declined."[5] Their differentiated approaches were examined for their abilities to accomplish similar levels of change and innovation. That report would spur discussions among five of the institutions' college presidents as well as those at six additional universities who were eager to find a way to develop partnerships that would enhance their students' success and in closing the achievement gap.[6]

The eleven University Innovation Alliance (UIA) universities are all public institutions, and that is not a coincidence. UIA has both a sense of opportunity in taking on the challenge of graduating more students and an obligation to ensure that a high-quality education is accessible and

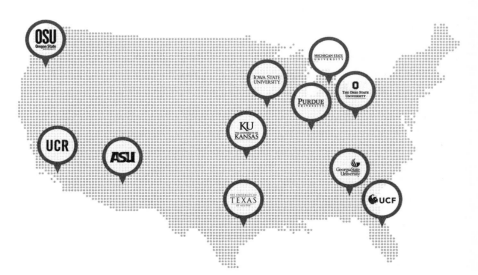

University Innovation Alliance member institutions.

The University Innovation Alliance and "Next Generation" Institutions

Arizona State University
Georgia State University
Iowa State University
Michigan State University
Ohio State University
Oregon State University
Purdue University
University of California, Riverside
University of Central Florida
University of Kansas
University of Texas at Austin

affordable for middle-class families. Another commonality among these universities is that they serve at least 20,000 students each; several enroll more than 50,000 students. The institutions represent all major regions nationally, with some still evolving in mission, some categorized as land-grant universities, and others—like ASU—recognized as state flagships. It is the first time a group of public research universities has self-organized across state and conference lines specifically to test and scale solutions to the challenges of access and graduation in higher education. The UIA's vision is "that by piloting new interventions, sharing insights about relative costs and effectiveness, and scaling those interventions that are successful, the UIA will significantly increase the number of low-income Americans graduating with quality college degrees and will, over time, catalyze systemic changes in the entire higher education sector."[7] In sum, the UIA's aim is to develop "next generation" institutions through a technology-enhanced partnership model that leverages the scale and diversity of higher education to serve larger numbers of low-income students, and models the practices—and commitment—necessary to succeed at scale.

The Georgia State Advantage: Predictive Analytics

The University Innovation Alliance's first large-scale initiative leverages technology to transfer predictive analytics knowledge and best practices from an "exemplar institution"—in this case, Georgia State—to the other member schools. Georgia State has successfully used predictive analytics and proactive advising interventions to keep students on track for timely graduation. This approach has resulted in an increase of 5 percent for semester-to-semester retention and an almost half-a-semester reduction in time to degree for graduating students. If the other ten UIA institutions are able to implement Georgia State's system with comparable gains, up to 19,000 more students could stay enrolled, with UIA graduates saving almost $200 million in tuition and fees every year. Taxpayers would save $100 million in educational costs, and, over five years, these innovations could produce more than 61,000 additional graduates from UIA institutions and save almost $1.5 billion in educational costs to students and taxpayers.

Furthermore, if the innovations could be collaboratively scaled across *all* public universities nationally, they would help up to 335,000 additional students stay in college each year. This would produce $2.2 billion in saved tuition and fees annually for students, with an additional $1.4 billion in cost savings to taxpayers. As a series of institutional partnerships, the UIA is still young and somewhat untested, but it holds significant potential. Joining any group of high-profile, competitive higher education institutions is not without its challenges, but through the use of technology, innovation, and collaboration, partner institutions can help thousands of students earn an education with less cost while simultaneously helping the nation produce a more educated workforce.

Conclusion: The Benefits of New Technologies

EdPlus at Arizona State relies heavily on partnerships to broaden access to education, enhance the quality of teaching and learning, and ultimately increase graduation rates and student outcomes. EdPlus advances ASU's mission of inclusion, efficiency, and innovation into digital arenas, enabling learners' access to educational opportunities that were previously out of reach. Using collaborative and multifaceted online platforms, EdPlus at ASU delivers new educational models, working closely with corporate partners to reduce financial barriers, broaden access, and improve student learning outcomes, in part through increased research on these issues specifically. We have developed more than 150 technology partners to support our faculty in creating fully customized courses, as well as to challenge our thinking more broadly in refining the university's mission. These partnerships have taught us three useful lessons:

1. *Choose partners who share your values.* ASU sees its values reflected in the work of all the partners discussed in this chapter. ASU and Starbucks are driven to broaden educational access, while

ASU and the Mayo Clinic are committed to supporting medical education with new technologies that better serve their local and extended communities. Finally, ASU and its ten partner universities in the UIA are passionate about increasing graduation rates and outcomes success on a national, multi-thousand-student scale. Finding these shared core values is essential in selecting organizations with which to partner, and if your values align, the changes can be transformative.

2. *Working together is better than standing alone*. Through its strategic alliances, ASU has learned repeatedly that it can accomplish much more collaboratively than it would ever be able to achieve on its own. Using the eventual strategic plan with the Mayo Clinic, for example, ASU had no plans or interest in building a medical school, and the clinic was not that interested in creating an instructional design or online learning enterprise. Yet each institution learned to stay within its own area of expertise, and together they were able to transform a curriculum and advance how future medical professionals are educated.

3. *Successful partnerships are long-term marriages*. ASU has signed on to these partnerships for the long term, and the university's leadership is pragmatic in acknowledging that partnerships include challenges and obstacles that must be overcome for the participants to thrive. Faculty members and administrators are also aware that higher education is being disrupted—sometimes by technologies—more than ever before, but there is also a greater need for a more educated workforce than ever before. Ironically, as funding for online programs is dramatically rising, technology-enabled learning is still in its infancy, and what it will look like five years after this book is printed is increasingly difficult to imagine. Still, we close with two predictions: soon there will be more digitally enabled students than undergraduates living on campus at numerous premier universities, and higher education as we know it today will hardly be recognizable tomorrow.

Notes
1. Adkins, *International Learning Technology Investment Patterns*.
2. "A Partnership between ASU and Starbucks Raises the Bar for the Role a Public Company Can Play in Support of its Employees' Life Goals," ASU Online, Arizona State University, accessed April 10, 2016, https://asuonline.asu.edu /starbucks-and-arizona-state-university.
3. Education Trust, *Pell Partnership*.

4. Vaughan, "Healing Partnership."

5. Selingo et al., *Next Generation University*.

6. The additional six universities are: Iowa State University, Michigan State University, Ohio State University, Oregon State University, Purdue University, and the University of Kansas.

7. Burns, Crow, and Becker, "Innovating Together."

A Disruptive Opportunity: Competency-Based Education as a Shaper of Successful Partnerships

Paul LeBlanc and Kristine Clerkin

Higher education and the employer community have long been in conversation, but the tone of that conversation has taken on more contentious and frustrated notes over the past ten years. Increasingly, employers complain that colleges and universities are not producing graduates ready for the workplace, while educational institutions complain that employers are not doing their part, that is, hiring and accepting that they need to do some training. The disconnect has become a chasm, with one recent survey revealing that 96 percent of chief academic officers believe their graduates are prepared for employment, while only 11 percent of employers agree.[1] Whatever grains of truth exist in their respective narratives, that yawning gap speaks to genuine disconnect.

Competency-based education (CBE) provides an opportunity to close the gap through partnerships between institutions and employers because it gives both parties a shared vocabulary to talk about the challenge. Employers do not think about curriculum and courses—they think about what people can do in terms of their competencies. CBE programs do the same, shifting from what students know to what students can do with what they know. Moreover, because CBE starts with clarity around those competencies, it forces education providers to look hard at what employers need to make sure the competencies are the right ones, will lead to job offers and workplace success, and can be defended. To accomplish those goals, higher education institutions developing CBE programs can and should partner with employers and other organizations in meaningful ways.

Competency-based education has been hailed as the next "disrupter" of higher education. With hundreds of institutions in the program design phase or about to launch new CBE programs, the wave of change

*What is the greatest challenge facing a leader developing
a higher education partnership this year?*

The greatest challenge is in finding a partner who has the necessary chemistry
with your institution and the willingness to actually build a strong and durable
agreement. This partner also has to have needs that your own institution can fill.
Finally, both partners need to commit the necessary resources to fill those needs.

seems real. Policy makers, administrators, and faculty either talk about
CBE as a necessary force of disruptive change or bemoan it as the latest
fad. In our work, we have learned that students do not much care whether
their education is disruptive. The older, working adults we serve want a
form of higher education that is affordable, flexible, highly supportive,
relevant to their work, and helps them move forward in life. Once fully
engaged, many see only a model that works for them. Our students do
not use the words "personalized" or "adaptive," either; rather, they talk
about flexibility, high levels of support, and being debt-free. To be truly
disruptive, higher education must serve these students well with a cost-
effective model, offer a streamlined user experience, be highly scalable,
and provide an avenue for finding underserved audiences. Partnerships
and strategic alliances clearly offer higher education institutions a number of opportunities to build these capabilities.

This chapter describes CBE and then discusses how it shapes, requires,
and thrives on successful partnerships, networks, and co-ventures. We
discuss four types of alliances with examples we have seen in our work
at College for America (CfA) at Southern New Hampshire University
(SNHU). The same study cited above found that only 29 percent of businesses partner with higher education institutions on any initiatives.[2] We
believe this is a lost opportunity and thus conclude with some thoughts
about what makes those partnerships successful as well as how institutions might think about developing their own networks.

What Is Competency-Based Education?

Competency-based education allows students to earn credit and progress toward degrees and credentials through demonstrating *competence,*
or what they can do (skills) with what they know. Most CBE models
require students to show *mastery* of knowledge and skills at a high level
and many, such as ours, have no grades, only the bilateral "yes" (mas-

tered) or "not yet" (try again). Students submit their work; they learn from fast, targeted feedback, and resubmit. They soon overcome their fears of failure and learn to use feedback, developing the "growth mindset" described by Carol Dweck.[3] The goal is to help students become "self-directed" learners who can vary pace but not lose momentum while maintaining steady progress toward the degree.

Many programs make use of assessments in the form of projects rather than tests to demonstrate the application of knowledge. Students move at an individual pace in the program and across topics; the time required to earn a degree depends entirely on each student's ability, motivation, prior knowledge, and schedule. Rigorous method and skill are required to build valid, reliable assessments. Best practices in CBE program design begin with the careful construction of required competencies based on well-established frameworks, labor market data, and analysis of learning outcomes in traditional programs. The design moves backward to construction of assessments that allow demonstration of specific competencies, to rubrics that guide the assessment, and finally to learning resources that precisely help the student gain knowledge and skills. Faculty reviewers must be trained and monitored to provide substantial, timely feedback that can guide the student.

Because most competency-based programs are built on an applied framework that first asks what do students need to know and do in order to be educated citizens and employees, program designs usually incorporate the well-accepted Degree Qualifications Profile (DQP) created by the American Association of Colleges and Universities with the Lumina Foundation. CBE programs can also incorporate cross-cutting skills from an analysis of various occupations and workforce sectors. In College for America's associate of arts degree (stackable to all its bachelor of arts programs), built on the DQP, students are required to master competencies across the three dimensions of content knowledge, foundational skills, and personal and social skills by demonstrating the following:

- Access information

- Analyze data

- Apply economic theories

- Build teamwork through marketing

- Chart the evolution of media

- Confront culture

- Consider the environment

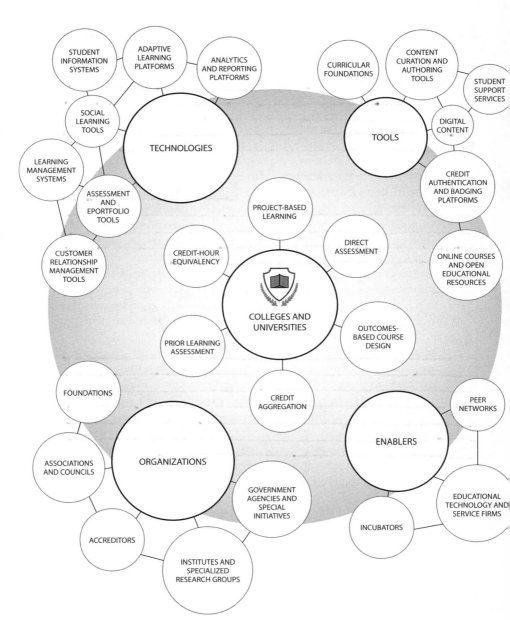

The competency-based education landscape. *Source:* Fleming, "Mapping the Competency-Based Education Universe."

- Decode media
- Develop a budget
- Establish a professional presence
- Evaluate popular psychology
- Examine ethical perspectives
- Experience art
- Experiment with psychology
- Explore writing
- Investigate business ethics
- Leverage business tools
- Manage people
- Plan for success
- Solve problems

Mastery at a high level is demonstrated through project-based assessments that make sense to career-focused students. Despite the chasm in perception about the effectiveness of higher education, CBE shows there is strong consonance between the competencies required of educated citizens and of well-prepared employees.

Competency-based education models are not new in postsecondary education, though CfA was the first program to get approval for Title IV financial aid in April 2013 based on direct assessment of learning rather than credit hours. What is new is that online delivery systems and the use of learning analytics make CBE programs scalable beyond career-technical areas to almost any field of study. It is now possible to track the progress of perhaps thousands of students, all starting at different dates and moving at varied, personalized paces. This capacity for great scale and personalized learning sets the stage for new kinds of partnerships.

Four Partnership Models

What are the elements of successful partnerships? Most successful organizations in any sector can map a complex network of strategic alliances, partnerships, and vendor relationships that serve their interests. What, then, are the elements of successful higher education partnerships, and how do they differ from simple transactional relationships? We have found these four indicators to be useful in assessments:

1. Does the relationship have *strategic value* beyond the value of any contract, such that in combination or individually both parties can more easily or effectively achieve their goals?

2. Is there a *business value* beyond the value of the transaction? Does the partnership help either party to reach new markets, create revenue, or reduce costs?

3. Are the parties' *missions aligned*?

4. Do *trust, investment,* and *accountability* characterize the relationship?[4]

Officially launched as a separate unit of SNHU in October 2013, CfA has developed partnerships that fit one or even all of these criteria and are critical to its business and education models. The concept for a low-cost, competency-based offering was developed in an Innovation Laboratory in 2012 at SNHU. The initial planning group received a Next Generation Learning Challenge grant from Educause and the Bill and Melinda Gates Foundation in June 2012, and was charged with launching a pilot no later than January 2013. Between June and January 2013, the staff expanded slightly to include an assessment expert, a couple of software developers, an instructional designer, two learning coaches, a partnership developer, and a marketing director. The project moved quickly through five iterations of curriculum, assessment, technology, and student experience with new student cohorts. Given CfA's target of a low-cost ($2,500 per year) subscription model, expensive marketing was out of the question, so the team decided to work with and through employers to enroll students. An initial group of twenty-five employers agreed to partner to enroll small numbers of employees in the program. As of 2016, CfA has a variety of partnerships with more than one hundred organizations that fit loosely, yet with productive overlap, into four categories.

1. Workforce Alignment, Talent Management, Retention, and Career-Planning Partnerships

The first type of partnership is primarily with employers to increase workforce alignment, talent management, retention, and career planning. Through strategic employer partnerships, competency-based education models can offer institutions a direct connection with local and national employers and a rich student pipeline. CBE makes clearly visible to students and employers the competencies they have mastered, even upon completing a general education program. Many CBE programs offer students both a competency transcript and a credit transcript to help make

this achievement meaningful to employers. CBE program design method-
ology aligns curriculum to important, cross-cutting competencies that prepare students for multiple jobs. If there is a "skills gap," one reason may be
that employers and applicants do not speak the same language about the
skills and competencies they already possess or need to acquire. CfA offers
its low-cost CBE programs only to employees of corporate partners
because of the special strategic value of such a program for employers and
the value it offers CfA in helping find qualified, new students.

One of these first partners was Anthem Blue Cross Blue Shield of
New Hampshire. Anthem CEO Lisa Guertin was convinced that her
employees would take advantage of an opportunity to get a college degree paid for by the company. She had a hunch that having a group of
employees working on the program would activate a learning culture in
the company even among employees who had been in their jobs for a
long while. The competencies required to complete CfA's associate of
arts in general studies degree would prepare these employees well for
that changing business model.[5] Anthem had one of the first cohorts of
about forty employees in CfA's pilot phase. During this nine-month period, students were not charged tuition but were full-fledged students of
SNHU. CfA staff worked with these students directly to implement a
number of changes as curriculum and technology features were rolled
out. Most of the students were customer service representatives, but a
few were team leaders and administrators for whom a college degree
had become increasingly important in order to advance in Anthem, the
nation's second-largest health insurer.

Anthem national headquarters in Indianapolis started to pay attention to the New Hampshire–based pilot. They liked the initial results
and, given the program's low cost, believed that they could offer the
benefit to many nondegreed frontline employees who normally do not
benefit much from tuition-assistance programs. The top leaders saw industry consolidation ahead (Anthem agreed to buy Cigna, the fourth-
largest health insurer in the summer of 2015) and wanted to attract and
retain the best employees. Of Anthem's 55,000 employees, some 34,000

*What is the most important piece of advice you could offer to
a president or provost now designing a partnership?*

Start with partnership discussions at the board level and explore areas where
there may already be connections. Then leverage these connections and focus on
bringing leaders into the conversation who have the energy to follow through.

did not have a college degree. CfA and Anthem estimated that perhaps 15 to 20 percent would express interest and that over time as many as 10 percent of nondegreed employees might enroll in the program. As of September 2015, over 6,000 Anthem employees have expressed interest in the program, and nearly 2,000 have enrolled. The partnership with Anthem provided strategic value to the company in that it sees education benefits as a way to improve and retain a quality-focused workforce. CfA gained the opportunity to reach thousands of potential students in a cost-effective manner that aligns with its mission to aid in the career development of frontline workers.

2. Subject Matter Expertise and Learning Resources Partnerships

The second driver of CBE partnerships includes subject matter expertise and learning resources. Most online CBE programs offer extensive learning resources, faculty feedback, coaches or advisors, mentors, and learning communities, but students can also expect to learn from many other sources as well. An increasing number of employees learn through massive open online courses (MOOCs), take skills courses from training providers during boot camps, or participate in training programs. Though most offer extensive, curated learning resources, CBE programs do not prescribe or require where or how people learn. CBE partners thus have the opportunity to engage experts from the workplace in the development of resources and customized programs to point to industry training materials, and to use free, open resources—all on an as-needed, just-in-time basis to help with the assessment at hand.

An early CfA partner that provided subject matter expertise is Partners Healthcare in Boston. Partners is the largest private employer in Massachusetts, with 65,000 employees, and the operator of some of Boston's most well-known hospitals, including Mass General and Brigham and Women's. Partners Director of Workforce Development M. J. Ryan had long worked with many postsecondary providers to build and retain a high-quality workforce for Partners. She and her team saw the challenges of shifting to a more competitive, patient-centered, community model over the next decade and knew they would need a more flexible workforce. Ryan saw few options that would offer employees a useful, affordable program aligned to Partners' needs and the needs of its frontline workers to move ahead in their careers.

CfA had already begun to focus on healthcare, and its workforce strategy team prepared an analysis of the skills needed for the fastest-growing healthcare occupations.[6] Partners and CfA applied jointly for a grant from the Commonwealth of Massachusetts Healthcare Transformation Fund to pilot the project, and CfA curriculum designers and a team at Partners began to collaborate on a certificate degree program for nonclinical healthcare workers. The certificate credential would stack into an associate's degree in healthcare management, and then into a bachelor's degree in healthcare management for those students wanting to progress. The grant would pay for the first fifty students, with a full rollout to follow for all Partners employees and to CfA's numerous other healthcare partners.

The certificate program was only one piece of a larger relationship with Partners. In the spring of 2015, Partners announced that it would pay $2,000 annually for any employee to pursue a degree with College for America. The alliance with Partners has obvious strategic and business value for both sides. Both teams' missions are entirely aligned around creating educational opportunities for frontline employees, and there is long-term planning and investment.

3. New Student Outreach Partnerships

The third driver is the need and opportunity to reach new students through new channels. Competency-based education changes the dynamic of higher education from administrator or faculty centered to student centered, and can offer an attractive platform for partners who want to serve nontraditional students in new ways. Such partners may want personalized, on-the-ground services to provide additional structure and complement an online program. In a sense, these offer the possibility of bringing college to students in their communities rather than requiring students to go to colleges that may not be organized to serve their specific needs. Organizations seeking partnerships with higher education institutions include community-based nonprofits and youth organizations, charter schools, trade unions, and membership associations.

When the staff at Match Education in Boston inquired about a partnership, the CfA team was interested in experimenting to connect with this student audience. Match operates highly successful pre-K–12 public charter schools in Boston that target at-risk urban youth. Match's value proposition is that, through a chain of high achievement through their schools, they will generate far better four-year college completion rates than similar schools in Boston, and to date Match has produced outstanding rates: approximately 80 percent of its high school graduates go on to college and, of those about 50 percent graduate within six years. But the Match leaders were troubled by the 30 percent who drop out, most within the first year. Their analysis was that a mix of financial, social, and cultural factors contributed this dropout rate. These students were prepared to do college work but floundered at local community colleges and public institutions because they began in demoralizing developmental education courses, suffered financial setbacks, needed transportation or childcare, or experienced family crises. Almost all are first-generation students and eligible for Pell grants, and thus are in challenging financial circumstances.

Match saw CfA's flexible, low-cost model as the beginning of an answer for these students. They appreciated the alignment with workforce competencies because the goal of the new program, Match Beyond, became not just college success but career success. Match decided to invest in a program that offered a range of counseling, mentoring, financial, and career-planning services tailored to each student. They rented study space in downtown Boston convenient to public transportation and extended their "no excuses," mission-driven culture to the pilot group of college students. CfA's program offered the flexibility their students needed to move at a varied pace and to receive extra help where needed.[7] The Match team set high goals of 80 percent associate degree graduation rate within two years. As the partnership with Match evolved, a strategy to serve this new audience of students began to emerge. These partnerships are still in early stages, but a number of partnerships with large, national organizations to bring college to the community have good potential for scale. Potential partners are asked if they have the willingness and capacity to invest people and resources, to make a long-term commitment, and to be accountable for results.

4. Scalable Technology Partnerships

Early providers have mostly offered online, flexibly paced programs in some kind of subscription or unlimited consumption model. As such, there may not be courses, credits, grades, sections, or syllabi, and faculty roles may operate differently. These new requirements can cause challenges with traditional learning management systems (LMSs), such as Blackboard and Canvas, for example. New providers like Salesforce, Regent, Workday, and Flatworld Learning offer more flexible, configurable solutions adaptable to CBE. Well-funded learning analytics companies such as Civitas see benefit in ground-floor CBE relationships that are structured as vendor relationships but usually go beyond, as development teams must work together closely to build requirements. The strategic and business value of these relationships in creating new solutions goes beyond the price of the contractual agreement.

In 2012, in looking for a system to accommodate its online program, CfA faced the "build or buy" question of which LMS would accommodate CBE. Most LMSs on the market are oriented to the typical delivery model of courses, credits, sections, and assignments. Salesforce, a $4 billion global software company with 2.5 million current users, offers a highly configurable customer relationship management system that the CfA team chose for student records. They attempted to adapt a market-leading LMS (Canvas) for the student learning platform. Salesforce worked beautifully to track student information of all kinds, but adapting the traditional LMS to competencies created a confusing student experience. So the CfA team began to experiment with building an LMS on Salesforce. Salesforce provides a highly secure, cloud-based solution and an open architecture for bolting on customized applications and solutions, many of which could help CfA provide a seamless student experience. Salesforce Foundation nonprofit pricing allowed CfA to keep costs down and plan for thousands of users.

Most CBE programs require modification of an existing LMS or the creation of a new one, and all are challenged to integrate with university student information systems. Financial aid disbursement presents another set of systems challenges. The burgeoning CBE field has responded with some organized outreach to established and new systems vendors. The Technical Interoperability Project, organized by the Competency Based Education Network, is building interoperability standards for CBE systems among the various established vendors such as Blackboard, D2L, Ellucian, Pearson, and Oracle.[8] The vendors and the institutions pledge resources to build interoperability prototypes that will help CBE institutions with their systems planning. Other institutions are now developing strategic partnerships such as CfA's with Salesforce. Technology partnerships are not new in higher education; Arizona State University, profiled in chapter 9 of this volume, has implemented scores of them. But CBE typically requires highly customized work in building an application best suited to the model that the institution offers.

As interest in CBE has grown, a number of new providers have entered the market. SNHU spun off its Salesforce platform in 2015 as a separate nonprofit company, Motivis Learning. The University of Texas System CBE initiatives have designed TEX, a "full-stack" solution of technology platforms that operate in coordination, while Northern Arizona University has co-ventured with Pearson to build both technology and curriculum. Many of the "first-mover" CBE institutions are working with Regent Education for financial aid packaging or with Workday on their new CBE-aligned student information systems. At first glance, these technology partnerships look a lot like vendor relationships; however, the strategic and business value often far exceeds the dollars being exchanged. Institutions can often negotiate favorable arrangements as

> ## Successful Partnerships: Four Action Steps
>
> 1. Define how partnerships might help fulfill strategic or mission objectives.
> 2. Analyze existing partnerships to determine whether there are ways to leverage them more broadly.
> 3. Hire business development people who know how to talk with employers and design a partnership contract.
> 4. Determine whether and where the institution can build customized credentials and programs.

these vendors compete to build new solutions or modify existing products for a new market. Mission alignment, trust, and investment are core values for success because development of these solutions can take more time and money than anticipated.

How Institutions Can Build Successful Partnerships: Four Action Steps

In conclusion, we recommend four best practices in the development of successful partnerships based on CBE programs:

1. *Define how partnerships might help fulfill strategic or mission objectives.* The plan to develop deep or wide networks with employers and other partners is a key strategy. Such a plan may require investment, perhaps moving resources from another area, so it is important to have a shared understanding of the whys. Lay out clear goals and metrics for the initiative.

2. *Analyze existing partnerships to determine whether there are ways to leverage them more broadly.* We know of several colleges and universities that have deep, local employer relationships for program development but have not leveraged them on a national level to build a network of partnering organizations. In our experience, companies that offer internships to students should also be a deep pipeline for customized credentials and employee populations.

3. *Hire business development people who know how to talk with employers and design a partnership contract.* Each may be a bit different and require separate financial and contractual work, so it will be wise to determine whether the general counsel's office has the expertise to review these contracts, or whether outside help is

required. Use a customer relationship management system or other systems to track these relationships, as there may be multiple approaches to the same partner.

4. *Determine whether and where the institution can build customized credentials and programs.* CBE programs can fine-tune the development of competencies and real-world-looking assessments in ways that resonate strongly with employers and career-oriented students. Some colleges have a workforce development branch that does this work. Many potential partners will eventually be eager to talk about developing programs that meet their current and future workforce needs.

In sum, a "feel good" advisory committee of local employers that meets once a year is no longer enough. They are being replaced by strong data, nonstop planning, and substantial inquiry. The institutions that get this right will be the ones most in demand. Their graduates will secure jobs and then promotions, while the college or university thrives on new ideas and programs. As much as any other social need, higher education is today expected to address the need to place people in more and better-paying jobs. To meet this challenge as educators, we need partnerships and alliances that support both the supply and demand sides of the equation, a plan for scale to attract new students, and a broader concept of our how our institutions can operate more effectively within local, national, and global networks.

Notes

1. Jaschik and Lederman, *2014 Inside Higher Ed Survey of Chief Academic Officers*; Lumina Foundation and Gallup, *What America Needs to Know about Higher Education Redesign*.

2. Lumina Foundation and Gallup, *What America Needs to Know about Higher Education Redesign*.

3. Dweck, *Mindset*.

4. These draw on the four dimensions of alliance fit described in Greve, Rowley, and Shipilov, *Network Advantage*.

5. Alssid and Shields, "College in the Call Center."

6. Goldberg and Alssid, *Nonclinical and Frontline Healthcare Roles Continue to Rise*.

7. Crawford, "Bringing a Charter-School Approach to College."

8. Resources produced by the Competency-Based Education Network can be found at "Resource Library," Competency-Based Education Network, accessed April 2, 2016, http://www.cbenetwork.org/resource-library/.

CHAPTER ELEVEN

International Objectives: The Benefits and Challenges in Developing Branch Campuses and Partnerships Abroad

Michael Jackson and James Larimore

In 2004, the global management consulting firm Booz Allen Hamilton published a list of "the world's ten most enduring institutions of the twentieth and twenty-first centuries in the areas of arts and entertainment, business and commerce, government, nonprofits, and academia."[1] Listed alongside the Modern Olympic Games, the US Constitution, General Electric, Sony, and the Rolling Stones were two universities, Dartmouth College and Oxford University. The common denominator among this diverse array of entities was the capacity to innovate and adapt to significant changes in their external environments. It is instructive that universities on two continents were included on this list, as if to remind us that colleges and universities in the United States are also part of a larger, interconnected global web of exchange that carries both risk and opportunity.

This chapter provides an overview of how and why so many US colleges and universities have sought to internationalize their academic programs, faculty, student bodies, and fundraising efforts, through alliances and coventures with institutions on other continents. The themes here are familiar ones: expanding the relentless search for talent, strengthening institutional capacity for innovation, building relationships with partners in industry and government, providing students with opportunities to learn and acquire experiences that will enable them to compete for jobs and other resources, and shoring up finances through new markets.

The views and ideas presented in this chapter represent the distillation of the authors' experiences over three decades of senior leadership at Stanford University, Dartmouth College, the University of Southern California (USC), Swarthmore College, Amherst College, and New York University–Abu Dhabi. Collectively, our work has taken us to several-dozen destinations where American colleges and universities are developing collaborations with foreign institutions, alumni, and businesses, including: Shanghai, Beijing, and Shenzhen in mainland China; Taiwan; Hong Kong; Tokyo, Japan; Dubai and Abu Dhabi in the United Arab Emirates (UAE); Jakarta, Indonesia; Seoul and Incheon in South Korea; and Bangkok, Thailand. In addition, we have worked with delegations from Australia, Malaysia, England, and South Africa.

While not a comprehensive treatise on the reasons why American institutions of higher education might now engage in international partnerships and strategic alliances, we hope that these perspectives will provide presidents and provosts, in particular, with insights and action steps that will help them proceed in developing, expanding, and solidifying international activities by their institutions.

Starting Point: Reasons for the Growth in Study Abroad Programs

The number of US college students studying abroad has more than tripled since 1994, with nearly 300,000 US students participating in some form of study abroad during the 2012–13 academic year.[2] While the percentage of US college students who participate in these programs is still relatively small with respect to total US postsecondary enrollment, the Institute of International Education (IIE), an organization with over 1,200 member institutions worldwide, launched the Generation Study Abroad campaign in 2014 with the goal of doubling the number of students who study abroad by the end of the decade.[3]

Work remains to be done to enrich the learning experience for students who study abroad. For many years, the international activities of many colleges and universities focused on sending students overseas to study, particularly during the middle to latter part of the twentieth century. This is not to say that individual campus leaders or faculty did not have international involvements, as many did, particularly those engaged in area studies of certain regions of the world, such as Africa, Asia, and Latin America. While institutions supported and valued these internationally focused academic activities, however, they were not as prominently marketed as they are today. In most cases, these activities were not promoted as key programs to distinguish an institution from its peers and to attract students, star faculty, potential donors, and overseas partners.

Schools without the resources to develop self-contained international programs often encouraged their students to take advantage of partnership programs sponsored by consortia like the Council on International Educational Exchange or to enroll directly in universities in foreign countries for a semester or academic year. More wealthy schools, particularly

What is the greatest challenge to developing a successful international higher education partnership?

Successful international partnerships are not unlike other key alliances maintained by the college or university. They require honest and ongoing communication about interests, expectations, and desires, as well as a willingness to devote time, attention, and other resources to their assessment and refinement.

those located in the eastern United States, leased villas or large estates in or near major European cities—including Berlin, Florence, London, and Rome—to house students and the professors who accompanied them to teach classes related to the country in which they were staying.

As more students have the opportunity to study abroad, institutions will need to clarify their intentions and goals for study abroad programs and ensure that academic, social, and cultural priorities are aligned to create experiences that are more than an opportunity to travel outside of the United States. From our vantage point, international experiences have significant positive benefits for students and their institutions as globalization continues to change the way the world connects and works.

The Impact of International Free Trade Agreements

Perhaps it should be no surprise that the number of US students studying abroad has grown so dramatically since the early 1990s. As international free trade regimes became more prominent in the 1990s, the American and world economies became more globalized and connected, and companies and businesses started looking for talent from other countries, particularly in science, engineering, and computer science. As a result, colleges and universities began to embrace a similar approach to finding new, talented, ambitious faculty, students, friends, and donors from around the world. The US government also supported this activity by increasing the number of visas available to companies sponsoring uniquely educated and talented foreign professionals in fields that served to enhance the US economy, particularly in medicine, information technology, engineering, and the sciences.

Altbach and Knight summarized this evolution in 2007 in their article "The Internationalization of Higher Education": "The contemporary emphasis on free trade stimulates international academic mobility. Current thinking sees international higher education as a commodity to be freely traded and sees higher education as private good, not a public responsibility. Commercial forces therefore have a legitimate or even a dominant place in higher education, which comes under the domain of the market."[4]

As active participants in this international talent exchange, we would expect colleges and universities in the United States to expand their interests in looking abroad for potential students, and we might expect to see dramatic increases in enrollments from countries where family incomes have risen and families have the opportunity to choose among both universities in their home countries and those located in other nations.

Implications in the Growth of our International Student Population

The number of international students in American colleges and universities has increased dramatically in the last fifteen years, rising 72 percent, from 514,723 in 1999–2000 to 886,052 in 2013–14. The contribution of international students to the US economy is thus three times what it was fifteen years ago, up from $9 billion to $27 billion dollars in tuition, room and board, books, travel, and other costs.[5]

These increases also represent a direct response to the global recession, which put enormous stress on the global economy. As a result, many prominent institutions increased the number of full-paying international students to strengthen their finances. At first, only private schools made this strategic move, but now even the large public systems in states like California, Illinois, Michigan, and Wisconsin have increased enrollments of international students. In 2011, the *Seattle Times* reported that almost 18 percent of the entering freshman class at the University of Washington was from another country, with more than half of international students coming from China. According to the *Seattle Times*, it was a dramatic increase from six years earlier, "when only two percent of the school's freshmen came from other countries."[6]

Broadly speaking, these students have good experiences and accomplish their goals of developing and mastering skills and expertise in their chosen fields of study. Some stay in the United States after graduation, find employment, and are sponsored by the companies for which they work. The vast majority, however, return to their home countries after completing a practicum year of working in their field of study. They do so with an affinity for and connection with their alma maters, the cities in which they have lived and traveled to for other matters, and for the United States in general. In our experience, these students and alumni also want to continue to be engaged by their colleges and universities, and many look for opportunities to work with American and other multinational companies. As those of us in the United States think about the potential for US students to serve as global ambassadors, we should not overlook the opportunity to engage international alumni, and their families, as collaborators in identifying new opportunities or thought partners in considering potential solutions to complex or vexing issues.

Looking beyond Europe: The Association of Pacific Rim Universities

As American higher education institutions broadened their international activities to include the pursuit of talent and opportunities for collaboration in other parts of the world, these efforts have been especially focused in science and engineering, medicine, computer science, and the arts. In this process, presidents and provosts have become less parochial in their views of international institutions with whom they might affiliate. Traditionally, universities cultivated relationships with European universities, particularly in France, Germany, Great Britain, Italy, and Russia. More recently, however, schools in Asia and beyond—especially in Australia, China, Hong Kong, India, Japan, Malaysia, Singapore, and Taiwan—have started receiving attention as the economies of these nations expanded, and as evidence mounted to demonstrate their excellence and innovation in fields that promoted shared economic growth, or focused on tackling large-scale and seemingly intractable problems like water, energy, the functioning of megacities, and security.

In the mid-1990s, a major shift occurred in the western United States, which had broad implications for the internationalization of institutions in America and the development of branch campuses and new partnerships abroad. Four leading Association of American Universities research universities boldly partnered to create a new association called the Association of Pacific Rim Universities (APRU). APRU was an original idea of the then president of USC, Steven B. Sample. In 1997, he partnered with the presidents of the California Institute of Technology; the University of California, Berkeley; and the University of California, Los Angeles, to start APRU. APRU's vision evolved from seeing the rapid economic integration of the region and the formation of Asia-Pacific Economic Council (APEC). The founding presidents' vision was to establish a premier alliance of research universities as an advisory body to international organizations, governments, and businesses on the development of science and innovation in the Asia-Pacific region, as well as on the broader development of higher education. The vision now encompasses creating and fostering new knowledge on the global challenges affecting the region, and the impact of the region on global challenges.

Since its founding, APRU has grown to include forty-five top-tier research universities from the US states of California, Hawaii, Oregon, and Washington, as well as the countries of Australia, Canada, Chile, China, Hong Kong, Japan, Malaysia, Mexico, New Zealand, the Philippines, Russia, Singapore, South Korea, Taiwan, and Thailand. It includes seventeen APEC economies, including the world's three largest economies. More than 140,000 faculty teach at APRU member institutions, enrolling more than two million students annually. APRU organizes forums that regularly bring together senior administrators, deans, faculty, graduate and undergraduate students, and senior administrators to focus on topics like education and research, teaching, intellectual property and commercialization, and policy research papers on topics of common interest. Activities are also organized for Asia-Pacific student leaders, Asia-Pacific women in leadership, doctoral students, and early career research networks for professors. APRU presidents have a well-attended annual two-day meeting to provide leadership and guidance to the APRU Secretariat.

The strategic development of a multinational network of institutions like APRU provided a learning community that set the stage for how US universities in the West approached further development of international partnerships and the option of a branch campus overseas. These institutions and their leaders now had visible and reliable potential partners who were sharing information, and with whom they developed reciprocal, bilateral, and multilateral topic-based collaborations that focused on defined needs and common interests. Importantly, faculty from member schools were not limited only to working with colleagues at other member institutions; rather, they could be connected to an even larger network of potential collaborators and thought partners. The establishment of APRU did not go unnoticed by schools in other parts of the United States, and after a long period of focusing on partnerships principally in Europe, there was now much more credibility and direct experience in exploring affiliations with universities in the Asia-Pacific region, in part because ten American universities of the forty-five institutions in the association are also members of the prominent Association of American Universities, which includes sixty-two leading research universities in the United States as judged by the federal research dollars they are awarded each year.

APRU universities located outside of the United States are more quickly recognized as credible by other leaders in American higher education, who are learning that these institutions share with their US counterparts a number of key academic and institution values focused on teaching, research, and service. Additionally, several countries in the

Middle East—including Abu Dhabi, Dubai in the UAE, Jordan, and Saudi Arabia—have invested heavily in their own national institutions and sought out partnerships with universities from other countries, particularly the United States.

Recent Trends in International Partnership Development

During the late 1990s and early 2000s, a variety of institutions from across the United States explored a range of affiliations with foreign governments and colleges and universities located in other countries. US schools also shifted their emphasis on what they wanted domestic students to learn as a result of attending overseas programs and interacting with international students on their home campuses. Schools now encouraged students to understand themselves as global citizens, not just tourists or visitors to other countries, and, as emerging global citizens, student preferences shifted toward opportunities to live among the local citizenry in apartments, homes, and institutional facilities in town, not as members of a separate enclave of short-term visitors. An increasing number of students sought internships in businesses operating in the countries where they studied, and participated in focused, short-term programs to gain a variety of exposures to help them see and experience how things worked on a practical level in their host countries. As one best practice, elite business schools such as those at Harvard, USC, and Yale began to require that all students seeking a master of business administration degree participate in international experiences that included case studies about specific businesses, and present their ideas to the actual leaders of those companies. This curricular innovation was rapidly seen as a desirable experience, and is now more common among the top-rated business schools in the United States.

On a broader scale, American universities—particularly those engaged in research and with fairly well-developed relationships with international alumni, donors, and government agencies—were being invited to open branch campuses in other countries, particularly in the Middle East and China. Schools sent their campus leaders overseas to explore such opportunities, and also hosted delegations from potential host countries. Some American university leaders and representatives of the aspiring host countries presented and discussed alternative visions for the campuses, potential development sites, ideas about how to initially finance these new ventures, and how local and national governments might assist in the development of such campuses. For our purposes, we define a campus as a physical location with buildings, dedicated staff, student residences, and other amenities that one would commonly find on a typical college or university campus. Alternatively, some universities explored opening offices in foreign capitals or economic centers where they already had strong networks of alumni, donors, and trustees. Such offices were typically small, two-person operations that concentrated on establishing and maintaining connections between faculty and deans and local universities, potential donors, admission prospects and their parents, and alumni. In 1997, USC—after appointing non-American voting trustees in 1994, the first higher education institution in the United States to do so, and after taking all trustees on a fact-finding trip to the Asia-Pacific region—opened small offices to promote connections with their constituencies in Hong Kong, Jakarta, Seoul, Shanghai, Taipei, and Tokyo.

Over the next decade, a variety of approaches took root. Universities like Syracuse, Notre Dame, and USC chose to open small offices to promote connections with their constituencies in cities like Hong Kong, Jakarta, Shanghai, Taiwan, and Tokyo. In contrast, Northwestern (journalism and communication), Cornell (medicine), Texas A&M (chemical, electrical, and petroleum engineering), Carnegie Mellon (business, computer science, and information systems), Virginia Commonwealth (arts), and Georgetown Universities (foreign service) decided to establish programs in Qatar as part of the Education City initiative supported by the Qatar Foundation for Education, Science and Community Development. Following a similar model, the Incheon Global Campus (IGC) in South Korea near the capital city of Seoul houses operations for programs offered by George Mason University, Ghent University, the State University of New York at Stonybrook, and the University of Utah in a dedicated facility built by the government and Incheon Metropolitan City. The purpose of IGC is to innovate the education system of Korea and to nurture the next generation of leaders in the fields of education, economics, industry, culture, and arts. It has been estimated that $1 billion will be invested in the campus, although global financial trends could affect the final result.

As an example of the vulnerabilities even major, well-established institutions can experience, the turmoil caused by global financial recession greatly affected the plans of Michigan State University (MSU), which opened a campus for undergraduates in Dubai just before the financial crisis. It closed it two years later as the enrollments they anticipated did not materialize. MSU now maintains a small graduate program there. George Mason also had a presence in Dubai, but decided to close it for financial reasons and concentrate on its IGC program. Both schools had

> *What is the most important piece of advice you would offer to a higher education leader developing an international partnership this year?*
>
> Be prepared to put yourself in the other partner's shoes and learn about the cultural, political, and economic factors that are shaping their perspectives internationally as well as their perceptions of opportunities and constraints. Remain open to possibilities.

counted on the government of the Emirate of Dubai to provide the resources to help them through the lean start-up years and until enrollments were sufficient, but the faltering global economy led the government of Dubai to unexpectedly scale back its ambitions.

In an unusual model most likely difficult to replicate, New York University opened a selective institution in Abu Dhabi, the capital city of the United Arab Emirates, that is primarily sponsored by the crown prince of the UAE with the financial backing of the UAE government. NYU Abu Dhabi (NYUAD) recruits talented students from around the world, offers a generous program of financial aid to retain them, and provides a broad array of academic offerings taught by NYUAD faculty and enhanced by visiting faculty from NYU's campus in New York. NYUAD welcomed its first cohort of undergraduates in the fall of 2010, and four years later former US President Bill Clinton addressed the inaugural class of 2014 at its graduation ceremony. NYU's global strategy, as articulated over time by its former president John Sexton, evolved from a traditional US research campus connected to a set of fourteen international study abroad centers to a system with two "portal campuses" in New York and Abu Dhabi through which a student can enter this "global network university" as it encourages the free movement of scholars and students through its various physical and online properties. Overall, however, as many US universities have pursued opportunities abroad, they have also continued to support robust international programs based in faculty research and scholarship, such as important scientific research centers like the Stanford Linear Accelerator Center (SLAC) and the University of Chicago's Argonne National Laboratory. Yet the sobering realities of the recent recession and global economic slowdown have made even elite institutions much more cautious about attempting to open full campuses overseas.

Additionally, key characteristics of the US college and university system can be difficult or even impossible to replicate in foreign countries, including democratic governance, academic freedom, publicly supported state universities, transparent financial systems, government incentives for tax-deductible charitable contributions, and the support of agencies like the National Science Foundation or the National Institutes of Health, which provide direct grants to schools to pursue projects based on peer review, to name a few.

The above examples include relatively large, well-financed research universities. Small colleges have been understandably more cautious about establishing their own branch campuses. Many have instead implemented more focused partnerships and alliances with colleague institutions abroad that allow their students to explore their academic interests internationally, to gain exposure to other cultures, and to become global citizens as they return to campus to share these experiences. A large number of schools promote conversations, readings, and programs to help students draw more from what they learned abroad. Liberal arts institutions such as Dickinson and Grinnell Colleges have focused on global study and engagement as strengths that distinguish them from their competitors. Dickinson, for example, describes its approach to global study as "pervasive," "integrated," "continuous," and "active," characterizing its rural Pennsylvania campus as "the hub of the College's worldwide network of study and research centers."[7] At Grinnell, located in rural Iowa, nearly 60 percent of students participate in off-campus study programs that are tied to broad curricular themes such as global health, global economics and regional development, migration and diaspora, or human rights and social justice.

As noted in *Internationalization in U.S. Higher Education*, published by the American Council on Education in 2005, "high quality education must prepare students to live and work in a world characterized by growing multiculturalism and diminishing borders. Higher Education institutions across the country are rising to this challenge [through] . . . internationalization strategies."[8] As of 2015, the US State Department estimates that about 37 percent of Americans now have valid passports, roughly eight times more than in 1991.[9] The State Department also estimates that approximately 6.8 million Americans were living outside of the United States in 2012.[10] US institutions of higher education have been and will continue to evolve strategies to adapt to opportunities and challenges in the global economy, respond to preferences of US students for greater opportunities to live and study abroad, and capture new opportunities for enrollment revenue and collaboration with foreign governments, businesses, and educational institutions.

Conclusion: Choosing the Right Model for Your Institution

There is little doubt that the increase in international partnerships and co-ventures is here to stay. Higher education institutions that ignore this phenomenon are doing themselves as well as current and prospective faculty, students, and alumni a disservice, as opportunities to strengthen institutions will be missed. Organizations like the Association of Pacific Rim Universities, the National Association of Foreign Student Advisors, Student Affairs Administrators in Higher Education, and the Consortium for the Financing of Higher Education, to name a few, provide information, ideas, and case studies about international activities in higher education. As well, these associations can provide the opportunity to talk directly with peers at other schools about what they have learned, what they are currently doing, and what they are planning. Schools must also be sure that whatever strategies they decide to employ are based on several core concepts:

- Institutional adherence to mission
- Support from trustees, senior administration, and faculty leaders
- Building on traditions and strengths
- Clear-eyed assessment of benefits and risks
- Support of alumni networks, donors, and possibly parents in potential host country
- Understanding of laws, rules, politics, local customs, accreditation and licensing requirements, and other aspects of how to do business in foreign countries
- In-country support

During the early years of the Internet and mass access to computers, colleges and universities struggled with how to keep up with current technology. Leaders talked about wanting institutional technology to be on the "cutting edge" but not the "bleeding edge," where financial resources and human capital were wasted with risky investments. The same holds true for international activities. What is right for one school may be wrong for another. Decisions about international involvements must be made after thoughtful research, planning, and strategizing. The ultimate goal should be to strengthen a school's academic, research, and service programs in ways that build on faculty strengths and that engage students, alumni, and supporters, exciting them and solidifying their long-term relationship with their college or university.

Notes

1. Booz Allen Hamilton, *Word's Most Enduring Institutions.*
2. "Fast Facts on the Open Doors Report on International Students in the U.S., 2014," Institute of International Education, accessed April 3, 2016, http://www.iie.org/Research-and-Publications/Open-Doors.
3. "Generation Study Abroad," Institute of International Education, accessed April 11, 2016, http://www.iie.org/Programs/Generation-Study-Abroad.
4. Altbach and Knight, "Internationalization of Higher Education."
5. "Fast Facts."
6. Long, "Foreign Enrollment Skyrockets for US."
7. "Global Study and Engagement," Dickinson College, accessed April 3, 2016, http://www.dickinson.edu/global.
8. Green, *Internationalization in U.S. Higher Education*, 111.
9. Bureau of Consular Affairs, *Who We Are and What We Do.*
10. Costanzo and von Koppenfels, "Counting the Uncountable"; Association of Pacific Rim Universities website, accessed April 3, 2016, http://apru.org/; Hudzik, *Comprehensive Internationalization*; Peterson and Helms, *Challenges and Opportunities for the Global Engagement of Higher Education.*

CHAPTER TWELVE

Public-Private Partnerships: Models That Work

John Ottenhoff

Some would argue that it is competition that makes American higher education great. The United States has not only a superb collection of state-supported universities but also competition within those systems. And, unlike most countries, alongside that array of public colleges and universities stands a "distinctively American"[1] group of residential liberal arts colleges, not to mention an array of private research universities, that are among the richest and most powerful in the world.

Competition drives innovation, but competition is also costly. In an increasingly difficult struggle for state funding, historic divisions between "flagship" and "land-grant" institutions have become more complicated with an explosion of new doctorate and master's-level universities and two-year colleges that often compete for the same students. Take Michigan, for instance, where the University of Michigan must not only reckon with Michigan State University but also with Northern Michigan, Central Michigan, Western, and Eastern Michigan Universities—and more than twenty-five two-year colleges. And for Michigan's small privates—Albion, Alma, Aquinas, Calvin, Hope, and Kalamazoo, just to name a few—they must appeal to students who compare not only programs and amenities but also location, sticker prices, and aid packages. While the scope and resource base of the ninety-plus higher education institutions within the state vary greatly, recruiting the right students—who often submit multiple applications across the spectrum—remains a concern of all. Cooperation in this environment makes sense and is worth the effort, but it has been a continuing challenge.

But while Michigan remains a worthy yet complex environment for competition between private and public institutions, other states such as North Carolina have found research partnerships—in the Research

Triangle encompassing Duke, North Carolina, and North Carolina State Universities—to be effective ways of bringing together private and public universities and the private and public sectors, as well. Emory and Georgia Tech Universities in Georgia and the University of Pittsburgh and Carnegie Mellon University in Pennsylvania have shaped similar partnerships. And some programs, such as Preparing Future Faculty (PFF), have focused on cooperation between different kinds of institutions and in the process brought together publics and privates. PFF recognized that cooperation made perfect sense for the institutions educating future professors and the many nondoctoral colleges and universities who would employ them. Over its 10 years of existence, the project engaged 53 private institutions, 167 state and local colleges and universities, 58 religiously affiliated institutions, 4 American Indian tribal colleges, and 1 military academy.[2] In fact, PFF stands as a creative prototype for how cooperation can increase the effectiveness of institutions large and small, public and private, while enhancing conditions for student learners and the professoriate.

So, in this challenging environment, why would a small private liberal arts college choose to collaborate with a large state-funded university? What might a state university with over 14,000 students seek in a collaboration with a private college of 1,100 undergraduates on the other side of the state, and what might these potential partners see in each other that would lead to overcoming deeply ingrained competitive instincts in favor of cooperation? The collaboration between the College of Idaho and Idaho State University arose through recognition of complementary strengths, a history of successful partnerships, and a moment of opportunity. While these may not all be required ingredients for a successful private-public higher education collaboration, they are centrally important ones.

Like many small, tuition-dependent institutions, the College of Idaho (C of I), a private liberal arts college founded in 1891, has been seeking new sources of revenue for two decades or more. With two small graduate programs in education, new master's degree programs seemed a likely avenue for growth, and, with changes coming in state and regional healthcare systems, a program in physician assistant (PA) studies seemed especially promising. The college has become known regionally for quality academic programs in the sciences. Fully a third of the student body graduates with majors in the sciences within an innovative curriculum requiring a major and three minors across the traditional liberal arts divisions and one professional area.

Idaho State University (ISU), a Carnegie-classified doctoral research high and teaching institution founded in 1901, is the state's lead institution in health professions and medical education. With its main campus in Pocatello, in southeastern Idaho, ISU has sought to broaden its reach and has opened branch campuses to the north in Idaho Falls, to the west in Twin Falls, and Meridian—in Idaho's Treasure Valley, the population center of the state. ISU has been active in working with partners like C of I in creating cooperative programs in nursing, pharmacy studies, and occupational therapy. Recently, the university aggressively expanded its Meridian facility with state-of-the art biotechnology laboratories and new facilities for pharmacy, dentistry, and several other health programs.

Framed in this way, it made good sense for a large state university known for its healthcare programs to partner with a small college known for its strong science programs. C of I offered the established ISU program a record of excellent teaching and a network of C of I–trained doctors throughout the state—especially important in securing clinical rotations for PA students in training. The C of I campus offered PA students another option—a site closer to Boise than the main Pocatello campus, with the amenities of campus life that the Meridian facility lacked—and cooperation was preferable to competition for a small institution seeking to quickly establish a new program while navigating the complex, and expensive, terrain of medical instruction, clinical training, and accreditation. Even though C of I might have seen more profit in going it alone, ISU's experience in training PAs and the university's reach regionally made it wise for C of I to seek collaboration rather than becoming a competitor.

The existing partnerships have also been helpful, as the lead planners knew each other from previous agreements, grasped the dynamics of the different campuses, and had established a foundation of trust. Negotiating and updating memoranda of understanding (MOUs) on a yearly basis confirmed the necessary academic quality on both sides, with C of I students performing well in graduate programs and ISU delivering a combination of superior programming and high rates of success. Leaders at both institutions acknowledged that the PA program agreement would not have happened without that history of trust.

Additionally, economic workforce conditions were timed almost perfectly, with physician assistants constituting one of the fastest-growing occupations in the nation. The Idaho Department of Labor estimates that the number of PA positions in the state will increase by more than 40 percent between 2008 and 2018. A projected shortage of physicians, an aging population, and implementation of the Affordable Care Act of 2010 also are expected to drive the demand for physician assistants. ISU's program, which began in 1995 as an undergraduate program, moved to the master's level in 2004 and expanded to the Boise area in 2007. The

What is the greatest challenge facing a higher education leader developing a public and private partnership this year?

Tight budgets, while a strong incentive to partner, are also the greatest challenge to successful, long-term agreements, especially between public and private institutions. For public-private partnerships to work in the first place, planners need to think imaginatively and expansively beyond familiar calls for austerity, and to convince colleagues that partnerships of this nature can be one of the best ways to address fiscal pressures.

addition of the Caldwell site brings the total to seventy-two available seats and offers better healthcare to a largely rural state in need of more primary care. Demand remains strong: the program received over 650 applications in the most recent admission cycle.[3]

Building a Better Bridge: A Six-Step Plan for Public-Private Partnerships

While the Idaho State University–College of Idaho collaboration reflects some special circumstances, its planners developed a set of action steps for those considering other public-private affiliations:

1. *Start small.* It helps to start small and then build. The cooperative programs in nursing and occupational therapy helped to establish relationships and understanding. The financial stakes in the cooperative programs were minimal, making it easier to work together on this larger program. Scaling up the joint PA program remains the goal, as preliminary ideas for other collaborations are being entertained.

2. *Complementarity is not similarity.* It is necessary to think carefully about complementary strengths and different roles, and then to articulate them carefully. What does our small campus add to the program? How can both parties become stronger through this collaboration? Once the private and public institutions can get past the point of clarifying and noting—even accentuating—their differences, they can concentrate on how those differences can be useful and constructive. Public and private partnerships will often involve different scales and different levels of resources, but it will still be critical to establish a balance and avoid the perception of "junior" or subservient relationships for the smaller institution.

3. *Make memoranda of understanding intentionally broad.* MOUs need to be broad and give overall shape to the agreement, as partners cannot anticipate all the eventualities of the program once it is launched. For example, C of I and ISU had not fully worked out the implications of having different campus policies and schedules—a lesson learned when the first "snow day" was declared last winter on the C of I campus. On a larger scale, tuition levels posed an especially tricky issue, with the C of I private school tuition being slightly lower than the ISU public, yet out-of-state, tuition. While the business plan made the difference clear, explaining that differential to potential students could have been better handled based on our first-year observations.

4. *Collaborate with accreditors.* Accreditation issues can be challenging and represent the true test of the partnership's durability. ISU's bid to expand introduced several unknowns into a program that was solidly established and had a strong record of success; C of I needed to be continually clear about academic standards and support. Conversely, C of I's business plan called for rapid expansion of the Caldwell program, but the accrediting agency mandated a five-year period before further growth could happen. Strategic cooperation and patience were important.

5. *Communicate successes and failures.* Clear and direct communication is essential. Problems happen, especially in a program dependent on distance learning technology, as ours is. It is tactically wise for leaders on both sides to be in close contact and to approach problem solving as much as possible in face-to-face meetings. As noted, unexpected challenges and problems *will* emerge, and responses need to be forthcoming even more promptly than on a single-campus institution.

6. *Seek a cooperative and creative, rather than competitive, partner.* Finding the right level of complementarity in the partnership is a foundational element of success, especially if one partner is joining a successful preexisting program. ISU has maintained control over the admission process and the curriculum. The twelve students at the C of I site will receive dual degrees, and while faculty members in the C of I program remain under contract with ISU, they are subject to C of I campus policies because they are considered C of I faculty. Both institutions provide leadership for the advisory board for the program. While many of these issues can be stipulated in MOUs, it is also important for professional relation-

Partnering with For-Profit Colleges: Four Benefits

PAMELA GOAD

1. *Centrally located campuses*. For-profit institutions tend to be in centralized transportation areas or downtown, which can be especially useful for publics and nonprofits located at a distance from public transportation systems or land locked on their current campuses. Excess capacity will sometimes exist at these facilities, which tend to be newer and technologically sophisticated, and classroom spaces can be leased as needs rise and fall.

2. *Adjunct teaching opportunities*. For-profit faculty are often employed in industry and have restricted teaching schedules. Thus there is the opportunity for adjunct faculty from private and public institutions to secure additional teaching income and professional development.

3. *Bookstore and library access fees*. For-profit colleges are often interested in partnering with public and nonprofit institutions for bookstore and library access that will supplement the traditional institutions' auxiliary income levels.

4. *General education curriculum and faculty needs*. Articulation agreements to meet general education course requirements are also typical areas for which for-profit institutions seek private and public partners to provide sequences of courses and experienced faculty according to annually negotiated fee structures.

Pamela Goad is vice president of the Northwest Commission on Colleges and Universities and was formerly chief academic officer of the Art Institute of Seattle, a for-profit institution.

ships to develop and build. Informal and social gatherings, outside the scope of a formal MOU, can make a significant difference in shaping and then reinforcing the partnership.

Partnering with Foundations: A Different Approach to Public-Private Affiliation

A different set of collaborations between private and public institutions is taking shape with support from the Andrew W. Mellon Foundation, specifically among the fourteen member colleges in the Associated Colleges of the Midwest (ACM) consortium and the Committee on Institutional Cooperation, which includes the fourteen members of the

Big Ten Conference and the University of Chicago. Both entities have long traditions of working cooperatively, but within a circle of like institutions. The Mellon Foundation's suggestion that the two groups work together was at first met with dubiousness, yet several strong initiatives have rapidly emerged. The leadership of the foundation offers this initial view:

> In spite of obvious differences in scale, research universities and liberal arts colleges have a mutual interest in resisting specialization, sustaining their commitments to general education, demonstrating that teaching and research are integrally linked, and controlling costs. Research universities have the resources and infrastructure to enable liberal arts colleges to expand their curricular offerings and to build intellectual community, and liberal arts colleges have much to share with their university colleagues about getting undergraduates involved in research and community engagement, and in introducing new PhDs to the intimacy and professional opportunities available in a residential liberal arts community. Another incentive for the research universities is the opportunity to recruit liberal arts college students into their graduate programs.[4]

This collaboration is based on the formula of complementary strengths, a history of successful partnerships, and a moment of perceived opportunity. Initially, partnerships have been based among institutions in the same states, Grinnell College and the University of Iowa, or Lawrence University and the University of Wisconsin, as examples. The Midwest Faculty Seminar sponsored by the University of Chicago is another vehicle through which both kinds of institutions are working in sustained partnership. In working with the two consortia, the Mellon Foundation sought to highlight those complementary strengths. In a pilot program called Enhancing the Midwest Knowledge Ecosystem, or EMKE, the ACM and the Council of Independent Colleges (CIC) are exploring areas of common intellectual interest—the digital humanities and languages, especially less commonly taught languages, language pedagogy, and opportunities for language sharing.[5] A call for collaboration was issued for projects that would help faculty gain perspectives from the other institutions and teaching environments, to create cross-consortial learning communities that will contribute to personal and professional development, and to expand resources available to faculty through sharing. The goal was to bring together colleagues who most likely shared graduate school training and parallel academic interests to find projects that gained strength from their complementary perspectives.

While the results of the EMKE project are still being realized, the initial conversations have resulted in a new Mellon-funded Fellows Pro-

> *What is the most important piece of advice you would offer a
> president or provost now beginning to develop a public-private
> higher education partnership?*
>
> A successful public-private partnership must be driven by shared trust and knowl-
> edge, and the best way to achieve these goals is by forming multiple layers of collab-
> oration, including ongoing social interaction.

gram that responds to another current need: the diversification of college
faculty. As the ACM points out, "Throughout higher education, changing
demographics are re-defining the student landscape, posing new challenges and opportunities for institutions to enhance the education of all
students by encouraging diversity in the pipeline that feeds the professoriate while also providing support that will better enable diverse
undergraduate students to succeed and thrive."[6] The new program attempts to build on the collaborations started through EMKE using three
components:

1. *Undergraduate fellowships* to support graduate school exploration among students from ACM colleges.

2. *Tenure-track faculty fellowship appointments* at ACM campuses
   for new scholars with terminal master's or doctoral degrees.

3. *Biconsortial meetings on creating nurturing academic settings*
   for a diverse faculty and hiring and promoting to diversify the
   professoriate.

Major financial support from an organization like the Mellon Foundation obviously makes building partnerships such as the ACM-CIC
arrangement much easier; generous funding has a way of erasing doubts
about cooperation, but this kind of partnership does not have to depend upon external funding. Colleges and universities should recognize
the historically strong record of liberal arts colleges in producing a dispro-
portionate number of PhDs. With an emphasis on small classes, independent work, and faculty-student research, liberal arts colleges constitute
an important partner for *both* public and private universities. Cooperation across the public-private divide in preparing future faculty leaders
and creating pipelines for employment make obvious sense, and emphasizing complementarity as the cornerstone in identifying long-term partnering prospects is the wisest way forward.

The Mellon Foundation highlights something we all know: higher education is a competitive business. Our institutions compete for students, for reputation, and for funding. As a result, public-private initiatives like those between the College of Idaho and Idaho State University, and, on a larger scale, the members of the Associated Colleges of the Midwest and fifteen international research universities, also reflect what the foundation views as a "growing recognition that collaboration must become an important part of future planning."[7]

What is necessary for the Mellon Foundation's prediction to become a reality? Perhaps fear will be a key—fear of declining state support and rising tuition at the private colleges creating unsustainable, separate, and duplicative programs, with each supporting its own staffs and physical plants. Perhaps economic necessity will force institutions to reconsider whether sharing assets like library collections, scientific equipment, or programs might be worth the effort such cooperation requires. Perhaps increasingly strenuous demands for good assessment of student learning and better articulations of the value in a college degree will create more collaborations such as Preparing Future Faculty, and perhaps students who are increasingly moving among various institutions at all levels will demand articulation among curricula, thus making it easier for them to complete their degrees. As all of these things begin to happen, it follows that successful collaborations between privates and publics like those described in this chapter will become more frequent and influential.

Notes

1. See Koblik and Graubard, *Distinctively American.*

2. See "Who's Involved in PFF," Preparing Future Faculty, accessed April 3, 2016, http://www.preparing-faculty.org/PFFWeb.History.htm.

3. For information about the program, see the Idaho State University Department of Physician Studies website, accessed April 3, 2016, http://www.isu.edu/PAprog/.

4. Andrew W. Mellon Foundation, *Grantmaking to Support Collaboration in Higher Education.*

5. "ACM and 'Big Ten' Explore Ways to Collaborate through Mellon-Funded Planning Workshops," Associated College of the Midwest, June 18, 2012, http://www.acm.edu/features/news/358.

6. "Undergraduate and Faculty Fellows Program for a Diverse Professoriate," Associated Colleges of the Midwest, accessed April 3, 2016, http://www.acm.edu/professional_development/Funding_Opportunities/Fellows_Program.html.

7. Andrew W. Mellon Foundation, *Grantmaking to Support Collaboration in Higher Education.*

III

Consortium: New Benefits, Changing
Purposes

CHAPTER THIRTEEN

A New Way to Design and Deliver Higher Education Consortia

Phillip DiChiara

American higher education has given birth to more than one hundred consortia, and the overwhelming majority focus on academic collaboration. In contrast, the Boston Consortium for Higher Education (TBC) was specifically designed in 1995 by the chief financial officers of Boston College, Massachusetts Institute of Technology, Northeastern University, Tufts University, and Wellesley College, with a focus on reducing nonacademic operating costs. After its incorporation as a 501(c)(3) not-for-profit institution in 1998, they were subsequently joined by Babson College, Bentley University, Berklee College, Boston University, Brandeis University, College of the Holy Cross, Emerson College, Harvard University, Olin College of Engineering, Rhode Island School of Design, Suffolk University, and Wheaton College. While created by financial executives, the methods used to co-create solutions to shared problems were not solely financial, and the use of behavioral tools has helped to develop both bottom–up and top–down innovations as the appetite for larger and more complex projects has continued to grow over the past twenty years.

The consortium movement in higher education was initiated in California in 1925 with the creation of the Claremont University Consortium providing centralized services to a cluster of (now) seven institutions. In 1958, the Committee on Institutional Cooperation (CIC) was formed as an academic counterpart to the Big Ten Athletic Conference membership. The Five College Consortium in western Massachusetts—including Amherst, Hampshire, Mount Holyoke, and Smith Colleges along with the University of Massachusetts—began efforts to collaborate in the 1950s and incorporated in 1965.[1] As noted in other chapters in this book, the idea of organized collaboration has continued to gain momentum, with periods of growth and shrinkage a function of the economy of the particular period and the willingness of the participants to cede some level of absolute individual sovereignty to the group and, theoretically, the greater good.

It was an American Council on Education Conference in 1965 titled "Formation of a Professional Organization of Consortia" that led to the creation of what has since become the Association for Collaborative Leadership and a national platform for consortia to share ideas, resources, and project expertise. Even for the consortia that predated this conference and the subsequent association, movement and public awareness began to grow for the Associated Colleges of the South (founded 1952), Associated Colleges of the Midwest (1958), New Hampshire College and University Council (1966), Associated Colleges of the Twin Cities (1972), Virginia Tidewater Consortium (1973), Southeast Pennsylvania Consortium for Higher Education (1993), Five Colleges of Ohio (1995), and the Colleges of the Fenway in Boston (1996). As the business model for higher education is increasingly challenged, collaborative options provided through consortia are growing in importance.

As additional consortia formed, some accumulated multiple successful programs and solutions and became sustainable entities. Others failed, often because the investment by the participating members was deemed to be excessively high relative to the return they received. Some of this may have been a failure of management to develop among the governing board an understanding of the deeper requirements of genuine collaboration, and the fact that this work often requires years to develop the necessary relationships. Creating an organization with a single full-time staff member and little if any infrastructure or capital, and then charging it with primary or sole responsibility for multiorganizational change, is soon viewed as unrealistic.

While conveying a networking relationship between two or more entities, traditional collaboration also implies a democratic, participatory method of conducting business. Many are quick to use the term "collaboration," as it conveys images of egalitarian behavior and equitable mutual gain. Yet the quest for achievement in a collaborative enterprise will be negatively affected when we devalue the techniques and processes that engender the genuine skills required. It is too easy to fall back on command-control and authoritarian styles of management, couched though they may be in gentle and civil discourse, simply because they may work well outside of a consortial relationship. While this may continue to be the de facto and default style of management in Western culture, it is also what makes consortial organizations such a challenge both to operate and sustain. In fact, this approach sets up a consortium

Communities of Practice as the Basic Dues Investment-Facilitating Collaboration

Basic support *provided by dues to* **create the opportunity** *to find solutions to problems that members agree to address collectively*

- Mutual learning and best-practice exchange
- Exposure and assessment of range of practices
- Formal educational opportunities to address shared challenges

- Early warning system for regulatory change
- Development of shared interest, courage, and trust to engage in an initiative

Application of Decision Gate
Winnowing down to the serious participants

- Searches for possible solutions via fact-finding, analysis, and discussion
- Pay-to-play project development based on individual school risk versus reward expectations
- Building support for corrective action   • Develop a broad set of options

Project Implementation and Management

- Independent financial structure, e.g., the self-sustaining business units
- Voluntary participation

Continued Project Development, Improvement, and Expansion

- Optimal leverage of member scale to achieve significant cost reductions and/or service improvements

The Boston Consortium for Higher Education's value proposition: What drives value?

for failure. By their nature, collaborations are voluntary and relatively fragile. Interpersonal trust must be generated, applied, and upon successful outcome recycled into future efforts. The possibility to amplify and increase the results of collaboration over time is the one attribute that should not be compromised in a race to achieve desired short-term goals and objectives.

Starting Out: Five Guidelines for Consortium Developers

The higher education community in Boston was relatively late to adopt the consortium model, partly because of the long individual history of each university, and partly as a result of a comfort with informal means of working cooperatively. The abundance of research universities encouraged a fair amount of academic collaboration, but back-office business collaborations were notably absent.

Initially supported by the Mellon Foundation, the regional Davis Educational Foundation became the primary benefactor of efforts to achieve the stated mission.[2] While the member schools covered all of TBC's administrative costs, it was the provision of venture capital from Davis to experiment and try new approaches that made the difference and subsequently led to programs and ventures that have been extended to the participant schools and beyond in the years since. With a mission of cost management of academic institutions, and an original governance team of chief finance officers, it was primarily a matter of creating trusting relationships and advancing an approach of enlightened self-interest. But the path to that level of mutual comfort has been long and often difficult.

As an external resource, the Association for Collaborative Leadership has endeavored in recent years to codify the methods and experiences of our colleagues in the form of an annual institute dedicated to increasing the sophistication in how these entities operate. Ultimately, trust is the basis for all collaboration. When trust is in short supply, the scale and sophistication of solutions to shared concerns and problems

Five Things One Needs to Know When Creating a Consortium

1. *It is not necessary to incorporate a consortium before undertaking a collaborative project.* Wait until the inevitable issues of varying interpretations of governance principles play out over time, possibly as long as two or three years. Being too quick to create legal or technical constraints places a burden on the emergence of a culture of collaboration.

2. *Suggest a gesture of commitment.* After two or three investigatory meetings considering the creation of a collaborative partnership, ask potential members for a modest equal contribution to sustain early, if limited, overhead costs. When the difficult realities of change management become apparent, such a move can separate the serious from the not so serious.

3. *Have a third-party facilitator take notes of meetings.* Let someone handle the necessary but burdensome scheduling and research requirements of a start-up consortium. Volunteerism will be required for projects to provide proof of concept, so don't waste it on administrative duties that can be outsourced in the short term and eventually borne by dues upon agreement that shared needs can be addressed collectively.

4. *Communicate an intent to research a collaborative enterprise as broadly public as the circumstances permit.* Neither faculty nor senior executives should find about such an exploration in the local newspaper . . . or at the water cooler.

5. *Review the implications of logical incrementalism.* Logical incrementalism speaks to the reality of managing change against competing demands for time, financial, and political resource.*

*Quinn, "Strategic Change."

will necessarily be limited. With a working model of mutual respect and understanding, opportunities are surprisingly broad. As more than one consortium leader has succinctly stated, dialogue leads to relationships, relationships lead to trust, and out of trust comes opportunity.

The mission of TBC is to reduce nonacademic operating costs and improve the quality of our institutional operations. Principally, this mission is accomplished by leveraging both economic and intellectual scale, understanding the role of human and organizational behavior, and thinking systemically about the challenges that member schools are confronting. In retrospect, the key insight of the founding members was to view the consortium as a means to offset the inherent risk aversion of most colleges and universities. They created a third-party vehicle to experiment and provide pilot or demonstration projects. In effect, when the project was successful and adapted, the member institutions genuinely deserved the credit. If the project failed, it was just the consortium doing what it was set up to do: experiment.

The larger leap of faith involved accepting a temporary, short-term loss in order to position oneself for a larger, long-term gain. For governance dominated by seasoned financial executives, this was a difficult concept to accept. What if the short-term loss did not lead clearly to the larger solution? How long must I invest in a collaborative enterprise before I will see a return on my investment? Will I be delayed in achieving my objectives if other institutions move more slowly than I do? Finally, on a deeper level, are we truly collaborating or merely cooperating with subsets of the membership who have discovered overlapping common ground, and does this matter? Numerous members of TBC found over the years that co-creating new solutions that require real change and significant financial investment carries major challenges, and that, as some have joked, for all of its altruistic benefits, collaboration can be an unnatural act.

1. Leverage Human Behaviors

While many of the founding members of the Boston Consortium had existing relationships and knew one another through the National Association of College and University Business Officers (NACUBO) and other peer professional organizations, most understood that moving to a more intricate level of collaboration was going to require careful nurturing over time.[3] To begin, it seemed to be a practical and positive way to develop our skills by targeting apparent low-hanging fruit. At that time, we had three committees working on different "back-office" opportunities: purchasing, human resources, and environmental health and safety. It was understandable that financial executives would place emphasis on matters of purchasing early on, but in fact it is a particularly complicated function despite what might superficially appear to be a straightforward task. Nonetheless, we sought a few commonly shared items to determine the opportunity: standard 8.5×11 white paper seemed simple enough.

In fact, antitrust regulations limit access to pricing information across multiple institutions. Consortium management spent a fair amount of time with our attorney ensuring that we would not stumble into an illegality. To add to the complication, there was no consistent standard for paper among the member schools: some needed white paper, others needed recycled paper, still others expected desktop delivery by their vendor, some insisted their logo be on the packaging, and so on. Pricing? No one could disclose, except through a blind survey submitted to the consortium with an agreement about confidentiality. We were confident that suppliers offered different pricing to individual schools; after all, in our society, we operate in a free marketplace. Worse, we believed few of the eleven members would switch vendors based on the price of a single category of item, nor should they; however, the inquiry began to peel back the layers on addressing optimal pricing, with hundreds of thousands of items with stock-keeping units, or SKUs.

As a solution, we asked each school to submit it's pricing to the consortium office using a blind study. We discovered that most institutional pricing fell within a range of plus or minus $4 per case, or within a margin of about 8 to 10 percent. There were two exceptions for which pricing was two standard deviations more than the others. Without mentioning names, the result was reported to the board of the consortium. The board members asked the managing director what action was planned, and the response was nothing other than to share the blind information to the procurement professionals. At the time, that did not sit well with any of them. They were told that we would report back in six months.

The pricing survey was conducted a second time six months later. The pricing from the two outlier schools had changed. The leadership's assessment was that managers tend to act in their own interest, and upon distribution of the pricing range, procurement heads realized that their CFOs could discover the disadvantaged pricing. In fact, the disparity may have been created by some product specifications exceeding others, not a failure to effectively negotiate, and not every institution had the scale to obtain optimal pricing.

The lesson for our membership was that human behavior, and not just economic scale, must be leveraged. Return on investment is important, but if incentives are not in place, a strong business case can be inadequate and unachievable. Nonetheless, simply identifying inefficiencies or redundancies is not solution implementation. Rather, that requires a process of solution co-creation, where members invest their staff time in formulating a plan. Some may recall the popular advisory from the 1960s: "If you are not part of the solution, you are part of the problem."[4] That is actually incorrect in this case. Rather, we learned that "If you are not part of the problem, you can't create a workable solution to it." It would be many years before we had both the necessary skills and fundamental understanding of how to achieve this across multiple organizations. Collaboration is a long-term investment.

2. Expect Candor

Bringing all of the stakeholders from across the full membership to a single, professionally facilitated discussion raised candor dramatically. When a functional manager and supervisor sit at the same table, there is and should be a level of respect and an appropriate openness of thought. The reality is that we do not typically express our deepest or most radical ideas in a public forum when a supervisor is present. Interestingly, we also observed that managers from other organizations are not as intimidated in telling someone else's boss exactly how they feel.

The facilities working group was also charged to find a way to reduce the cost of heating oil, a major expense item in Boston and New England. Once again, the expected specification options presented themselves: use of #2 fuel oil versus #3 fuel oil, use of fuel oil versus natural gas, central plant versus multiple-site delivery, and preference for minority vendors, as examples. It appeared likely to be a pricing stalemate. When the working group assembled and discussion began one winter afternoon, the first forty-five minutes were engaging, but the second forty-five minutes became tense. The culmination of the session came when one energy manager said to the CFO of another university, in a tone of deep frustration, if budget managers did not push for desirable longer-term predictability in the fuel oil pricing, they would not need to establish fixed or guaranteed prices for the term of the agreement. A financial executive from another school responded with incredulity, asking whether that institution in fact transferred risk to the vendor, unfavorably affecting pricing when a contingency fund could be established instead. It was immediately apparent that, over time, an unspoken assumption had crept into the acquisition process. At a result, several institutions eventually saved several hundreds of thousands of dollars through the group's collective action.

Candor, properly facilitated, can be a force to tease out downstream assumptions that need updating. That would appear to be particularly effective in a setting across multiple institutions where sacred cows are not part of consortium collaborative culture.

3. Acknowledge and Work with Free Riders

As project successes lead to a greater appetite for more complex undertakings, a new dynamic may creep into the group process. While project management must include guidelines to proceed from opportunity identification to the order of magnitude of the potential return, different colleges and universities face buy-in decisions at varying paces. For those institutions that move quickly to participate and develop a shared solution, it can be frustrating when an uninvolved member chooses to participate only after the work has been done by others. This "free rider" syndrome may not begin intentionally, but, given the varied appetite for risk, it is hard for an institution to turn away from a solution that works, particularly when the cost of consortium overhead is shared.

For TBC, an effective solution has been found in a practice of acknowledging and emphasizing that, over time, different subsets of schools have played the lead role in achieving our collaborations. Not every school will be interested in every initiative, but once a portfolio of successes has accumulated, it will show a distribution representative of the whole, and with this more sophisticated understanding—and appreciation—of teamwork in place, remaining quid pro quo attitudes typically soften.

4. Eliminate Middle Management Fear

When consortium leaders drive project development from the top down without sufficient consideration for the contributions of middle management, trust may be jeopardized, and the long-term participation of these volunteers will diminish. If middle managers and department heads see the consortium and its working groups as a threat to their job security, or even their personal influence, this resource will evaporate before it is applied. Colleagues in charge should not overlook the explicit and implicit knowledge they bring to common work and shared assignments. Within a consortium, with multiple cross-institutional influences, such inclusion is essential.

5. Reinforce Good Citizenship

Creating a bond among professionals is a role that many national and international peer professional organizations do with varying levels of success. Local and regional consortia have the potential to do this in

Time →

Opportunity discovery, discussed — Opportunity bounded, broadly defined — Value established, preliminary ROI established — Individual school-specific decision whether to implement

First Decision Gate

Identification of an idea/undertaking that is supported by several members.

Requires:
Board agreement to commit modest amount of TBC and member time to establish a preliminary level of interest, feasibility, and potential ROI.

Intention:
Low-cost or no-cost analysis to better articulate nature of opportunity.

Outcome:
Opportunity bounded in broad terms, possibly suggesting alternate paths to organize opportunity.

Progression:
If early feedback suggests value, interested schools may choose to make a second investment involving more time and cost.

Second Decision Gate

Early investigation within the first decision gate suggests adequate the merit to justify continued investigation and financial investment, including grant funds and/or a "pay-to-play" investment by several schools.

Requires:
Board willingness to commit additional funds even if only a minority of members feel the value is adequately significant to justify.

Intention:
Invest modest funds to provide deeper level of understanding about the feasibility and order of magnitude of ROI.

Outcome:
Preliminary financial and operational parameters established.

Progression:
Make-or-break stage.
Before commitment of major funds, invest adequately to establish potential value in implementation. Some members may opt out of continued investigation after determining a poor fit in their particular circumstance.

Third Decision Gate

Second level of analysis is encouraging, and detailed planning and a school-specific ROI are required in order to make a final go/no-go decision to implement.

Requires:
Individual members invest significant funds to complete a business plan of appropriate detail. Grant funds may or may not be available, but commitment of TBC staff time is likely significant.

Intention:
Individual schools invest significant funds in addition to possible grant support.

Outcome:
Financial and operational considerations provide as much detail as necessary to make a final decision.

Progression:
At the end of this stage, theoretically several or all schools still active in this stage of investigation intend to implement unless business plan specifics fail to meet minimum expectations. Some members may opt out.

Participation is always voluntary. Individual schools may opt out at any time. Schools may opt back in at the consent of the core group as formed at Second Decision Gate.

The Boston Consortium for Higher Education's initiative investigation using multiple decision gates.

a forceful and effective manner while serving as a powerful driver of change in campus operations.

Building the momentum for increasing collaboration begins simply by scheduling meetings a year in advance. Within a given group of professionals—facilities managers, for example—some may attend only one or two of the four meetings scheduled, but it is better to avoid the complications of short-term meeting planning. We have found that by providing a quality meeting space, good food, and a dedicated professional facilitator, those who are inclined to collective action will assemble and start working with one invitation.

Good citizenship behavior is a recognized phenomenon in group processes. Over time, participants vote with their feet, and what remains are the innovators and early adopters. As a result, what senior managers can harvest is an enhanced set of operational practices for their institutions. We have found that this is what members want from their consortium: leaders who have created a safe space to experiment with new approaches and networks supported by adequate funding and accompanied by little individual risk.

The Characteristics of a Successful Consortium

While project and program development is the output that members seek, and defines the value provided by a consortium, what distinguishes a successful consortium is sometimes reflected in its governance and business model:

- *Firm governance*. Founding members of a new consortium must establish prudent governance practices. One example is that a strong case can be made for dues costs to be evenly distributed: all schools should have an equal voice and equal opportunity to participate in individual projects, but no one is required to do so. The recurring overhead of consortium management must be equally borne. Avoid "gaming" of dues based on variables such as student or employee count, or plant size, or budget scale. Because no institution will always benefit or benefit equally, avoid the temptation to put in place the seeds of destruction, when debates about dues equitability might emerge when they should be emerging over action strategies for constructive output.

- *Common economic guidelines*. As important are the economic guidelines established before formulation of the entity. If dues are set equally, engagement in operational projects or program development must be funded on a pay-to-play basis. It may be a further advantage to stage project costs in multiple decision points so that initial interest is not thwarted, but those who see the project moving away from an earlier ideal application in the case of a single school can opt out before final costs are fully assumed.

- *Clear revenue streams.* Every expense item should be tied to a particular revenue stream. Most successful consortia have a version of this in place. With TBC, the standing overhead costs to operate and maintain consortium staff are alone tied to annual dues. Administrative operating costs are identified separately from project development costs. Project costs are covered by the pay-to-play requirement, with the possible addition of grant support. Once a project or program is implemented, ongoing costs are shared by those member schools utilizing the service. Additional revenues may be provided by charging nonmember schools a premium over the ongoing shared costs. Grant support is used to augment individual pay-to-play contributions in order to take some of the first-dollar risk off the table from the schools. In effect, soft revenues from grant support act as venture capital for new ideas, not as support for the core consortial vehicle.

- *Rational size.* The number of members forming a consortium is also worth pondering. Some believe that a smaller enterprise—say, six or fewer—enhances the chance of deeper collaborations. Others believe that a larger enterprise—say, eight to a dozen or even more—increases the likelihood of sharing specific common problems but also adequate scale to create a workable solution. One size does not fit all, however deep the relationships and the sense of common ground.

- *Local geography.* Of course geography plays a role. There are advantages to being within a radius of five to ten miles. While some consortia like CIC have been consistently successful and extend across multiple states, longer-distance consortia require a different and disciplined approach. Some may argue that such large entities begin to cross the line of traditional consortia and approach something closer to corporate alliances, but what counts is productive output. Collegiality at the middle management level will be far more difficult to achieve, but the necessity of senior management engagement in cases like this may cut through resistance to change.

- *Lunch included.* Potential members of the governing body will need to compare their objectives and assess their ability to work as an effective board. Nothing takes the place of increasing familiarity

Trust with Intrinsic Reward: Resilient Partnership
- No promise in immediate reward, but shared belief in the alliance
- Willing to make sacrifices toward mutually shared vision
- Common values and goals
- High potential for significant shared accomplishment
- The journey is as important as the outcome; partnership transcends mere business relationship

Mutual Trust: Shared Investment
- Trust to honor commitments even if they are unequal or delayed
- Collaboration is easy within only loosely defined boundaries
- Sensitive to broken commitments, in turn creating high fragility for ongoing partnerships in face of past failures versus growing resilience in face of past successes

Contingent Trust: Scorecard Reciprocity
- You owe me in the future for indulging your need of my partnership
- Partner overvalues their own contribution but undervalues others
- Becomes hostile if perception is that the score is uneven
- Relationship is unstable and often brief or limited to certain transactions

Low Trust: Quid Pro Quo
- "Partner" must have benefits equal or greater than the other party
- Reward of collaboration must be certain
- Partner will not support others without an assumption of complete payback
- Viewpoint is the immediate short term
- Relationship is artificial and circumstance based
- Partner exhibits strict risk aversion

No Personal Trust Involved: Free Market Transaction
- Minimum expectation of service, as shopping at a "big box" store
- Minimum loyalty; incidental to who has the lowest "price" today
- Does not qualify as a collaboration or alliance

Process Trust: Auctioneer Mentality
- Adversarial between competing consumers; the vehicle of exchange is a financial auction
- Even the transactions are handled in a transactional fashion
- No trust in the individual, full trust in the process

Level of Capacity for Collaboration

Level of Trust

The Boston Consortium for Higher Education's collaboration quotient. Based on ideas from Hoffman, "Connections with and comfort with your partners, including simple courtesies such as meals, parking, and preprinted agendas. Pay attention to the inevitable sense of peer influence; no one should feel pressured to participate. Anticipating that there may be unwilling participants is important to future success.

Conclusion: Essential Actions

In the coming five to ten years, a number of new consortia will form. Scaling up is often a productive tool for gaining efficiencies, but the necessity of learning how to collaborate across multiple organizations is quite different from working within one entity. Several newly established consortia will likely fail as a result of not investing in the development of trusting relationships and the use of nonhierarchical skills. Command-control is an effective managerial technique, but it must not be the only approach.

Collaboration is about voluntarily ceding some organizational authority—in specific, useful circumstances. No group of institutions will always agree that a shared service or program has equal value to every member school. It is this process of finding common ground that is at the essence of successful collaboration. To be successful requires time and facilitated dialogue. Room for changes of mind, last-minute revisions, and cold feet should be expected and tolerated, for the failure to achieve agreement and subsequent implementation is not an existential threat unless it poisons the well of goodwill within the group. If that happens, pause and begin again.

Notes

1. In 1914, formal collaboration began among the colleges and universities of the Connecticut River Valley in western Massachusetts (Amherst, Mount Holyoke, and Smith Colleges; YMCA International College, later renamed as Springfield College; and Massachusetts Agricultural College). The Committee on University Extension of the Connecticut Valley Colleges lasted until 1958, doing the following:

- Arranged the first wireless broadcast of collegiate courses (by radio) in the United States.
- Offered leadership training courses for mill workers in Chicopee, Holyoke, and Springfield.
- Helped to organize Holyoke Junior College (which later became Holyoke Community College).
- Provided consultants to the Pittsfield Engineering Program and to the Westover Air Force.
- Started student and faculty exchanges in the 1930s.

2. The Davis Educational Foundation, established as a public charitable foundation in 1985, supports the undergraduate programs of public and private, regionally accredited, baccalaureate degree–granting colleges and universities

throughout the six New England states. Elisabeth K. Davis and Stanton W. Davis cofounded the foundation after Mr. Davis's retirement as chairman of Shaw's Supermarkets Inc. The foundation is an expression of the couple's shared support and value for higher education and has provided close to $98 million in grants to more than 157 institutions. For more information, visit http://www.davis foundations.org/def.

3. NACUBO is a membership organization representing more than 2,500 colleges, universities, and higher education service providers across the country and around the world. NACUBO specifically represents chief business and financial officers through advocacy efforts, community service, and professional development activities. The association's mission is to advance the economic viability and business practices of higher education institutions in fulfillment of their academic missions. For more information, visit http://www.nacubo.org/.

4. Adapted from William Torbert, PhD, Carroll School at Boston College, Chestnut Hill, Massachusetts.

CHAPTER FOURTEEN

Where Partnerships Begin: A Fresh Look at the Purpose and Outcomes of Liberal Arts College Consortia

R. Owen Williams

Liberal arts colleges are approaching a crisis. In 2012, Bain & Company published a study suggesting that one-third of colleges and universities were on an "unsustainable financial path."[1] In 2013, Moody's published a negative outlook for the entire higher education sector, after which they downgraded several decidedly respected liberal arts colleges.[2] In a 2013 survey of higher education chief financial officers by *Inside Higher Ed* and Gallup, only 27 percent were strongly confident in the viability of their institution's business model over five years, and an even smaller 13 percent were strongly confident in their business model over the next ten years.[3]

The liberal arts business model—expensive infrastructure and tuition dependence, among other vulnerabilities—seems near a breaking point. The amount of personal attention given to students is higher than can be afforded at many public institutions: student-to-faculty ratios are low, the number of staff committed to students' needs is high, and the quality and quantity of facilities on some campuses border on luxurious. As a result, the median tuition at private liberal arts colleges is three times the median tuition of public universities. In 2010, fewer than ten liberal arts colleges charged over $50,000 per year for room, board, and tuition; today over thirty charge more than $60,000 per year.[4] When those numbers are matched to the median annual income in the United States—$51,939—one can see why even wealthy families are complaining that a private liberal arts college costs too much.[5]

The liberal arts *educational* model, in contrast, deserves to be preserved. Graduates of the small, private, residential, academically rigorous institutions, such as those in the 130-member Annapolis Group, make up

What is the greatest challenge for a higher education leader in developing a consortial relationship this year?

Getting college administrators to look beyond the walls of their own campus is always difficult, particularly when consortium members see each other as competitors, but it has become even less likely at a time when senior administrative turnover is so high. At the Associated Colleges of the South, where we have sixteen member institutions, eleven of our colleges have had new presidents (and twelve have had new provosts) over the past two years; these college officers tend to spend at least a year getting to know their own institutions, thus limiting their appetite for consortial activities.

barely 1 percent of all college graduates, yet they have played a disproportionately large role in shaping American culture through their numerous eventual leadership achievements in corporations, nonprofit boards and agencies, and the educational and healthcare sectors. Still, as wonderful as their results tend to be, their business model is unsustainably expensive. So how can liberal arts colleges maintain their extraordinary excellence without pricing themselves out of existence? As many of the chapters in this book demonstrate, partnering through consortia, alliances, and new types of affiliation has become both a strategy and a necessity, even for elite institutions.

For more than two decades, multiple liberal arts colleges have been working together, primarily to enhance the quality of education they offer. Through regional organizations such as Associated Colleges of the South (ACS), Associated Colleges of the Midwest (ACM), and the Great Lakes Colleges Association, to name three, liberal arts colleges are bringing faculty and administrators together to design and implement best practices and innovative programs. The National Institute for Technology in Liberal Education accurately described the nature of these arrangements in a document titled "Collaboration Continuum" as the pyramidal movement from networking to coordination to cooperation to collaboration to integration.[6] Each step represents an increased level of commitment to combining with other institutions so as to improve the quality of liberal arts education.

Collaborating in these ways is not simple or smooth, however. Effective partnerships like consortia require their members to relinquish a natural tendency to proprietary control. Collaboration requires courage,

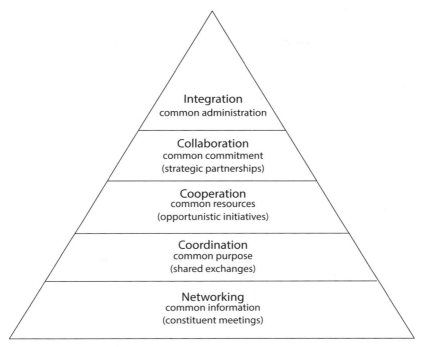

The Collaboration Continuum.

the willingness to pursue new directions, and confidence simultaneously in one's own institution and in potential partners. For the liberal arts business model to be sustainable, these collaborations will need to move more aggressively toward cost-reduction initiatives. Over the coming decade, some small number of liberal arts colleges will continue business as usual, some will close their doors, and many will begin to collaborate in ways previously unknown by all but a few institutions. In this chapter, I examine five ways that liberal arts colleges can partner using consortial agreements, not just to survive but also to thrive.

Centralized Services: The Largest Challenge

The most important step will be the hardest to take: consolidating joint services. Joint purchasing is something colleges have done for years, typically in state organizations such as the South Carolina Independent Colleges and Universities, which has created "a purchasing coalition to leverage economies of scale to reduce the cost of purchasing common goods and services."[7] Conversely, joint services—combining campus activities like information technology or human resources—is far more demanding. It is also far more promising as to cost reductions. Liberal arts colleges have the opportunity not just to contain costs, but also to reduce them by providing these vital services more efficiently. On this issue, Phillip DiChiara in chapter 13 in this volume, on the Boston Consortium, shares a similar view.

The single largest budget item at most colleges pertains to personnel costs, faculty and staff.[8] I return to the cost of faculty below, but first let us consider the growth in staff at liberal arts colleges, which is sometimes called "bureaucratic bloat." According to a 2010 study by the Goldwater Institute, most of the increase in college costs comes from administrative bloat, with administrative staff growing at more than twice the rate of instructional staff.[9] It is true—college staffs have grown significantly in past years, in part because of government regulations (e.g., Title IX officers and psychological counseling), but this growth is also substantially attributable to the hunt for revenue; colleges have added admissions counselors to locate new students and their tuition revenue, and new development officers to identify new sources of philanthropic support. So long as these new employees generate revenue, there should be no reason for concern. But when staff size goes up in areas that have no offsetting revenue, such as in information technology, human resources, financial aid, or international programs, then the need to reevaluate presents itself.

Assuming those services and the number of staff employed to provide them are necessary, it may be wisest to consider consolidating this work with the same work being done with other colleges. The Claremont University Consortium has done this quite successfully since the early twentieth century; the consortium provides twenty-eight essential services for the Claremont Colleges (Claremont Graduate University, Claremont McKenna College, Claremont University Consortium, Harvey Mudd College, Keck Graduate Institute of Applied Life Sciences, Pitzer College, Pomona College, and Scripps College), which, according to their

Key Liberal Arts College Consortium Partnerships

- Centralized services
- Collaborative financial aid strategies
- Virtual academic departments
- Shared professional development
- Coordinated budget design

website, includes "campus safety, a central library, health and counseling services, ethnic centers, central bookstore, physical plant and facilities support, payroll and accounting, information technology, human resources, real estate, risk management and employee benefits."[10] While proximity obviously matters in some of those areas, we can hardly tell our students to prepare for a global stage when their colleges are unwilling to operate across boundaries.

Financial Aid: Building the New Model

Most liberal arts colleges provide a significant amount of financial aid, and, at many of them, almost all students receive some amount of financial assistance. Financial aid tends to be the second-largest line item in the college budget, smaller only than personnel costs. But the stated price of tuition, room, and board is typically quite different from the cost incurred by most students. For the majority of undergraduates, the price is discounted by some variable amount that gets them to their actual "cost," an amount that is different for every student. While liberal arts colleges attempt to level the playing field through financial aid, ironically, they often end the process by providing advantages to wealthy families in a manner that actually perpetuates income inequality in America.[11]

Many colleges have become obsessed with rankings, and rankings have created a vicious cycle in which colleges must enroll a critical mass of superior students in order to attract the rest. The challenge for many liberal arts colleges is therefore to convince prospective applicants that the admissions process is more competitive than it is, and they do this by effectively buying their best applicants with "merit-based aid," as opposed to "need-based aid," which has the effect of running up the average scores on the Scholastic Aptitude Test (SAT) as well as grade point averages. Looked at another way, the institution's "full-pay" students essentially cover the cost of education for themselves, and for the smart students who could not afford that institution. Demand for the best colleges and universities allows them to avoid this strategy, but most colleges have to compete for students, especially the students most likely to succeed, and it is by working together through strategic alliances and consortia that new, more collaborative and less competitive approaches to financial aid will emerge.[12] At the Associated Colleges of the South, enrollment officers are currently looking for ways to address this issue.[13] The problem of merit-based aid is much too big for any one college to tackle alone, as is the practice of tuition discounting, yet, by working together as a consortium, it might prove possible to significantly reduce these costs.

The Wisdom of Virtual Departments

One of the greatest advantages of a liberal arts education is the frequent contact and easy access students have to faculty, but the cost of this access is rising beyond the grasp of some middle-tier colleges. Faculty members are retiring later, teaching fewer courses, and receiving increasingly expensive benefits. Also, the number of faculty members is also growing. From 1970 to 2010, the number of college students grew from 8.5 million to 20.5 million, yet the number of faculty grew at an even faster rate, nearly tripling. As of this writing, there are 1.4 million faculty members in the United States, half a million of whom are tenured or on the tenure track. At liberal arts colleges, almost 95 percent of faculty members are tenured or on track to it, which means that the faculty represents a large, fixed line item in college budgets. As a result, some colleges are now partnering virtually to address the rising costs of the entire faculty enterprise specifically through more efficient, collaborative departmental structures.

As the founder of a virtual classics department, Sunoikisis, ACS's membership is directly addressing this challenge. Small academic programs at liberal arts institutions often face two major difficulties: a lack of breadth in the courses they offer and an environment that is too comfortable to be truly rigorous. The homogeneity, comfort, and small scale of the liberal arts experience can inhibit academic rigor because the challenges students face are mitigated by an environment that is entirely too familiar.[14] In addition, not every institution can afford to have a major in Arabic or Russian, for example; however, through the creation of virtual academic departments like Sunoikisis, many more colleges could offer what have traditionally been lower-enrollment majors, expanding educational opportunity beyond the borders of what a single institution can affordably offer.

The professors in a virtual department hold their department meetings via Skype, and some classes are taught online. Unfortunately, anything "online" can sometimes be viewed as anathema at well-established liberal arts colleges, yet there is an abundance of evidence that online courses can yield superior results compared to traditional delivery methods. Liberal arts colleges have begun to "flip" courses, offering lectures out of class and more discussion in class, so there is no reason not to offer some courses completely online. An important near-term opportunity is in virtual departments as consortia like ACS expand the boundaries of collegiality and serve more students more effectively in the process.

Raising Academic Standards through Shared Professional Development

Our focus thus far has been principally on the ways collaboration can reduce institutional costs, assuming those institutions are willing to loosen the reins of proprietary control. Another option increasingly being utilized is collaborating directly to improve academic standards. Nationally, consortia are considering new models of assessment and learning outcomes. At ACS, for example, all sixteen member colleges send faculty to a summer teaching workshop that has been transformative in the view of several sets of participants. For a week of recorded sessions, professors take turns observing and being observed in classrooms with their peers as students. One of the larger findings from these workshops has been to begin to make online courses more widely available to ACS students.

In partnering to address issues of academic quality, members are developing new strategies to expand their academic calendars and to blend online with on-campus learning options. Employers increasingly expect college graduates to be conversant and adept in the technologies employed in online classes, and they expect students to be able to collaborate across distance and conduct online research. Liberal arts colleges are not alone in capturing the ways that online courses enhance students' critical thinking, reading, listening, and discussion skills by pushing them beyond the familiar boundaries of traditional classrooms. Online classes can also provide a more diverse learning experience than traditional classes at small liberal arts institutions while simultaneously reducing costs if managed carefully. Some of the multi-institutional corporate-based collaborations now being considered are those offered by Coursera, Udacity, and EdX. The liberal arts are noted for their development of "critical thinking" skills, but our members have observed that even seasoned liberal arts professors are challenged to articulate what those skills are or how they are actually developed. Former philosophy

What is the most important piece of advice you would offer to a president or provost now developing or joining a consortium this year?

Be open to the possibilities: the consortial opportunity to reduce costs while also enhancing outcomes is enormous.

professor Tim van Gelder has extracted six lessons from cognitive science that help instill critical thinking, including skills transfer and argument mapping, and ACS members have come to depend on the constructive, candid exchanges found in their joint teaching workshops to serve as the platform for these key academic collaborations.[15]

Sharing Governance and Sharing Budgets

There is another critical way in which liberal arts colleges can and need to work together more effectively: budget development. Given the many challenges facing the liberal arts sector, it is time to rethink budget development and to offer faculty members more structured opportunities to understand the financial management of their institutions, as happens at the Associated Colleges of the Midwest.[16] Although most colleges make some form of budget and financial information available to their faculties, there is a need for more systematic and purposeful dissemination of financial data, accompanied by the cultivation of the skills and perspectives necessary to understand and work effectively with that data among professors no matter what their rank at an institution.

Additionally, misunderstandings about the finances supporting the liberal arts business model contribute significantly to a related misunderstanding about "shared governance," a concept that many involved in higher education appear to misinterpret. Joanne Creighton, president emeritus of Mount Holyoke College, tackled the issue of governance with candor: "Faculty members have a great wealth of knowledge to impart to students and deeply held commitments to academic standards, but they can be naïve about how their institution exists in a competitive world."[17] Bill Bowen echoed Creighton's view in a 2015 *Chronicle of Higher Education* article, saying, "We need new ways, maybe even radically new ways, of engaging faculty members and administrators in discussions of options, and how to seize them, that will cut across departmental lines and at times across campus and even institutional boundaries."[18]

The real issue is that most classroom teachers are never taught the definition of shared governance or how to develop a budget from its basics. Colleges, and especially liberal arts colleges, need to address both issues with more depth and structure. In the case of governance, a good start is now being accomplished through a partnership sponsored by the Academic Leadership and Innovation Institute conducted by the Great Lakes Colleges Association and funded by the Mellon Foundation.[19] By bringing liberal arts faculty and administrators together from multiple campuses at a remote location, it becomes possible for all parties to think differently and, perhaps, better understand the governance—and financial—imperatives facing their sector. Finally, the issues of shared governance and budget development are hardly limited to the institution's faculty members. Creighton accurately identifies another challenge facing many institutions: "Although many trustees have highly developed business acumen, they can be impatient and simplistic about how to get things done in an academic environment."[20] Yet few trustees will ever admit their lack of knowledge about leading the institution, and this is an abrogation of their fiduciary responsibility to the college or university. At ACS, we are about to begin a program for trustees in conjunction with the Association of Governing Boards, much like the institute ACM offers member faculty, that will provide higher levels of orientation, training, and accountability.

Conclusion: Partnering for Survival

In a 1990 report, the economist David Breneman asked, "Are We Losing Our Liberal Arts Colleges?"[21] The shift to professional education was, he insisted, driving liberal arts colleges out of existence. Since that report, the number of liberal arts colleges has declined significantly, from 540 to the current 130, as was recently reported in the "Education Life" section of the *New York Times*.[22] Will that number be further reduced in the coming years?

Simply said, for the liberal arts model to survive, much depends on the ability of these colleges to build strong alliances and affiliations. College administrators already network and communicate about such things as presidential transitions, presidential mentoring, provost-to-president transitions, and legislative lobbying, but they also will need to achieve efficiencies of scale and nonduplication of programs in order to preserve the quality of what they offer. Through intentional partnerships, liberal arts colleges are accomplishing new models of success in instruction, consolidated services, virtual departments, online instruction, budget development, and participation in shared governance. The paths forward for their institutions can move from vulnerability to strength by expanding on these agreements.

Notes

1. Denneen and Dretler, "Financially Sustainable University."

2. Moody's Investor Service, "2013 Outlook for Entire US Higher Education Sector Changed to Negative," January 16, 2013, https://www.moodys.com/research /Moodys-2013-outlook-for-entire-US-Higher-Education-sector-changed--PR_263866. On Moody's liberal arts downgrades, see Rivard, "Downgrading Elite Colleges."

3. Lederman, "CFO Survey Reveals Doubts about Financial Sustainability."

4. I am not the first to see this looming crisis in higher education. See, for example, Zuckerman, "America's College Crisis"; Taylor, *Crisis on Campus*; and Putman, *Our Kids*. See also Mitchell, "Chart," for statistics on the recent rise in college costs.

5. US Census Bureau, "Income, Poverty and Health Insurance Coverage in the United States: 2013," news release, September 16, 2014, http://www.census.gov/newsroom/press-releases/2014/cb14-169.html.

6. Hagood and Pang, "Collaboration"; "The Collaboration Continuum [Adapted from the Work of Arthur T. Himmelman]," Collaboration Toolkit, accessed April 4, 2016, https://sites.google.com/a/nanfitoandassociates.com/collaboration-toolkit/home/where-are-you-in-your-current-collaboration/collaboration-continuum.

7. "Programs," South Carolina Independent Colleges and Universities, accessed April 4, 2016, http://www.scicu.org/about-scicu/programs/.

8. According to the Commonfund Higher Education Price Index, "the bulk of education costs are related to personnel, mainly college faculty." "Questions and Answers: Higher Education Price Index," Commonfund Institute, accessed April 4, 2016, https://www.commonfund.org/CommonfundInstitute/HEPI/Pages/default.aspx.

9. Reynolds, "Degrees of Value."

10. "About CUC: An Overview," Claremont University Consortium, accessed April 4, 2016, http://www.cuc.claremont.edu/aboutcuc/.

11. As it turns out, many of the "best students" come from wealthy families that can afford to buy homes in good school districts, summer camps, test-prep courses—all the things that lead to high grade point averages and test scores—so those kids don't necessarily need financial aid. Children from the highest quintile of wage earners in the United States are fourteen times more likely to attend selective colleges than children from the lowest quintile. Sixty percent of all students at Dartmouth College come from families with annual incomes of $200,000 or more. Rich kids get into the best colleges, after which they get the best jobs, then make the most money, and on and on.

12. In this instance, "success" means "to graduate." Here again, students from wealthy families are far more likely to graduate in four years, partly because they come from homes that expect that, but mostly because they don't have to hold down jobs while attending college.

13. Because this is an effort to lower rather than raise prices, it seems unlikely that antitrust issues will arise, but legal counsel are also involved in this project.

14. Associated Colleges of the South, "Sunoikisis."

15. van Gelder, "Teaching Critical Thinking."

16. "Professional Development," Associated Colleges of the Midwest, accessed May 4, 2016, http://www.acm.edu/professional_development/index.html.

17. Creighton, "Orchestrating Shared Governance." 70.

18. Bowen, "Toward a Shared Vision of Shared Governance."

19. Hanover Research, *Institutionalizing Innovation in Higher Education*.

20. Creighton, "Orchestrating Shared Governance," 70.

21. Breneman, "Are We Losing Our Liberal Arts Colleges?"

22. Treaster, "Liberal Arts, a Lost Cause?"

IV

Merger: The Right Reasons to Consider One

Why Mergers Are (Quietly) Increasing among Colleges and Universities: A Review of the Pros and Cons

Susan Resneck Pierce

In unprecedented ways, those in higher education leadership positions are now genuinely worried both about the viability of many colleges and universities and the possibility that a good number of those that survive will be damaged. A few statistics illustrate the seriousness of the financial problems facing many of this country's higher education institutions:

- In the fall of 2013, after surveying 1,700 colleges and universities, Bain & Company and Sterling concluded that one-third of all "colleges and universities are in real financial trouble" because, the report explained, "their operating costs are rising faster than revenues and investment returns can cover them."[1]

- In April 2014, Moody's Senior Vice President Susan Fitzgerald put it starkly, "What we're concerned about is the death spiral—this continuing downward momentum for some institutions. We will see more closures than in the past."[2]

- In the fall of 2014, Moody's reported that between 40 and 45 percent of all colleges and universities would suffer enrollment declines in the 2015–16 academic year.[3]

The litany of problems facing many private colleges and regional universities is well known to readers of this volume: declining enrollments; untenable tuition discounts; unsustainable debt; decreasing net tuition revenue; structural deficits; and growing skepticism on the part of students, their families, and elected officials about whether the value of a college education is worth the cost. In this climate, it is not surprising that an increasing number of presidents and trustees now think that merging with another institution may be their best road to fiscal stability and survival.

At the same time, mergers are difficult to achieve. Despite the potential benefits, there are also any number of potentially negative consequences in merging for faculty, staff, students, alumni, and even local residents. There are some happy exceptions, but these have been small in number. Moreover, the most successful mergers have either been between institutions that were strong in their own right and believed that a merger would bring them benefits without sacrificing their current mission, or between institutions in which each partner contributed complementary elements to the new entity.

My role as president of the University of Puget Sound during the 1993 decision to transfer our law school to Seattle University has led a number of presidents and trustees to speak to me about possible mergers in the years since. We made this important mission decision for Puget Sound even though the law school was bringing us $750,000 a year in overhead. Moreover, unlike many prospective mergers today, this was one of those decisions that benefitted both institutions, and one in which no one lost a job or compensation. Specifically, Seattle University agreed to honor all rank and tenure for faculty, to retain all staff, and to offer comparable compensation. The law school also remained in its location in Tacoma for five years, until Seattle University built a new facility that was far more desirable than the Puget Sound location. Even so, the decision was highly contentious at the time, leading to at least one lawsuit, angry editorials and cartoons in the local newspaper, distressed alumni, and a few outraged elected officials. Today, most parties celebrate that decision, which ultimately benefitted both institutions.

Successful Mergers: Five Recent Examples
1. Rutgers and the University of Medicine and Dentistry of New Jersey

Perhaps the most dramatic and complex merger to date has been that between Rutgers and the University of Medicine and Dentistry of New Jersey (UMDNJ), which took effect on June 30, 2013. With this merger, officials said at the time, "Rutgers is officially absorbing most of the state's medical university, a sprawling enterprise that includes hospitals, clinics and institutes, as well as eight professional schools spread across five campuses. Rutgers' annual budget will leap by more than forty percent to nearly four billion dollars as it acquires most of the University of Medicine and Dentistry of New Jersey—a deal that will bring the state university coveted medical and dental schools and a renowned cancer institute."[4] The arrangement also elevated Rowan University in Glassboro, New Jersey, to the status of a research university, absorbing as well UMDNJ's School of Osteopathic Medicine.[5]

This merger attracted its share of protests, including a failed attempt by the president of the New Jersey State Senate to abolish the existing Rutgers board. It also required significant changes in governance and budgeting, and the practical details that needed to be resolved were monumental. According to Christopher Molloy, the interim chancellor of Rutgers' new Health Sciences Division, "At Rutgers alone, there was a checklist with more than 4,600 tasks that needed to get done, and hundreds of employees served on integration teams. More than 1,000 university policies and 3,000 vendor contracts had to be reviewed while decisions had to be made about everything from campus parking rates to the dimensions of diplomas."[6]

2. Georgia State System

The Georgia State Board of Regents in January 2013 began a process of mergers. At that time, they consolidated eight of their institutions into four, moving from thirty-five institutions to thirty-one. Although none of the campuses closed, the consolidations were intended to save $6 million in administrative costs annually. Two years later, in January 2015, the regents approved a proposal to merge two more pairs of colleges.

3. George Washington University and the Corcoran College of Art and Design

In February 2014, George Washington University and the Corcoran College of Art and Design announced that George Washington would assume ownership of the Corcoran building and operate the art college, which had been struggling financially. The National Gallery of Art would acquire much of the Corcoran's collection. A few trustees from each institution confidentially negotiated an agreement that resolved issues ranging from the ownership of the art collection and of the facilities to the role of the college faculty within the framework of George Washington. In response to a lawsuit, a District of Columbia Superior Court judge on August 18, 2014, approved the merger.

Corcoran board member Michela English, who was a member of the negotiating team, stressed the importance of having clear principles guide the process throughout: "In order to be able to fairly evaluate our options, the Corcoran Board of Trustees established three clear criteria that any alternative needed to meet: to provide a path to long-term financial sustainability for the College, to ensure that the Corcoran art collection was available for viewing by the public, and to preserve and renovate the Corcoran's historic building across from the White House. Having these criteria proved very valuable in evaluating prospective merger partners and strategic alternatives." She also emphasized that "maintaining strict confidentiality was important to the Corcoran Board, GW, and the National Gallery. All Board members signed confidentiality agreements, and we were reminded by counsel at the beginning of each meeting how important it was that all negotiations be considered confidential. We all received numerous calls from the press but all were referred to a designated spokes person so that messaging could be carefully managed."[7]

4. The University of New Haven and Lyme Academy College of Fine Arts

The Lyme Academy College of Fine Arts and the University of New Haven announced in April 2014 that Lyme would become the sixth University of New Haven college and its first bachelor of fine arts program. An article in *The Day* explained that the academy will, in the words of University of New Haven President Steven H. Kaplan, be "semi-autonomous" and maintain its current mission. Lyme students will have access to the University of New Haven's liberal arts programs; its campus in Florence, Italy; its career counseling office; and its library. The University of New Haven will oversee Lyme's finances, and its admissions staff will now recruit for Lyme. The university will also in the early years subsidize Lyme until its enrollments grow to an anticipated level that would allow Lyme to become financially self-sufficient.

President Kaplan provided the following insights into the merger process, stressing the importance in this case of moving quickly:

> Once the University of New Haven decided to acquire the Lyme, it was clear to me that it was best to move as quickly as possible to complete the merger so we could turn around the college's losses, which were about to become our losses, as quickly as possible. We thus completed the entire process from our first conversation to the closing in about six months. This was the right thing to do because we were quickly able to introduce significant staffing reductions in Lyme, leading them closer to a balanced budget, and dramatically increase enrollments with our much larger recruitment resources. A disadvantage to moving so quickly was that in such acquisitions, even if the acquirer has the best of intentions, the entity being acquired is going to have a certain level of apprehension for a given time among faculty and staff mem-

bers. Nevertheless, by investing in campus improvements, increasing enroll-ments, and allowing their board and faculty to remain autonomous, it took us less than a year for the necessary levels of trust to be built.[8]

5. The Berklee College of Music and the Boston Conservatory of Music

The Berklee College of Music and the Boston Conservatory of Music have announced that they will merge in 2016. Because the campuses are only two blocks apart, the institutions have decided to merge their physical spaces into one downtown "four-block shared campus," as conservatory president Richard Ortner characterized it.[9]

A Different Approach: Consolidated Higher Education System

Since 2009, we have also seen the emergence of the Community Solu-tion Education System (TCS), a nonprofit organization of five previously independent college or universities that have affiliated. Although each institution has its own board, presidents, and accreditation, a single sys-tem board and a system president ultimately govern all the campuses. Founded as a not-for-profit education system in 2009, an inspiration of Michael Horowitz, then president of the Chicago School of Professional Psychology and now president of TCS, the system today includes the following members:

- The Chicago School of Professional Psychology, which offers more than 20 degree programs and many international opportunities in psychology and related behavioral and health sciences for more than 4,000 students in Chicago, Washington, DC, and California.

- The Santa Barbara and the Ventura Colleges of Law.

- Saybrook University in San Francisco, which focuses on humanis-tic studies offering advanced degrees in psychology, mind-body medicine, organizational systems, and human science.

- The Dallas Institute of Nursing, which offers an associate degree and vocational nursing programs.

- Pacific Oaks College, which offers bachelor's completion, master's, and certificate programs in human development, counseling, edu-cation, early childhood education, and teacher credentialing on its main campus in Pasadena and satellite locations.

What differentiates TCS from most nonprofit education systems is that it provides a broad, overarching mission consistent with each member college's mission and also shared services for all institutions. Approximately 150 staff members are located in TCS space in Chicago and Irvine, California, providing support for international services, legal affairs, admissions operations, financial aid, technology, finance, marketing, human resources, and institutional research. This model allows the TCS schools to offer a level and quality of support that no one institution would be able to afford.

The TCS model has several other distinctive characteristics. Most campuses are located in urban areas where there are plentiful services available to students, such as inexpensive restaurants and access to public transportation, so that TCS does not need to invest in amenities. The system's focus is mainly on the adult student who, on average, is a 35-year-old woman seeking a professional degree or completion of a bachelor's degree. Although TCS has had the opportunity to add additional schools, the current leadership has deliberately slowed that process, recognizing that growth for its own sake is not their goal. As President Horowitz explains,

> Affiliation to The Community Solution means you share a common mission and institutional culture that is maverick, global in perspective and focuses education on professions that make communities stronger and better. We view ourselves as a higher education community of colleges and universities not a service provider. It's for that core mission reason we have rejected colleges that might need our services yet don't fit our culture and community. It is the shared mission that creates a sense of team and colleagueship that gives extra energy to our work on behalf of our colleges and creates a community across all levels of our system: trustees, faculty, students, alumni and staff.[10]

Why the Plan Fails: Examples of Unsuccessful Mergers and Merger Explorations

The examples that follow illustrate key reasons why mergers fail, such as abiding concerns about whether one of the partners would bring too much liability; unresolvable disagreements about the location of the merged campus; failure to come to terms an governance; or a fear of protests by faculty, students, and alumni. To preserve confidentiality, these three cases, all actual situations, have altered identities. None is a project on which I have worked.

Two Small Northeastern Colleges

A small number of board members from a small northeastern college with a primarily local student body engaged in preliminary, confidential discussions about potentially merging with an institution with a similar mission located ten miles away. Both colleges, which have a number of cross-applicants, had not met their budgeted enrollment numbers for six years. Both had been spending down their endowments in order to fund ongoing operations, and their leadership teams estimated if they continued on their current paths, they would be forced to close within five years or sooner. They believed that by merging and sharing back-office operations they could create important economies of scale. Trustees also recognized that it would make sense to close one of the campuses, but fearing alumni and community protests and potential legal liabilities, they were unwilling to put that on the table. In lieu of closing one of the campuses, they then discussed limiting courses and majors to only one campus rather than offering the same courses and majors on both campuses in order to reduce the overall size of the combined faculty. Once again, concern about protests led them to abandon this notion. It appears unlikely as of this writing that these two institutions will merge.

A Faith-Based College and a Research University

The president of a once-selective, private, faith-based college in the Midwest facing declining enrollments and escalating tuition discounts shared his private vision that the flagship Research I university located in the same city, now turning down many qualified in-state applicants, would acquire his campus to enable the university to accept more applicants. He further specified that although his college would become nonsectarian, in all other ways it would be true to its current mission, with the same faculty and staff offering the same curriculum. At the same time, he feared that the university might not want to assume either the significant amount of deferred maintenance on his campus or its level of debt. He also worried that because most of his faculty colleagues did not meet the university's more rigorous research expectations, they might not be retained.

After worrying for many months about how he might begin to engage in such conversations with the university without risking making public information that he believed would damage his college, he shared a concept paper with key board members and the president of the university that made the best case he could for the merger. Although this group seriously weighed his proposal, his fears turned out to be correct. The university did not wish to take on the financial liabilities of the college, and it was particularly reluctant to assume the obligations involved in hiring the college's entire faculty.

A Polytechnic University and a Liberal Arts College

The president of a small private liberal arts college west of the Mississippi that had enjoyed stable enrollments indicated that her institution was now "barely holding its own" in terms of recruitment, and that to achieve the desired number of students it had increased its financial aid discount rate to 55 percent, which produced the institution's first operating deficit. She and the president of a polytechnic university located two hours away entered into preliminary conversations about a merger that would enable them to become a comprehensive university rather than separate institutions offering more limited ranges of programs. Both recognized that, for a merger to make sense, they would need to consolidate programs on one campus, and, understandably, they both wanted their campus to be the one to survive. Each also wanted to remain as president, and both believed that most of their board members would want to remain active. Because they could not resolve these fundamental issues between them, and because each was nervous about what it would mean if their casual conversations became public, they ultimately decided to abandon the concept of merging.

The Twelve Issues Leaders Need to Consider First

1. Two campus operations
2. Institutional loyalty
3. Legacy preservation
4. Restricted endowments
5. Accreditation requirements
6. Creditor obligations
7. Severance responsibilities
8. Joined faculty guidelines
9. Board of trustee authority and continuance
10. Presidential selection
11. Future degree nomenclature
12. Institutional name

The Twelve Issues Leaders Need to Consider First

The examples considered in this chapter pose a variety of issues for presidents, trustees, and faculty to consider at the *start* of their merger planning and discussions:

1. *Two campus operations.* Potential partners need at the earliest possible moment to address the critical question of whether both campuses will remain open or whether one will close in order to reduce operating and capital expenses. Even if the two institutions agree that one campus is to close, they then need to consider major questions such as deferred maintenance and desirability of location when deciding which location will close or whether *both* campuses will close and a new site identified.

2. *Institutional loyalty.* If two campuses with low enrollments merge and one campus is then closed, what reason is there to believe that students who were interested in the now-defunct campus would now enroll at a new merged institution in a different location?

3. *Legacy preservation.* If one campus is to close, what is its board's responsibility in maintaining its legacy?

4. *Restricted endowments.* If two campuses merge, how will the merger affect the use of restricted endowments? Additionally, if one campus closes, to what extent can that campus use restricted endowment for the transition or to fund the operations of the new institution? In such a circumstance, the institutions need to understand state law as it pertains to releasing restricted gifts. As a beginning point, the institution needs to determine whether the state in which it resides has adopted the Uniform Prudent Management of Institutional Funds Act (UPMIFA), which provides procedures for unrestricting restricted gifts. In addition to donor consent to a change, institutions can under certain circumstances release restrictions (usually on small gifts that are more than twenty years old) and in other circumstances petition the attorney general or the courts to release description on newer and larger gifts.

5. *Accreditation requirements.* If a campus closes or merges, what does it need to do to meet the requirements of its accrediting association? Perhaps most importantly, how will the students from that campus be accommodated in terms of finding new academic homes and receiving comparable financial aid?

Five Action Steps

1. Hire experienced legal counsel
2. Anticipate unanticipated costs
3. Engage crisis communications professionals
4. Assess costs and benefits
5. Monitor the emotional impact

---

6. *Creditor obligations*. If a campus closes or merges, what are its obligations to creditors?

7. *Severance responsibilities*. Similarly, what is the institution's obligation to its faculty and staff in terms of severance?

8. *Joined faculty guidelines*. Assuming that the merger is intended to create economies of scale, who decides, and on what basis, which faculty and staff members will be retained and who will be let go? Also, who decides which academic programs will continue and which will be closed?

9. *Board of trustee authority and continuance*. What will happen to the boards of the merging institutions? Will they merge into a combined board with a certain percentage of board members from each institution, or will a new board entirely be constituted, and who will choose the members, whatever the model?

10. *Presidential selection*. If two campuses merge, who will be the president of the new entity, and how will she be chosen?

11. *Future degree nomenclature*. What degree will graduates receive going forward, and will alumni have the opportunity to change their degree-granting institution to the new entity?

12. *Institutional name*. What name should the merged entity carry?

Conclusion

In closing, the following paragraphs outline five action steps those approaching a merger might consider based on successful plans in this writer's experience:

1. *Hire experienced legal counsel*. Prior to embarking on any conversations, both institutions should engage legal counsel who have

significant expertise in higher education law. In the event that either campus closes or becomes part of a new entity, institutional leaders need particularly to understand the legal responsibilities to their students, to their faculty and staff, and to their creditors. Well-prepared attorneys will advise the institutions about any covenants in the founding charter that could limit the board's decision making. Legal advice should also include recommendations regarding accreditation, US Department of Education regulations, and the uses of restricted endowments.

2. *Anticipate unanticipated costs.* Closing or merging a college produces significant and often unanticipated costs. For example, are there any legal constraints that might prevent the board from selling the campus to other entities? If the campus is not salable, what arrangements need to be made to maintain it? And the disposition of the institution's assets—such as its library, art collection, scientific equipment, and furniture—will need to be decided.

3. *Engage crisis communications professionals.* Trustees contemplating changes of the magnitude of a merger would also be well advised to engage a crisis communications firm to help them craft their communications to both internal and external constituencies. They need to anticipate which of their decisions will be controversial and unpopular, and they will also need to anticipate the immediate and powerful impact of social media, in combination with the mainstream press, in shaping public opinion. Although conventional wisdom for years in higher education has been that parties to legal actions should not fight their battles in the press, successful social media campaigns relating to presidential tenure and to controversial board decisions have had an increasing impact on the ability of trustees to function effectively, and this fact should be taken into consideration. One needs only to take a single look at the virulent social media campaigns following votes of no confidence in the presidents of St. Louis, Florida Atlantic, and Transylvania Universities, or following Cooper Union's decision to charge tuition and Sweet Briar's near closure to understand the growing influence of this public conversation.

4. *Assess costs and benefits.* From the first considerations of a merger or closure, CFOs should individually and in collaboration determine the costs and benefits of each likely scenario, particularly for the trustee and executive leadership.

5. *Monitor the emotional impact.* In the event that merger discussions have been prompted by dire financial circumstances, the

leadership and planning teams need to recognize the genuine emotional impact their deliberations can have on the faculty, staff, students, alumni, and local community. In particular, they will need to remain mindful of the consequences for those employees who could lose their jobs, and a local community that could lose a long-standing, cherished institution. The president and the senior student affairs officer should thus be at the center of many conversations so that they can work through issues and concerns with their constituencies. The vice president for advancement will also need to assess carefully what this decision will mean to alumni, who may mourn the loss of a part of their past and present identities, as the vice president for enrollment weighs the impact of a merger on admissions and retention.

As a final recommendation, I urge all institutions contemplating a merger to begin simply by reading their mission statements because if both partners have comparable as well as complementary missions the process has a better chance of being a smooth one. Whatever their missions, all parties must have clarity about their similarities and differences because, in the end, they will need to play a skillful mental chess match as they anticipate the near- and long-term consequences of each of their choices.

Notes
An earlier version of this essay appears as "Merger Causes and Consequences," *Inside Higher Ed*, September 18, 2014.
  1. Marcus, "Higher Education Is Headed for a Shakeout."
  2. McDonald, "Small U.S. Colleges Battle Death Spiral as Enrollment Drops."
  3. Marcus, "US Colleges Projecting Decline in Revenue Despite Rising Tuition."
  4. Alex, "Rutgers' New Era Starts Today with UMDNJ Merger."
  5. Ibid.
  6. Heyboer, "Welcome to the New Rutgers."
  7. Michela English, telephone interview with Susan Resneck Pierce, July 2, 2015.
  8. Steven Kaplan, e-mail to Susan Resneck Pierce, July 3, 2015.
  9. Book, "Berklee College of Music and Boston Conservatory to Merge in 2016."
 10. Michael Horowitz, e-mail to Susan Resneck Pierce, June 27, 2015.

V

Closure: Hidden Costs
and Complexities

CHAPTER SIXTEEN

If That Moment Arrives: The Blueprint to Close a College

Michael Hoyle

When most Americans think of an organization closing its doors, they immediately think of small businesses. Most Americans do not think of a college closing its doors. US higher education, for most of the last one hundred years the envy of the world, is going through its first major core business challenge. Despite the reduced financial support from states to public universities, these institutions are increasing enrollment and expanding into new degrees. Small-to-medium-sized private colleges, however, are and will continue to be in danger. The door could close on many of them for good.

There are many reasons why these institutions are suddenly in danger. The threat of closure has been building for decades, however, and many higher education leaders still have their heads firmly planted in sand. In 2014, Moody's downgraded four times as many colleges in their financial ratings than they upgraded. Bain & Company's now-famous 2012 report found that one-third of US colleges have unworkable and unsustainable business models.[1] Many small private colleges think they are disguising their troubles by offering deep discount rates, yet this strategy only delays an inevitable day of reckoning. John Thelin, a professor of higher education at the University of Kentucky, notes that in the 1960s, the Carnegie Commission on Higher Education predicted as much as 25 percent of American colleges could close. That has not transpired, but the warnings persist. How did we get here?

The following are some of the most common trip wires sending many small colleges to the edge:

- High discount rates, approaching 45 to 55 percent in some cases, that decrease net tuition revenue per student.

199

- Outdated degree programs that do not lead directly to graduate employment.

- The race to turn campuses into amusement parks with fancy gymnasiums, hotel-quality residence halls, and professional-level playing fields.

- Low and declining endowments.

- Spending in operating budgets that exceeds revenues.

- Poor and inexperienced executive leadership.

- A campus location that is no longer desirable to student consumers.

- No online presence.

- Lack of graduate programs tied to the local and regional economies.

Moody's Investor Service published a report on September 15, 2015, with the subtitle *Small College Closures Poised to Increase.*[2] It projects that the number of closures and mergers will increase in the next few years because of low enrollments. The number of "closures of four-year public and private colleges averaged five per year from 2004–2014." Closures are likewise expected to triple in the next few years, putting the number at fifteen, which is substantial. The report attributes this acceleration in closures to a handful of key market and operational points. Many small colleges have failed to grow revenues above the rate of inflation, and with fixed cost structures and labor-intensive operations, no growth in revenues becomes a recipe for financial distress. Perhaps even more eye opening is the report's assertion that students are choosing larger colleges and universities over smaller colleges. The financial ability of larger institutions to reinvest in their physical infrastructure and to provide meaningful, current academic programs and contemporary student services for the children of helicopter parents are all factors involved in the value proposition that students are using to choose universities and larger colleges.

Smaller colleges are becoming increasingly inefficient economic operations as fixed costs grow and become spread over fewer students on a declining net revenue per student; eventually the institutional checkbook is left without a balance. The *Economist* in 2012 pointed out that financially challenged colleges faced situations whereby they were spending more money on principal and interest payments on debt as well as on the expansion of the physical infrastructure in the "Disneyification" of college campuses while paying no attention to the maintenance and renewal needs of the existing plant.[3] Eventually, all this deferred mainte-

When Things Get Rough: Five Cautions for Leaders Closing Colleges

1. *Students come first*. Use that as your guidepost and you will invariably make a higher percentage of correct decisions.

2. *Your regional accreditation body is your best friend*. Keep them close and informed, and you will strengthen the odds of closing successfully.

3. *Be visible*. You must be visible to all constituents every day, if possible, to reassure the community that someone is leading it during these moments.

4. *Recognize faculty and staff as much as possible*. This will help to keep their morale high and serve you well as you work through the process.

5. *Take care of yourself*. Closing a college is an emotional roller coaster for all involved. As the community counts on its leader perhaps more than it ever has before, it is wise for that leader to take time to care for his or her well-being.

nance catches up, and institutions find themselves as so many Americans did in 2009, with too many credit card balances and no cash.

New England has seen a private college close its doors every year since 2011. Across the country, there are many colleges in danger of closing, yet actually closing a college or university is not a simple, straightforward, or easy undertaking. The situation at Sweet Briar College is an excellent example. Unlike most major corporations that can look at the balance sheet and make a rational economic decision to go out of business, American colleges have an emotional element to the brand, history, experience, and governance structure that makes closures a surprisingly difficult road to navigate, especially for leaders with no experience at all in this type of decision making. The trustees of Sweet Briar believed that they had closed the chapter on the history of the college with the vote to close the college. But the alumni and current, soon to be former, students believed otherwise, and put their wallets to work to raise the $12 million to keep the college in operation for the present. Sweet Briar's new leadership is proud to assert that it never closed. It came close to closing, but technically its doors have remained open throughout the process. Rightly or wrongly, this has been viewed as a confirmation of the resiliency of higher education institutions that can, and will, survive on shoestring budgets while committed alumni donate just enough money each year to keep the operation going until the next group of alumni step up.

Even colleges that decide closure is their best option will sometimes resurrect themselves years later and open their doors once more. A

Inside the Sweet Briar Decision: An Interview with Chief Academic Officer Pam DeWeese

Sweet Briar made national news in 2015 by apparently closing and then reopening. In fact, Pam DeWeese, the college's current dean of faculty and chief academic officer, clarifies that Sweet Briar never closed at any point. Contrary to public perception, the close date announced by the previous administration was August 25, 2015. As part of the court settlement and mediation process, the former board elected the new board. The new board immediately elected Philip Stone as the new president, and the college's accreditation with Southern Association of Colleges and Schools (SACS) continued as before, and it was able to resume classes on August 27, 2015, as planned. Martin and Samels interviewed Dr. DeWeese in November and December 2015 about leadership lessons drawn from the Sweet Briar situation.

From the perspective of chief academic officer, what do you view now as some of the main reasons the Sweet Briar community was able to survive and move forward?
Sweet Briar was saved by the alumnae's immediate and well-organized response to the announcement on March 3, 2015, of the proposed closure. By enlisting the aid of attorneys, as well as the college and local community, lawsuits and a mediation process initiated by the Virginia Attorney General's Office impeded the closure process begun by the former administration and board. An unprecedented social media campaign allowed the alumnae to raise over $12 million in less than 100 days that demonstrated their commitment to keeping the college's mission alive and well.

Now that the college is moving forward again, what are its priorities? New programs? New faculty areas of expertise? New markets?
Sweet Briar's academic priority continues to be providing a superior liberal arts education for women based on quality instruction, mentoring, and research opportunities with an excellent core of faculty teacher-scholars.

Looking back, what are one or two lessons learned that could be shared with presidents and provosts who may be facing difficult decisions about their institutional futures? Is there a pitfall to avoid? Is there a high priority to focus on?
The lessons learned are that Sweet Briar's founding under the trust established by Indiana Fletcher Williams protected it, in the opinion of the courts, from the closure voted upon by the former board. The announcement of the intent to close galvanized public opinion against the closure, and the ability of alumnae and other supporters to organize immediately, raise money, and put into effect a plan to oppose the closing demonstrated the depth of support for the institution by alumnae and the campus community.

prime example is Antioch College, which closed in 2008 only to reopen in 2011 after sustained alumni donations made the reopening financially possible. One would think that this rising tide of closures would be causing governors, legislatures, and higher education association professionals to openly discuss how to avert the disaster of losing higher education as a leading American industry. That discussion has been surprisingly mute. Even in Massachusetts, where higher education is a major economic engine with more than 125 colleges and universities in residence, the business model should be a prime topic for debate.

Marion Court College in Swampscott, Massachusetts, announced in June 2015 that it would close its doors owing to low enrollment and continued projections of low enrollment, low application interest, and little financial means to stay afloat. The Massachusetts School of Acupuncture, rather than close for being so small and economically challenged, has announced plans to merge with the Massachusetts College of Pharmacy and Health Sciences. Not all mergers are possible. The efforts of the small Montserrat College of Art in Beverly, Massachusetts, to merge with the large Salem State University began and ended six months later when Montserrat decided to continue to go it alone. Salem State, being a public university, began to receive criticism about the cost of a merger. Mergers, the subject of several other chapters in this volume, particularly chapter 15 by Susan Resneck Pierce, are fraught with many of the same concerns associated with closures, not the least of which is an emotionally charged alumni base.

Closure: Seven Best Practices

Should a college or university find itself in the unenviable position of having to address the final question of closure, I offer these seven steps forward as a model that has been tested:

1. *Be candid.* The president and board first need to have that confidential discussion and actually ask openly: Should we close? Far too often, these small colleges continue year after year serving 100–500 students without accreditation agencies or trustees really looking in the mirror and asking: Are students actually receiving the value and quality they are paying for? Are we really doing our fiduciary duty? These are not trivial questions, and far too many times such questions are not asked, or they are asked but discarded too quickly. Boards will have alumni members, and these discussions can become emotional. Many times what make board meetings so enlightening are the alumni trustees with insights that

are authentic regarding mission. In a distressed financial situation, these alumni often stand in the way of a courageous and correct decision for the long term, only prolonging the inefficient use of resources and lowering the quality of education for students.

2. *Design a teach-out strategy.* Once the question is asked and answered and the answer is to close, the next question is: What program will the college offer so that current students can finish their degrees? Timing is important, so that students have time to make alternative arrangements. Trustees need to remember that the paramount thread running through any closure map is the student experience. Most importantly, the teach-out plan needs to be centered on student needs. Will this be a teach-out, meaning the college stays in operation while all the current students are taught to degree completion? This can be quite expensive for a four-year institution. If teach-out is not feasible, then what colleague institutions will be approached to take over various programs and the students associated with them, along with their revenue, to complete their educations? Once the question is answered regarding an in-house teach-out or collaborating with another institution or group of institutions, the college can proceed to developing the details of the closure plan.

3. *Design a comprehensive communication plan and stick to it.* The communication plan needs to be broken down into subsets and implemented immediately, with the board and the president relying on a core group of personnel to execute it and with a single institutional spokesperson to handle all external information. External stakeholders are important and cannot be surprised. The narrative needs to be crafted, marketed, and adhered to from the beginning of the announcement, and these external stakeholders need to be on the trustees' side: accreditation agencies; alumni; municipal leaders; state higher education coordinating bodies; and local, state, and federal elected representatives. Internal stakeholders are equally important and play a key role. These individuals, some long serving, will be there long after the first wave of students graduates and faculty and staff members depart. When it matters most, these faculty and staff members will be the ones to turn off the light switch, so to speak, and they need to be treated wisely and fairly.

4. *Speak to every employee individually.* A president needs to meet individually with every faculty member and every staff member. This attention to the human capital of the organization is integral

to the success of the students completing their degrees with honor and dignity. It is also essential to the faculty and staff members finishing their work with honor and dignity. Many presidents on today's campuses do not know personally all the employees. In a closure, this will need to change.

5. *Develop an action plan that is flexible and inclusive.* The registrar, chief academic officer, and director of human resources (HR) need to lock themselves in a room and develop the master plan of when and how students will complete their degrees, incorporating the decision about whether a colleague institution, or institutions, will complete the college's programs. The academic "map" of how each student completes a degree forms the basis for the plan of when faculty and staff depart the institution. Trustees, most importantly, will need to ensure that there are enough faculty and staff present to deliver the services that students will need to complete their academic studies. This is the most expensive part of the teach-out and often where leaders will be tempted to try and save money. Accreditation agencies have learned to be vigilant, and once this teach-out plan is approved, they will work to ensure that it is carried out as planned. Guaranteeing that the institution has set aside the resources needed to complete the teach-out is a key action step. Maintaining the principal focus on the quality of the student experience, state attorneys general should exercise their mandates and assist accreditation agencies in this endeavor.

6. *Adopt a new presidential role.* The president of the college needs to make a mind-shift at this point. He or she needs to walk the campus every day and meet and talk to as many faculty, staff, and students as can be located, and the interchanges, no matter how difficult, need to be authentic. If the president does this, faculty and staff will respond and students will follow, and the mission of the institution, however close to ending, will continue to hold value.

7. *Stay focused on details until the end.* The less than glamorous parts of the teach-out plan also need to be discussed while all the pieces above are being implemented. There are many details that can be overlooked during the strains of these discussions, including:

- All transcripts need to be scanned, stored, and deposited with the appropriate state agency or accreditation body.

- The disposition of the physical campus needs to be planned and approved by the board.

- A respectful layoff package needs to be created and explained to every faculty and staff member, before their employment ends, and then again on their last day on campus.

- Important institutional archives need a permanent home; local museums and other colleges are the best organizations to approach.

- Someone needs to document the story of the college's closure for inclusion in the archives as well as for the edification of other higher education leaders, some of whom will face the same decisions. As educators, we need to learn from the experiences of our peers so that the record can be enhanced and the future student experience improved.

Advice for Those Who Choose Not to Close

If the decision by trustees is not to close, there are several options, but it should be acknowledged that they are equal in risk to closing. They are nonetheless three compelling choices and ones that should be considered, as some institutions may turn one of these choices into a successful outcome:

1. *Strategic reevaluation.* Conduct a strategic reevaluation and reimagining of the institution, and consider the development of academic programs that students are unlikely to find at competitor schools.

2. *Partnership.* Develop a partnership with other colleges whereby the surviving academic enterprise sheds duplicative core courses that are performed by other colleges at a lower per student cost, thus changing the business model and focusing the mission of the college on the last two years of the degree program, as one example.

3. *Acquisition.* Enter into negotiations with another college to be acquired. This is often a sound decision, yet trustees still fail to take advantage of the window of opportunity they have as fiduciary stewards to exercise this choice. There is time still, even during an institution's downward slide, to negotiate from a position of strength. If the board waits too long, however, the window will close. In many cases, boards can approach some colleges about merging or being acquired and still preserve their institution's name and legacy. There is a wider range of potential structures than many realize, but trustees will need to act more quickly than they may be used to in order to have choices.

Conclusion: The Changing Structure of Institutions

The next decade will bring several significant shifts in American higher education. The changing economics of the country will force more educational institutions to examine the relevance of their program offerings with respect to today's economy and future student demand. Many colleges and universities will continue to be financially challenged, producing an increase in college and university mergers. These new agreements will run the gambit from full-scale mergers to changing the name of one or both of the institutions in more loosely defined collaborations. In some cases, two or more colleges may choose to keep their names and brand identities as they collapse parallel administrative functions into one enterprise, thereby changing the cost curve and becoming more economically efficient.

A second structural change coming to higher education will include groups of institutions deciding to form "super" nonprofits and collapse the administrative functions into one. The individual colleges will keep their own 501(c)(3) statuses and brand identities while taking advantage of scale to lower administrative costs. These models have sprung up in the last three years around a specific administrative function. Twelve colleges in New England have formed EdHealth, a nonprofit health insurance company. In Vermont, Champlain, Middlebury, and St. Michael's Colleges formed the Green Mountain Higher Education Consortium and are collectively purchasing office supplies and their P-Card program. Lasell College and Mount Ida College, in Massachusetts, formed a joint campus police force. These examples will become more prevalent, but the size of these collaborations will balloon into super-nonprofit collaborations that will offer everything from finance, HR, payroll, insurance, campus police, information technology, registrar, and financial aid, as examples, all under one nonprofit for multiple colleges.

Finally, higher education is going to see a major industry shift away from the bachelor's degree and more toward a "passport" of skills and competencies. The business model of providing bachelor's degrees as it exists now is too labor intensive for these enterprises to remain viable. A major restructuring is going to happen, and most likely the business community is going to initiate that change when corporations like Amazon, Apple, Ford, Google, Microsoft, and Tesla discard the notion that they require employees to have a bachelor's degree and instead begin to demand specific skill sets that can be addressed through three-, six-, or twelve-month certificates. Changes such as these will be difficult and may not be welcomed by some higher education leaders and trustees, who will be forced to make unprecedented decisions in transforming the structures of their institutions. As the process continues, colleges and universities in every sector will look to alter their cost curve to remain economically viable. Whether it will involve options like merger, closure, or more simply rethinking the bachelor's degree and developing deeper links with the global workforce, American higher education will continue to reinvent itself to maintain its value in our business, civic, and cultural life.

Notes

1. Denneen and Dretler, "Financially Sustainable University."

2. Gephardt et al., *US Higher Education*. For information about the report, see https://www.moodys.com/research/Moodys-Small-but-notable-rise-expected-in-closures-mergers-for--PR_335314.

3. "The College-Cost Calamity." *Economist*, August 4, 2012, http://www.economist.com/node/21559936.

Appendix A

Selected Mergers in Higher Education, 2000–2016*

James E. Samels and Arlene Lieberman, Samels Associates,
Attorneys at Law, and Liam Lair, College of St. Benedict/St. John's University

Alliant International University was the result of merger between *California
School of Professional Psychology* and *United States International University*,
California, 2001

Andover College merged with *Kaplan University*, Minnesota, 2010

Argosy University formed with the merger of three institutions: *American
Schools of Professional Psychology*, the *University of Sarasota*, and the
Medical Institute of Minnesota, Arizona, California, Colorado, Florida,
Georgia, Hawaii, Illinois, Minnesota, Tennessee, Texas, Utah, Virginia,
Washington, and Washington, DC, 2001

Barat College was absorbed by *DePaul University* in 2001 but closed in 2005;
the facilities and educational inventory were sold, and DePaul absorbed the
faculty and student body, Illinois, 2001

Berklee College of Music and *Boston Conservatory of Music*, Massachusetts,
2015

Big Sandy Community and Technical College was the result of a merger of
Prestonsburg Community College and *Mayo Technical College*, Kentucky,
2003

Briarwood College merged with *Clemens College* (*International College
of Hospitality Management /Bradley College*) to form *Lincoln College of
New England*, Connecticut, 2010

Community Solution Education System formed in 2009 by the consolidation
of the following institutions, which retain their own boards, presidents, and
accreditations and are ultimately governed by a system board and system
president:
- *Chicago School of Professional Psychology*
- *Dallas Institute of Nursing*

*SOURCE: "List of University and College Mergers in the United States," LiquiSearch,
accessed April 5, 2016, http://www.liquisearch.com/list_of_university_and_college
_mergers_in_the_united_states.

- *Pacific Oaks College*
- *Santa Barbara and Ventura Colleges of Law*
- *Saybrook University in San Francisco*

Daniel Webster was acquired by *ITT Education Services Inc.* Daniel Webster was originally established in 1965 and in 2009 was acquired by ITT Educational Services Inc., the parent company of the ITT Technical Institutes, and subsequently became a for-profit institution, New Hampshire, 2009

Davenport University was a merger of *Davenport College*, *Detroit College of Business*, and *Great Lakes College*, Michigan, 2000

Fordham University absorbed *Marymount College*, New York, 2002

Franklin Pierce Law Center merged with the *University of New Hampshire* to become the *University of New Hampshire School of Law*, 2014

George Washington University absorbed *Corcoran College of Art and Design*, Washington, DC, 2014

University System of Georgia actions taken from 2013 to 2016 included:

- *Augusta State University* merged with *Georgia Health Sciences University* to form *Georgia Regents University*, which was renamed *Augusta University*, 2015
- *Gainesville State College* merged with *North Georgia College* and *State University* to form the *University of North Georgia*, 2013
- *Macon State College* merged with *Middle Georgia College* to form *Middle Georgia State College*, which was renamed *Middle Georgia State University*, 2015
- *Skidaway Institute of Oceanography* was merged into the *University of Georgia*, 2013
- *Waycross College* merged with *South Georgia College* to form *South Georgia State College,* 2013
- The University System of Georgia Board of Regents voted in 2013 to approve a proposal to consolidate *Kennesaw State University* and *Southern Polytechnic State University*, effective January 2015. The merged university retained the name *Kennesaw State University*
- The board of regents voted to approve a proposal to consolidate *Georgia State University* and *Georgia Perimeter College* under the name *Georgia State University*, 2016
- The board of regents voted to consolidate *Albany State University* and *Darton State College*, 2015

Johnson University absorbed *Florida Christian College*, Florida, 2013

Lawson State Community College absorbed *Bessemer State Technical College*, Alabama, 2005

Longy School of Music merged with *Bard College* to become *Longy School of Music of Bard College*, Massachusetts, 2012

Middlebury College affiliated with the then-acquired *Monterey Institute of International Studies*, California and Vermont, 2010

New York University acquired *Polytechnic Institute of Brooklyn* in 2008, merged in 2014

Pennsylvania State University absorbed *Dickinson School of Law*, 2000

Rutgers University absorbed the *University of Medicine and Dentistry of New Jersey*, 2013

St. John's University (New York City) College of Business absorbed the *College of Insurance*, 2001

Temple Baptist Seminary resulted after the trustees of two Baptist colleges, *Tennessee Temple University* and *Piedmont International University*, voted to merge the institutions, 2015

Trenholm State Technical College formed by a merger between *H. Councill Trenholm State Technical College* and *John M. Patterson State Technical College*, Alabama, 2003

University of Massachusetts Dartmouth absorbed *Southern New England School of Law*, 2010

University of New Haven absorbed *Lyme Academy College of Fine Arts*, Connecticut, 2014

University of Texas Rio Grande Valley was the consolidation of the *University of Texas–Pan American* and the *University of Texas at Brownsville*, 2015

University of Toledo merged with *Medical University of Ohio*, 2006

University of West Los Angeles absorbed *San Fernando Valley College of Law*, California, 2002

Woodbury College merged with *Champlain College*, Vermont, 2008

Appendix B

Selected Closures in Higher Education, 2000–2016*

James E. Samels and Arlene Lieberman, Samels Associates,
Attorneys at Law, and Liam Lair, College of St. Benedict/St. John's University

Antioch College, Ohio, 2008 (reopened in 2012)
Atlanta College of Art, Georgia, 2006
Ave Maria College, Michigan, 2007
Baltimore Hebrew University Inc., Maryland, 2009
Baltimore International College, Maryland, 2011
Barat College, Illinois, 2005
Beacon University, Georgia, 2009
Bethany University, California, 2011
British-American University, California, 2006
Cascade College of Santa Fe at Albuquerque, New Mexico, 2009
Chester College of New England, New Hampshire, 2012
Christ College of Florida, 2005
Cleveland Chiropractic College of Los Angeles, California, 2011
College of Saints John Fisher & Thomas More, Texas, 2014
Dana College, Nebraska, 2010
Founders College, Virginia, 2008
Goshen College, Florida, 2005
Hebrew Union College–Jewish Institute of Religion–Cincinnati, Ohio, 2011
Hebrew Union College–Jewish Institute of Religion–Los Angeles,
     California, 2011
Interboro Institute, New York, 2007
Interface College, Washington, 2015
International Institute of the Americas, Arizona, 2006
Jones College–Miami Campus, Florida, 2010
Jones International University, Colorado, 2015
Katharine Gibbs–New York, 2008

*SOURCE: Gerhz, "When Colleges Close: Recent History"; Lyken-Segosebe and
Shepherd, *Securing Tennessee's Future*.

Lake College, California, 2009

Magnolia Bible College, Mississippi, 2009

Mary Holmes College, Mississippi, 2005

Marymount College of Fordham University, New York, 2008

McIntosh College, New Hampshire, 2009

McLeod Regional Medical Center School of Medical Technology, South Carolina, 2011

Metropolitan College, Oklahoma, 2006

New College of California, 2008

New York Institute of Technology–Central Islip, 2008

Pillsbury Baptist Bible College, Minnesota, 2008

President's College School of Law, Kansas, 2003

Puget Sound Christian College, Washington, 2007

Rabbinical Seminary of Adas Yereim, New York, 2009

Salem Bible College, Oregon, 2009

Sheldon Jackson College, Alaska, 2007

Southampton College of Long Island University, New York, 2007

Southeastern University, Washington, DC, 2009

Southern Catholic College, Georgia, 2010

St. Vincent Catholic Medical Center New York–Brooklyn and Queens, 2008

Taylor University Fort Wayne, Indiana, 2009

Vennard College, Iowa, 2008

Wesley College, Mississippi, 2010

Appendix C

Selected Partnerships, Strategic Alliances, Consortia, and Affiliations in Higher Education, 2000–2016

James E. Samels and Arlene Lieberman, Samels Associates,
Attorneys at Law, and Liam Lair, College of St. Benedict/St. John's University

Partnerships

COLLEGE-INDUSTRY PARTNERSHIPS

Massachusetts Bay Community College Automotive Technology Center and BMW (2003), Jeep/Chrysler (1990), General Motors (1985), and Toyota-Lexus (1987), Massachusetts

The Department of Automotive Technology offers programs that are underwritten by four major automotive brands, providing students with in-depth, product-specific automotive technology programs. MassBay's Automotive Technology Center in Ashland offers training on the most advanced diagnostic equipment and new cars in one of the premier automotive training centers in the New England region. Students have the opportunity to work in the real world and earn a real paycheck while in school through the paid cooperative education program. MassBay's automotive program has a 99 percent placement rate of graduates into full-time jobs by graduation.[1]

EARLY COLLEGE DUAL-ENROLLMENT PARTNERSHIPS

The Harper-Roosevelt CommUniversity Partnership, Illinois, 2014

The Dual Degree Program, a unique partnership between Roosevelt University and Harper College, provides an excellent pathway for full-time students to earn quality, accessible, and affordable associate and bachelor degrees close to home at Roosevelt's Schaumburg campus. A student accepted into the program will be guaranteed admission to Roosevelt after earning an associate degree.[2]

Innovations Early College High School and Salt Lake
Community College, Utah, 2012
Innovations Early College High School partnership with Salt Lake Community
College, Salt Lake City, is considered the "school of the future." Innovations
Early College High School is competency based. The physical setup allows
students to go back and forth between the high school and community college.
Students pursue most of their competencies online and any class beyond that
is treated as dual enrollment. There is integration across the curriculum and
comprehensive accessibility.

Innovations High offers students the ability to take courses as they choose,
whether in a blended learning environment using digital textbooks, or in a
traditional "brick and mortar" class, or through courses that provide industry
certificates that demonstrate employable skills. Local and national experts
say the approach of Innovations High may be one of the first of its kind in
the country—a regular public school that allows students to build their own
schedules by cherry-picking classes from Salt Lake Community College, the
district's career and technical center, the district's traditional high schools,
and the school's own face-to-face classes, which will be taught using digital
textbooks through which students can move at their own speeds, on and off
campus.[3]

Massasoit Community College and Norfolk Agricultural
High School, Massachusetts, 2015
The Massasoit-Norfolk Aggie compact provides for students to earn college
credits from a combination of high school coursework and dual-enrollment
opportunities in general education, veterinary technology, and animal science
specialty courses.[4]

FACILITIES AND EXCESS CAPACITY PARTNERSHIPS
Wheelock College–Cambridge Education Group, Massachusetts, 2012

Cambridge Education Group, a UK organization that prepares international
students for higher education, partnered with Wheelock College to launch
ONCAMPUS Boston, a college preparatory program for international students
aiming to earn an American college degree. In the first year of the program,
students were enrolled at Wheelock, offering them an experience of college
life. Upon completion of the university transfer program, students have the
opportunity to progress into the second year of degree courses at Wheelock
or any of the other ONCAMPUS Boston partner institutions.

NONPROFIT PARTNERSHIPS
Year Up Partnership with Colleges and Universities, 2010

Year Up aims to close the opportunity divide by combining hands-on skill development, college credits, and corporate internships to prepare students for success in professional careers and higher education. It is free and students receive a stipend, but the program requires strong motivation and hard work. Year Up students learn information technology and professional skills, and gain work experience during internships at top companies. Students earn up to twenty-four college credits, with classes taught by certified college instructors. Year Up academic partners include: Atlanta Metropolitan College, Baltimore City Community College, Bellevue College, Cambridge College, City College of San Francisco, Community College of Rhode Island, Florida State College at Jacksonville, Foothill College, Harold Washington College, Johnson & Wales University, Kaplan University, Maricopa Community Colleges, Miami Dade College, Northern Virginia Community College, Peirce College, SUNY Empire State College, and the University of Phoenix.[5]

CORPORATE PARTNERSHIPS
Arizona State University and Starbucks, 2013

In 2013, Arizona State University President Michael Crow and Starbucks CEO Howard Schultz partnered in a shared mission to equalize access to higher education. Together, the university and the corporation have developed a first-of-its-kind strategic alliance that tangibly increases the role a public company can play in supporting its employees' goals. The Starbucks College Achievement Plan (SCAP) enables employees (termed "partners") who work as few as twenty hours per week the opportunity to earn a bachelor's degree with full tuition reimbursement through one of ASU's online degree programs. Starbucks' partnership with ASU not only provided this opportunity to its partners but also elevated its brand with consumers. Ultimately, Howard Schultz's objective for SCAP was to create not just an employee benefit, but "a culture transformation and a new operating model."[6] Preliminary data on the return on investment for SCAP indicates that Starbucks baristas who enroll in the program are retained at a 12 percent higher rate than partners who do not enroll in the program.

General Education Outsourcing

UNIVERSITY OF NEW HAMPSHIRE AND CULTURAL
EXPERIENCE ABROAD (CEA), 2006

In 2006, University of New Hampshire President Steven H. Kaplan and CEA CEO Brian Boubek signed an agreement through which UNH became CEA's "school of record." Through this partnership, students who complete courses at CEA Study Abroad Centers—located in Barcelona, Buenos Aires, Dublin, Florence, Paris, Rome, Seville, and Shanghai—earn UNH credits on UNH transcripts.

Criteria for faculty hire, course design and approval, course credit and grading, and student assessment are consistent with those on the UNH campus and with the Commission on Institutions of Higher Education of the New England Association of Schools and Colleges, which approves the school of record agreement. In addition, a standing UNH committee reviews and approves:

• all faculty and directors at CEA's eight Study Abroad Centers,
• all CEA Study Abroad Center courses taught by CEA staff, and
• all significant course modifications.

CEA produces a self-study for each Study Abroad Center on a fixed schedule, followed by a rigorous on-site team review conducted by UNH and utilizing an external evaluator. As of 2015, CEA successfully completed the Quality Improvement Program through the Forum on Education Abroad and were found to be meeting the Standards of Good Practice for Education Abroad.

UNIVERSITY OF MINNESOTA AND CAPA INTERNATIONAL EDUCATION (2005), THE DANISH INSTITUTE FOR STUDY ABROAD, AND THE SCHOOL FOR FIELD STUDIES (2014)

The University of Minnesota acts as a school of record for the following institutions:

• CAPA International Education (London and Sydney sites)
• Danish Institute for Study Abroad
• School for Field Studies

The university uses the following criteria in determining the appropriateness of acting as school of record for a select number of educational partners:

• The program must be one that the University of Minnesota actively uses and supports for University of Minnesota students.
• The program must be one the university has confidence in and experience with, as well as a stake in the academic content and quality of the programs.
• The program must have appropriate oversight mechanisms in place, such as advisory boards or councils and review processes.

The program has been developed in consultation with the Forum on Education Abroad's Standards of Good Practice for Education Abroad.[7]

UNIVERSITY OF PENNSYLVANIA GRADUATE SCHOOL OF EDUCATION, THE UNIVERSITY OF CAMBRIDGE, AND NAZARBAYEV UNIVERSITY, KAZAKHSTAN, 2010

In 2009, a group of curriculum planners from the Alliance for Higher Education and Democracy (AHEAD) at the University of Pennsylvania's Graduate

School of Education (GSE) began working with higher education colleagues at Nazarbayev University (NU) in Kazakhstan tasked with establishing that nation's first research university. This early work led to the signing in September 2010 of a formal contract between Penn and NU's Centre for Educational Policy, a private, not-for-profit entity established under the laws of Kazakhstan and housed and operating within the university. The center became operational relatively quickly and eventually resulted in a three-way partnership among NU, the University of Cambridge, and Penn GSE's Higher Education Division. The planners framed a statement of principle informing the work of Cambridge and Penn faculty members as they worked together to establish Nazarbayev University's Graduate School of Education.

Strategic Alliances

WORLD FOOD LOGISTICS ORGANIZATION'S APPROPRIATE
POSTHARVEST TECHNOLOGY PROJECT AND VARIOUS PARTNERS, 2009

A yearlong World Food Logistics Organization project funded by the Bill and Melinda Gates Foundation has successfully assessed the current state of postharvest losses and quality problems in a range of developing countries. The goals of the project were to develop a set of recommendations for guiding future projects, and to assist the foundation in planning its overall horticultural strategy. Project partners include the University of California, Davis (USA), Amity University (India), Institut des Sciences Agronomiques du Rwanda and Kigali Institute of Science and Technology (Rwanda), Council for Scientific and Industrial Research (Ghana), Kwame Nkrumah University of Science and Technology (Ghana), Ghana PolyTechnical Institutes (Ghana), and International Institute of Tropical Agriculture (Benin). Symantha Holben and Richard Tracy of the Global Cold Chain Alliance International Department provided project support.[8]

UNIVERSITY OF MASSACHUSETTS LOWELL
AND AMITY UNIVERSITY, 2014

Professor Krishna Vedula, professor of chemical engineering and dean emeritus at the University of Massachusetts Lowell and executive director of the Indo US Collaboration for Engineering Education, organized a workshop on "Global Excellence in Engineering Education" for the faculty members at Amity University.[9]

Consortia

GLOBAL CITIES INITIATIVE INVOLVING THE CONSORTIUM OF
UNIVERSITIES OF THE WASHINGTON METROPOLITAN AREA, 2016

A coalition representing local government, business, and higher education leaders in the greater Washington, DC, area has been chosen to participate in the Global Cities Initiative, a joint project of the Brookings Institution and JPMorgan Chase. Launched in 2012, the Global Cities Initiative helps public and private sector leaders grow their metropolitan economies by strengthening international connections and competitiveness. The Metropolitan Washington Council of Governments, the Greater Washington Board of Trade, and the Consortium of Universities of the Washington Metropolitan Area are coordinating the effort. The project will create a data-driven market assessment, which will evaluate the region's current export economy, support systems, and opportunities for growth. The region will then integrate those findings into a comprehensive metropolitan export plan that aligns goals, strategies, tactics, and operational commitments.[10]

THE BOSTON CONSORTIUM, 1995

The Boston Consortium was established in the fall of 1995 by the CFOs of a group of Boston-area colleges and universities to develop collaborative strategies and solutions for nonacademic areas of higher education operations. The consortium is currently composed of the following institutions: Babson College, Bentley University, Berklee College of Music, Boston College, Boston University, Brandeis University, College of the Holy Cross, Emerson College, Massachusetts Institute of Technology, Northeastern University, Olin College, Suffolk University, Tufts University, Wellesley College, and Wheaton College. The institutions' diversity is reflected in their operating budgets, which range from approximately $37 million to $1.5 billion, and annual research expenditures, which range from $0 to about $351 million. The combined endowment of the fifteen consortium members totals more than $11 billion, and the total full-time equivalent (FTE) count is approximately 45,000 employees, making the group one of the largest employers in the area. The combined student headcount is approximately 122,000.[11]

Notes
1. From "Automotive Technology," MassBay Community College, accessed April 5, 2016, http://www.massbay.edu/automotive/.
2. "Roosevelt and Harper Dual Degree Program," Harper College, accessed April 5, 2016, http://goforward.harpercollege.edu/academics/transfer/roosevelt_dual.php; "Harper Announces New Partnership with Roosevelt University," Harper College, accessed August 20, 2014, http://goforward.harpercollege.edu/about/news/archives/2014/082014b.php.

3. Schencker, "New Utah High School One of the First of Its Kind."

4. "Massasoit Community College and Norfolk County Agricultural High School Announce Veterinary Technician AAS Partnership," *Massasoit News: News and Updates from Massasoit Community College*, January 15, 2015, https://massasoitnews.wordpress.com/2015/01/15/massasoit-community-college-and-norfolk-county-agricultural-high-school-announce-veterinary-technician-aas-partnership/.

5. "What Is the Opportunity Divide?" Year Up, accessed April 5, 2016, http://www.yearup.org/opportunity-divide/?location=national-us/; "History," Year Up, accessed April 5, 2016, http://www.yearup.org/about-us/history/?location=national-us/.

6. "A Partnership between ASU and Starbucks Raises the Bar for the Role a Public Company Can Play in Support of its Employees' Life Goals," ASU Online, Arizona State University, accessed April 10, 2016, https://asuonline.asu.edu/starbucks-and-arizona-state-university.

7. "University of Minnesota's Role as School of Record," University of Minnesota, accessed April 5, 2016, http://umabroad.umn.edu/professionals/intleducators/schoolofrecord.

8. Lisa Kitinoja, "WFLO Identifies Postharvest Technologies," Global Gold Chain Alliance, accessed April 5, 2016, http://www.gcca.org/cold-facts/wflo-identifies-postharvest-technologies/.

9. "'Excellence in Engineering Education Can Be Achieved through Active Learning amongst the Budding Engineers in Classrooms,' Suggests Prof. Krishna Vedula, Executive Director during Workshop on "Global Excellence in Engineering Education" at Amity University," Amity University Events, accessed August 20, 2014, http://www.amity.edu/events/eventdetails.asp?id=3302.

10. Megan Goodman and Anthony Fiano, "Greater Washington Region Accepted into Global Cities Initiative, Will Develop Metropolitan Export Plan," news release, February 10, 2016, https://static1.squarespace.com/static/54f72b94e4b05ca04000cf5c/t/56bbb34727d4bd23c4d9c862/1455141703667/GCI+Announcement+Press+Release+2016-01-10.pdf.

11. "What Is the Boston Consortium?" Boston Consortium for Higher Education, accessed April 5, 2016, http://www.boston-consortium.org/about/what_is_tbc.asp.

Bibliography

Adkins, Sam S. *International Learning Technology Investment Patterns*. Monroe, WA: Ambient Insight, 2015. http://www.ambientinsight.com/Resources/Documents /AmbientInsight_2015_Q1_Global_Edtech_InvestmentPatterns.pdf.

Alex, Patricia. "Rutgers' New Era Starts Today with UMDNJ Merger." *The Record*, June 30, 2013. http://www.northjersey.com/news/education/rutgers-new-era-starts -today-with-umdnj-merger-1.598236.

Alssid, Julian L., and Patricia Shields. "College in the Call Center." *Training and Development Magazine*, February 8, 2014. https://www.td.org/Publications /Magazines/TD/TD-Archive/2014/02/College-in-the-Call-Center.

Altbach, Philip G., and Jane Knight. "The Internationalization of Higher Education: Motivations and Realities." *Journal of Studies in International Education* 11, no. 3/4 (2007): 291.

Anders, George. "The Skeptic: Stanford's John Hennessy." *MIT Technology Review*, July 27, 2015. http://www.technologyreview.com/news/539146/the-skeptic-stanfords -john-hennessy/.

Anderson, Nick, and Susan Svriuga. "Sweet Briar to Close Because of Financial Challenges." *Washington Post*, March 3, 2015. https://www.washingtonpost.com/news /grade-point/wp/2015/03/03/sweet-briar-college-to-close-because-of-financial -challenges/.

Andrew W. Mellon Foundation. *Grantmaking to Support Collaboration in Higher Education*. New York: Andrew W. Mellon Foundation, 2015. https://mellon.org /programs/higher-education-and-scholarship-humanities/consortia/.

Associated Colleges of the South. "Sunoikisis: Building a Virtual Department." YouTube video, 1:06:03. April 17, 2014. https://youtu.be/pmla_vaoEu8.

Babbitt, Ellen M. "Closing an Academic Program without Litigation: Process Planning, and Pragmatism." In *Academic Program Closures: A Legal Compendium*, edited by Ellen M. Babbitt. Washington, DC: National Association of College and University Attorneys, 2002.

Babbitt, Ellen M., Peter G. Land, and Scott L. Warner. "Anticipating and Managing the Legal Risks of Academic Program Closures." *NACUA Notes* 9, no. 2 (November 3, 2010).

Bailey, Brandon. "Hewlett-Packard Is Splitting into Two Companies." *Huffington Post*, October 30, 2015. http://www.huffingtonpost.com/entry/hewlett-packard -is-splitting-into-two-companies_us_56337eafe4b0c66bae5c0a71.

Bailey, Darlyne, and Kelly McNally Koney. *Strategic Alliances among Health and Human Services Organizations: From Affiliations to Consolidations.* London: Sage, 2000.

Barringer, Bruce R., and Jeffrey S. Harrison. "Walking a Tightrope: Creating Value through Interorganizational Relationships." *Journal of Management* 26, no. 3 (2000): 367–403.

Baum, Sandy, and Jennifer Ma. *Trends in College Pricing.* New York: College Board Advocacy and Policy Center, 2012. http://trends.collegeboard.org/sites/default /files/college-pricing-2012-full-report_0.pdf.

Benson, Lee, Ira Harkavy, and John Puckett. *Dewey's Dream: Universities and Democracies in an Age of Education Reform.* Philadelphia: Temple University Press, 2007.

Berman, Jillian. "Why More U.S. Colleges Will Go Under in the Next Few Years." *Market Watch*, March 28, 2015. http://www.marketwatch.com/story/why-more -private-colleges-are-closing-2015-03-25.

Birge, James, Brooke Beaird, and Jan Torres. "Partnerships among Colleges and Universities for Service Learning." In *Building Partnerships for Service Learning*, edited by Barbara Jacoby. San Francisco: Jossey-Bass; New York: John Wiley & Sons, 2003.

Book, Ryan. "Berklee College of Music and Boston Conservatory to Merge in 2016." *Music Times*, June 28, 2015. http://www.musictimes.com/articles/41790 /20150628/berklee-college-of-music-boston-conservatory-merge-2016.htm.

Booz Allen Hamilton. *The Word's Most Enduring Institutions.* McLean, VA: Booz Allen Hamilton, 2004. http://www.boozallen.com/content/dam/boozallen/media /file/Worlds_Most_Enduring_Institutions.pdf.

Bowen, William G. "Toward a Shared Vision of Shared Governance." *Chronicle of Higher Education*, January 16, 2015, A22-23.

Brassard, Gilles, and Paul Bratley. *Algorithmics: Theory and Practice.* Englewood Cliffs, NJ: Prentice Hall, 1988.

Breneman, David. "Are We Losing Our Liberal Arts Colleges?" *American Association for Higher Education* 43, no. 2 (1990): 3–6. http://files.eric.ed.gov/fulltext /ED339260.pdf.

Bureau of Consular Affairs. *Who We Are and What We Do: Consular Affairs by the Numbers.* Washington, DC: US State Department, 2013. http://travel.state.gov /content/dam/ca_fact_sheet.pdf.

Burns, Bridget, Michael Crow, and Mark Becker. "Innovating Together, Collaboration as a Driving Force to Improve Student Success." *EDUCAUSE Review*, March 2, 2015. http://er.educause.edu/articles/2015/3/innovating-together-collaboration -as-a-driving-force-to-improve-student-success.

Cary, Kevin. *The End of College: Creating the Future of Learning and the University of Everywhere.* New York: Riverhead Books, 2015.

Cauley, Kate. "Principle 1: Partners Have Agreed-Upon Mission, Values, Goals, and Measurable Outcomes for the Partnership." In *Partnership Perspectives*, issue II, vol. 1, edited by Kara Connors and Sarena Seifer. San Francisco: Community-Campus Partnerships for Health, 2000.

Christensen, Clayton M., and Henry J. Eyring. *The Innovative University*. San Francisco: Jossey-Bass, 2011.

Clark, John B., W. Bruce Leslie, and Kenneth P. O'Brien, eds. *SUNY at 60: The Promise of the State University of New York*. Albany: State University of New York Press, 2010.

Cole, Jonathan R. "Building a New Research-University System." *Chronicle of Higher Education*, January 17, 2016. http://chronicle.com/article/Building-a-New /234906.

Costanzo, Joe, and Amanda Kiekowski von Koppenfels. "Counting the Uncountable: Overseas Americans." *Migration Information Source*, May 17, 2013. http://www.migrationpolicy.org/article/counting-uncountable-overseas -americans.

Crawford, Amy. "Bringing a Charter-School Approach to College." *Boston Globe*, March 26, 2015. https://www.bostonglobe.com/ideas/2015/03/26/bringing -charter-school-approach-college/CPSqaG8MEkfs589yEnGc3O/story.html.

Creighton, Joanne V. "Orchestrating Shared Governance." In *Remaking College: Innovation and the Liberal Arts College*, edited by Rebecca Chopp, Susan Frost, and Daniel H. Weiss. Baltimore: Johns Hopkins University Press, 2014.

Creswell, Julie, and Reed Abelson. "New Laws and Rising Costs Create a Surge of Supersizing Hospitals." *New York Times*, August 12, 2013. http://www.nytimes .com/2013/08/13/business/bigger-hospitals-may-lead-to-bigger-bills-for-patients .html?_r=1.

Crow, Michael, and William B. Dabars. *Designing the American University*. Baltimore: Johns Hopkins University Press, 2015.

Cullotta, Ann. "Arne Duncan Visits Harper College, Praises Scholarship Program." *Chicago Tribune*, September 9, 2015. http://www.chicagotribune.com/suburbs /elgin-courier-news/news/ct-arh-arne-duncan-harper-tl-0917-20150909-story .html.

DeMillo, Richard. "Gatekeepers No More: Colleges Must Learn a New Role." *Chronicle of Higher Education*, September 14, 2015. http://chronicle.com /article/Gatekeepers-No-More-Colleges/232975/.

Denhart, Chris. "How the $1.2 Trillion College Debt Crisis Is Crippling Student, Parents, and the Economy." *Forbes*, August 7, 2013. http://www.forbes.com/sites /specialfeatures/2013/08/07/how-the-college-debt-is-crippling-students-parents -and-the-economy/.

Denneen, Jeff, and Tom Dretler. "The Financially Sustainable University." *Bain Brief*, July 6, 2012. http://www.bain.com/publications/articles/financially-sustainable -university.aspx.

Doz, Yves L. "The Evolution of Cooperation in Strategic Alliances: Initial Conditions or Learning Processes?" *Strategic Management Journal* 17, no. S1 (1996): 55–83.

Dussauge, P., and B. Garrette. *Cooperative Strategy: Competing Successfully through Strategic Alliances*. New York: Wiley, 1999.

Dweck, Carol. *Mindset: The New Psychology of Success*. New York: Random House, 2006.

Eckel, Peter D., and Matthew Hartley. "Developing Academic Strategic Alliances: Reconciling Multiple Institutional Cultures, Policies, and Practices." *Journal of Higher Education* 79, no. 6 (2008): 613–37.

Eckel, Peter D., and Karla Hignite. *Finding the Right Prescription for Higher Education's Ills: Can Health Care Provide Answers?* Washington, DC: National Association of College and University Business Officers, 2012. http://www.nacubo.org/Documents/Leadership/ManagingChange_ExecSummary2012.pdf.

Economist Intelligence Unit. *Higher Education in the 21st Century: Meeting Real-World Demands.* Dallas, TX: Academic Partnerships, 2014. http://www.economistinsights.com/sites/default/files/EIU_AcademicPartns_WEBr1.pdf.

Education Trust. *The Pell Partnership: Ensuring a Shared Responsibility for Low-Income Student Success.* Washington, DC: Education Trust, 2015. https://edtrust.org/wp-content/uploads/2014/09/ThePellPartnership_EdTrust_20152.pdf.

Fleming, Brian. "Mapping the Competency-Based Education Universe." *Wake-Up Call,* February 17, 2015. http://www.eduventures.com/2015/02/mapping-the-competency-based-education-universe/.

Franklin, B. "Proposals Relating to the Education of Youth in Pennsilvania [*sic*], 1749." Reprinted in *Benjamin Franklin on Education,* edited by J. Hardin. New York: Teachers College Press, 1962.

Gephardt, Dennis, Edith Behr, Karen Kedem, Susan Fitzgerald, and Kendra Smith. *US Higher Education: Small College Closures Poised to Increase.* New York: Moody's Investors Services, 2015.

Gerhz, Chris. "When Colleges Close: Recent History." *Pietist Schoolman,* April 29, 2013, http://pietistschoolman.com/2013/04/29/when-colleges-close-recent-history/.

Goldberg, Melissa, and Julian L. Alssid. *Nonclinical and Frontline Healthcare Roles Continue to Rise: College for America Workforce Trend Report.* Manchester, NH: College for America, 2014. http://nfwsolutions.org/sites/nfwsolutions.org/files/College_for_America_healthcare_report_2014.pdf.

Green, M. F. *Internationalization in U.S. Higher Education: The Student Perspective.* Washington, DC: American Council on Education.

Greve, Henrich, Tim Rowley, and Andrew Shipilov. *Network Advantage: How to Unlock Value from Your Alliances and Partnerships.* Cornwall, UK: John Wiley, 2014.

Guerin-Calvert, Margaret E., and Jen A. Maki. *Hospital Realignment: Mergers Offer Significant Patient and Community Benefits.* Washington, DC: Center for Healthcare and Economics Policy; Washington, DC: FTI Consulting, 2014. http://www.fticonsulting.com/~/media/Files/us-files/insights/reports/hospital-realignment-mergers-offer-significant-patient-and-community-benefits.pdf.

Gulati, Ranjay, and Harbir Singh. "The Architecture of Cooperation: Managing Coordination Costs and Appropriation Concerns in Strategic Alliances." *Administrative Science Quarterly* 43, no. 4 (1998): 781–814.

Hagedoorn, John. "Understanding the Rationale of Strategic Technology Partnering: Interorganizational Modes of Cooperation and Sectoral Differences." *Strategic Management Journal* 14, no. 5 (1993): 371–95.

Hagood, Amanda, and Grace Pang. "Collaboration: A Primer." *Academic Commons for the Liberal Education Community,* January 6, 2015. http://www.academiccommons.org/2015/01/06/collaboration-a-primer/.

Hamel, Gary. "Strategy as Revolution." *Harvard Business Review,* July–August 1996. https://hbr.org/1996/07/strategy-as-revolution.

Hanover Research. *Institutionalizing Innovation in Higher Education.* Washington, DC: Academy Administration Practice, Hanover Research, 2013. http://www

.hanoverresearch.com/wp-content/uploads/2013/06/Institutionalizing-Innovation
-in-Higher-Education.pdf.

Harkavy, Ira, and Matthew Hartley. "Pursuing Franklin's Dream: Philosophical and
Historical Roots of Service-Learning." *American Journal of Community Psychology* 46, no. 3 (2010): 418–27.

Harkavy, Ira, and John Puckett. "Mediating Structures in University and Community
Revitalization: The University of Pennsylvania and West Philadelphia as a Case
Study." *Journal of Research and Development in Education* 25, no. 1 (1991):
10–25.

Hartley, Matthew, Bryan Gopaul, Aida Sagintayeva, and Renata Apergenova. "Learning Autonomy: Higher Education Reform in Kazakhstan." *Higher Education*
(October 2015): 1–13.

Hartley, Matthew, Ira Harkavy, and Lee Benson. "Looking Ahead: Franklin's Theory
of Education in the Twenty-First Century." In *The Good Education of Youth:
Worlds of Learning in the Age of Franklin*, edited by J. H. Pollack. New Castle,
DE: Oak Knoll Press, 2009.

Harvard University. *Harvard University Financial Report, 2012.* Cambridge, MA:
Harvard University, 2012. http://finance.harvard.edu/files/fad/files/2012fullreport
_2.pdf?m=1389978181.

Hensley-Clancy, Molly. "The New American University: Massive, Online, and
Corporate-Backed." *Buzzfeed News*, July 20, 2014. http://www.buzzfeed.com
/mollyhensleyclancy/the-new-american-university-massive-online-and-corporate
-bac#.quo6zBKjD4.

Heyboer, Kelly. "Welcome to the New Rutgers: School Makes History with UMDNJ
Merger." *NJ.com*, June 30, 2013. http://www.nj.com/news/index.ssf/2013/06
/welcome_to_the_new_rutgers_university_makes_history_with_umdnj_merger
.html.

Hoffman, Reid. "Connections with Integrity." *strategy+business* 67 (2012):
20–25.

Hudzik, John K. *Comprehensive Internationalization: From Concept to Action.*
Washington, DC: Association of International Educators, 2011.

Hussar, William J., and Tabitha M. Bailey. *Projections of Education Statistics to
2022.* Washington, DC: National Center for Education Statistics, Institute of
Education Sciences, US Department of Education, 2015. https://nces.ed.gov
/pubs2014/2014051.pdf.

Institute for College Access and Success. *Student Loan Debt and the Class of 2013.*
Washington, DC: Institute for College Access and Success, 2014. http://ticas.org
/sites/default/files/legacy/files/pub/classof2013.pdf.

Jacobs, Peter. "Here's How Many Colleges Have Closed in the Past 25 Years." *Business Insider*, March 12, 2015. http://www.businessinsider.com/college-closings
-chart-2015-3.

Jaschik, Scott. "Not a Tsunami, But . . ." *Inside Higher Ed*, March 16, 2015. https://
www.insidehighered.com/news/2015/03/16/stanford-president-offers
-predictions-more-digital-future-higher-education.

———. "Revolution in Higher Education." *Inside Higher Ed*, October 7, 2015.
https://www.insidehighered.com/news/2015/10/07/author-discusses-his-new
-book-revolution-higher-education.

Jaschik, Scott, and Doug Lederman, eds. *The 2014 Inside Higher Ed Survey of Chief Academic Officers.* Washington, DC: Inside Higher Ed; Gallup, 2014.

Johnson, Edward A., and Kent M. Weeks. "To Save a College: Independent College Trustees and Decisions on Financial Exigency, Endowment Use and Closure." *Journal of College and University Law* 12, no. 4 (1986): 455.

Johnson, Nate, and Takeshi Yanaguira. *How Did Revenue and Spending per Student Change at Four-Year Colleges and Universities Between 2006–07 and 2012–13?* Washington, DC: Association of Public and Land-Grant Universities, 2015. http://www.aplu.org/library/public-university-spending-per-student-between -2006-07-and-2012-13/file.

Johnson, S. Whealler, and John B. Noftsinger. "Getting a Grip on Strategic Alliances." *Trusteeship* 12, no. 4 (2004): 15–19.

Johnston, Francis E., and Ira Harkavy. *The Obesity Culture: Strategies for Change.* Cambridgeshire, UK: Smith-Gordon, 2009.

Kahn, Gabriel. "The Amazon of Higher Education." *Slate,* January 2, 2014. http:// www.slate.com/articles/life/education/2014/01/southern_new_hampshire _university_how_paul_leblanc_s_tiny_school_has_become.html.

Kingkade, Tyler. "MOOC Skepticism Persists among University Presidents, Despite Rapid Growth of Online Courses in 2012." *Huffington Post,* November 26, 2012. http://www.huffingtonpost.com/2012/11/26/moocs-skepticism_n_2191314.html.

Koblik, Steven, and Stephen R. Graubard, eds. *Distinctively American: The Residential Liberal Colleges.* Piscataway, NJ: Transaction Publishers, 2000.

Konnikova, Maria. "Will MOOCs Be Flukes?" *New Yorker,* November 7, 2014. http://www.newyorker.com/science/maria-konnikova/moocs-failure-solutions.

Lapowsky, Issie. "Why Free Online Classes Are Still the Future of Education." *Wired,* September 26, 2014. http://www.wired.com/2014/09/free-online-classes-still-future -education/.

Lebetter, Tammi Reed. "Grand Canyon Univ. Sold; Trustees in Advisory Role." *Baptist Press,* February 10, 2004. http://www.bpnews.net/17607.

Lederman, Doug. "CFO Survey Reveals Doubts about Financial Sustainability." *Inside Higher Ed,* July 12, 2013. https://www.insidehighered.com/news/survey/cfo -survey-reveals-doubts-about-financial-sustainability.

Lindquist, Sue, and Mary Ann Hilmes. "Policy Statement on Considerations When Closing a Postsecondary Educational Institution." *Handbook of Accreditation and Policy Manual,* Revised. Council on Postsecondary Accreditation, April 1982. https://archive.org/stream/ERIC_ED473680/ERIC_ED473680_djvu.txt.

Long, Katherine. "Foreign Enrollment Skyrockets for UW." *Seattle Times,* November 14, 2011. http://www.seattletimes.com/seattle-news/foreign-enrollment-skyrockets -for-uw/.

Lumina Foundation and Gallup. *What America Needs to Know about Higher Education Redesign: The 2013 Lumina Study of the American Publics Opinion on Higher Education and U.S. Business Leaders Poll on Higher Education.* Indianapolis: Lumina Foundation; Washington, DC: Gallup, 2014. http://www .luminafoundation.org/files/resources/2013-gallup-lumina-foundation-report.pdf.

Lyken-Segosebe, Dawn, and Justin Cole Shepherd. *Securing Tennessee's Future: Learning from Closed Institutions. Indicators of Risk for Small Private Colleges and Universities.* Nashville: Tennessee Independent Colleges and Universities Associa-

tion, 2013. http://www.ticua.org/public_policy/sm_files/Learning%20from%20
Closed%20Institutions.pdf.

Marcus, Jon. "Higher Education Is Headed for a Shakeout, Analysts Warn." *Hech-inger Report*, September 3, 2013. http://hechingerreport.org/content/higher
-education-is-headed-for-a-shakeout-analysts-warn_12996/.

———. "US Colleges Projecting Decline in Revenue Despite Rising Tuition." *Busi-ness Insider*, November 18, 2015. http://www.businessinsider.com/us-colleges
-projecting-decline-in-revenue-despite-rising-tuition-2014-11.

Martin, James, and James E. Samels. *Merging Colleges for Mutual Growth: A New
Strategy for Academic Managers*. Baltimore: Johns Hopkins University Press, 1994.

———. *Turnaround: Leading Stressed Colleges and Universities to Excellence*. Bal-timore: Johns Hopkins University Press, 2013.

McDonald, Michael. "Small U.S. Colleges Battle Death Spiral as Enrollment Drops."
Bloomberg Business, April 14, 2014. http://www.bloomberg.com/news/articles
/2014-04-14/small-u-s-colleges-battle-death-spiral-as-enrollment-drops.

Mitchell, Travis. "Chart: See 20 Years of Tuition Increase at National Universities."
U.S. News and World Report, July 29, 2015. http://www.usnews.com/education
/best-colleges/paying-for-college/articles/2015/07/29/chart-see-20-years-of
-tuition-growth-at-national-universities.

Moody's Global Credit Research. *US Higher Education: Sector Stabilizes with Mod-est Revenue Growth in Challenging Environment*. New York: Moody's Investor
Services, 2015.

Nelson, Libby A. "Summoned to the White House (Update)." *Inside Higher Ed*,
December 2, 2011. https://www.insidehighered.com/news/2011/12/02/obama
-invites-college-presidents-meeting.

Nelson A. Rockefeller Institute of Government. *How SUNY Matters: Economic Im-pacts of the State University of New York*. Albany, NY: Nelson A. Rockefeller
Institute of Government, University of Albany; Buffalo, NY: Regional Institute,
University at Buffalo, 2011.

Northwest Educational Council for Student Success. *Guiding Document for NECSS*.
Arlington Heights, IL: Northwest Educational Council for Student Success, 2012.
http://www.necsspartnership.com/wp-content/uploads/Guiding_Document.pdf.

Office of Institutional Research, Assessment and Effectiveness. *2014–2015 Drexel
Factbook: Undergraduate Postgraduate Outcomes One Year after Graduation*.
Philadelphia: Drexel University, 2014. http://www.drexel.edu/provost/irae/factbook
/post-graduate-outcomes/Class%20of%202013/.

Oliver, Christine. "Determinants of Interorganizational Relationships: Integration and
Future Directions." *Academy of Management Review* 15, no. 2 (1990): 241–65.

Pappano, Laura. "The Year of the MOOC." *New York Times*, November 2, 2012.
http://www.nytimes.com/2012/11/04/education/edlife/massive-open-online
-courses-are-multiplying-at-a-rapid-pace.html.

Perna, Laura W., Kata Orosz, and Zakir Jumakulov. "Understanding the Human
Capital Benefits of a Government-Funded International Scholarship Program:
An Exploration of Kazakhstan's Bolashak Program." *International Journal of
Educational Development* 40 (2015): 85–97.

Peterson, Patti McGill, and Robin Matross Helms. *Challenges and Opportunities for
the Global Engagement of Higher Education*. Washington, DC: Center for Interna-

tionalization and Global Engagement, 2014. https://www.acenet.edu/news-room
/Documents/CIGE-Insights-2014-Challenges-Opps-Global-Engagement.pdf.

Porter, Michael E. "What Is Strategy?" *Harvard Business Review* (November–December 1996). https://hbr.org/1996/11/what-is-strategy.

Pristin, Terry. "Drug Company Lease Gives Security to a College." *New York Times*, October 1, 2003. http://www.nytimes.com/2003/10/01/business/commercial-real-estate-drug-company-lease-gives-security-to-a-college.html.

Putman, Robert D. *Our Kids: The American Dream in Crisis*. New York: Simon and Schuster, 2015.

Quinn, J. B. "Strategic Change: Logical Incrementalism." *Sloan Management Review* 20, no. 1 (1978): 7–21.

Ray, Julie, and Stephanie Kafka. "Life in College Matters for Life after College." *Gallup*, May 6, 2014. http://www.gallup.com/poll/168848/life-college-matters-life-college.aspx.

ReadyNation. *Closing the Job Skills Gap with New Yorkers*. Washington, DC: ReadyNation, n.d. http://readynation.s3.amazonaws.com/wp-content/uploads/RN-NY-Skills-Brief.pdf.

Regan, Claire M. "Program Aims to Boost the Borough's Brain Power." *Silive.com*, August 23, 2015. http://www.silive.com/news/index.ssf/2015/08/boosting_borough_brain_power_p.html.

Reynolds, Glenn Harlan. "Degrees of Value: Making College Pay Off." *Wall Street Journal*, January 7, 2014. http://www.wsj.com/articles/SB10001424052702303870704579298302637802002.

Rivard, Ry. "Downgrading Elite Colleges." *Inside Higher Ed*, August 30, 2013. https:/www.insidehighered.com/news/2013/08/30/prestigious-liberal-arts-colleges-face-ratings-downgrades.

Roth, Michael. "What Is a University For?" *Wall Street Journal*, March 4, 2016. http://www.wsj.com/articles/what-is-a-university-for-1457130080.

Russell, Alene. *A Guide to Major U.S. College Completion Initiatives*. Washington, DC: American Association of State Colleges and Universities, 2011. http://www.isac.org/dotAsset/dbf0788e-4c9b-4ccd-8649-65361d6ff059.pdf.

Samels, James E. "Higher Education Mergers, Consolidations, Consortia, and Affiliations: A Typology of Models and Basic Legal Structures." In *Merging Colleges for Mutual Growth: A New Strategy for Academic Managers*, 22–41. Baltimore: Johns Hopkins University Press, 1994.

Schencker, Lisa. "New Utah High School One of the First of Its Kind in the Country." *Salt Lake Tribune*, August 6, 2012. http://archive.sltrib.com/story.php?ref=/sltrib/news/54590773-78/innovations-students-lake-salt.html.csp.

Selingo, Jeff, Kevin Carey, Hilary Pennington, Rachel Fishman, and Iris Palmer. *The Next Generation University*. Washington, DC: Education Policy Program, New American Foundation, 2013. https://static.newamerica.org/attachments/2318-the-next-generation-university/Next_Generation_University_FINAL_FOR_RELEASE.8897220087ff4bd6afe8f6682594e3b0.pdf.

Soares, Louis. *Community College and Industry Partnerships*. Washington, DC: Center for American Progress, 2010. http://www2.ed.gov/PDFDocs/college-completion/02-community-college-and-industry-partnerships.pdf.

Stone, Chad, Danilo Trisi, Arloc Sherman, and Brandon Debot. *A Guide to Statistics on Historical Trends in Income Inequality*. Washington, DC: Center on Budget

and Policy Priorities, 2015. http://www.cbpp.org/research/poverty-and-inequality
/a-guide-to-statistics-on-historical-trends-in-income-inequality.

Straumsheim, Carl. "Grinnell College and the University of Iowa Announce a Digital Humanities Partnership That May Be a First for the Andrew W. Mellon Foundation." *Insider Higher Ed*, January 30, 2015. https://www.insidehighered.com
/news/2015/01/30/grinnell-college-u-iowa-announce-mellon-funded-digital
-humanities-partnership.

Sussman, Jason, and Charles Kim. "6 Signs of Disruption: What Higher Education
Can Learn from Healthcare." *University Business*, April 2015. http://www
.universitybusiness.com/article/0415-sussman.

Taylor, Mark C. *Crisis on Campus*. New York: Alfred A. Knopf, 2010.

Thomas, Nancy. *An Examination of Multi-institutional Networks*. Paper 19. Boston:
New England Resource Center for Higher Education, 1999. http://scholarworks
.umb.edu/cgi/viewcontent.cgi?article=1018&context=nerche_pubs.

Tierney, William. "The Disruptive Future of Higher Education." In *Postsecondary
Play: The Role of Games and Social Media in Higher Education*, edited by William
Tierney, Zoë B. Corwin, Tracy Fullerton, and Gisele Ragusa. Baltimore: Johns
Hopkins University Press, 2014.

Treaster, Joseph B. "Liberal Arts, a Lost Cause?" *New York Times*, July 31, 2015.
http://www.nytimes.com/2015/08/02/education/edlife/liberal-arts-a-lost-cause
.html?_r=0.

Tuby, Kimberly, Susan I. Fitzgerald, Karen Kedem, Edith Behr, and Kendra M. Smith.
Slow Tuition Growth Supports Continued Negative Outlook. New York: Moody's
Investor Services, 2014. http://www.cic.edu/News-and-Publications/Multimedia
-Library/CICConferencePresentations/2015%20Presidents%20Institute
/20150105-The%20Financial%20and%20Strategic%20Outlook%20for%20
Private%20Colleges%202.pdf.

van Gelder, Tim. "Teaching Critical Thinking: Some Lessons from Cognitive Science." *College Teaching* 53, no. 1 (2005): 41–46.

Vaughan, Christopher. "A Healing Partnership: ASU-Mayo Collaboration Is Helping
Create the Next Generation of Health Science." *ASU Magazine*, December
2012. https://magazine.asu.edu/december-2012/articles/featured-articles/healing
-partnership.

Warrell, Helen. "Students under Surveillance." *Financial Times*, July 24, 2015. http://
www.ft.com/cms/s/2/634624c6-312b-11e5-91ac-a5e17d9b4cff.html#slide0.

Watson, Jamal Eric. "Merger Creates Higher Education Success Story." *Diverse Issues
in Higher Education*, July 20, 2015. http://diverseeducation.com/article/76423/.

Watters, Audrey. "6.003z: A Learner-Created MOOC Spins Out of MITx." *Hack
Education*, August 14, 2012. http://hackeducation.com/2012/08/14/6.003z
-learner-organized-mooc.

Weeks, Kent. "Creative Options: College Mergers and Institutional Reassessment."
Lex Collegii 11, no. 2 (1987): 3–4.

Womack, Brian. "Google Rises after Creating Holding Company Called Alphabet."
Bloomberg Business, August 10, 2015. http://www.bloomberg.com/news/articles
/2015-08-10/google-to-adopt-new-holding-structure-under-name-alphabet-.

Woodhouse, Kellie. "Discounting Grows Again." *Inside Higher Ed*, August 25, 2015.
https://www.insidehighered.com/news/2015/08/25/tuition-discounting-grows
-private-colleges-and-universities.

———. "Closures to Triple." *Inside Higher Ed*, September 28, 2015. www .insidehighered.com/news/2015/09/28/moodys-predicts-college-closures-triple -2017.

Yanci, Jim, Michael Wolford, and Paige Young. *What Hospital Executives Should Be Considering in Hospital Mergers and Acquisitions.* Charlotte, NC: Dixon Hughes Goodman, 2013. https://www.dhgllp.com/Portals/4/ResourceMedia/publications /HCG_Hospital%20MandA%20Whitepaper_ThoughtLeadership.pdf.

Zimpher, Nancy L., and Jessica Fisher Neidl. "Statewide University Systems: Taking the Land-Grant Concept to Scale in the Twenty-First Century." In *Precipice or Crossroads? Where America's Great Public Universities Stand and Where They Are Going Midway through Their Second Century*, edited by Daniel Mark Fogel and Elizabeth Malson-Huddle. Albany: State University of New York Press, 2012.

Zuckerman, Mortimer B. "America's College Crisis." *U.S. News & World Report*, May 29, 2015. http://www.usnews.com/news/the-report/articles/2015/05/29 /failing-the-college-test.

Contributors

JAMES MARTIN has been a member of the Mount Ida College faculty since 1979. Now a professor of English, he served for over fifteen years as the college's vice president for academic affairs and provost. An ordained United Methodist minister, he was awarded a Fulbright Fellowship to study mergers in the University of London system. Martin is also a senior academic advisor at the Education Alliance and a senior contributor and HigherEdJobs.

With his writing partner, James E. Samels, Martin has coauthored six previous books published by Johns Hopkins University Press: *Merging Colleges for Mutual Growth* (1994), *First among Equals: The Role of the Chief Academic Officer* (1997), *Presidential Transition in Higher Education: Managing Leadership Change* (2005), *Turnaround: Leading Stressed Colleges and Universities to Excellence* (2009), *The Sustainable University: Green Goals and New Challenges for Higher Education Leaders* (2012), and *The Provost's Handbook: The Role of the Chief Academic Officer* (2015). He cowrites with Samels a column on college and university issues, Future Shock, for *University Business Magazine*. Martin and Samels also cohosted the nation's first television talk program on higher education issues, *Future Shock in Higher Education,* from 1994 to 1999 on the Massachusetts Corporation for Educational Telecommunications (MCET) satellite learning network. A graduate of Colby College (AB) and Boston University (MDiv and PhD), Martin has written articles for the *Chronicle of Higher Education, London Times, Christian Science Monitor, Boston Globe, Trusteeship, CASE Currents,* and *Planning for Higher Education.*

JAMES E. SAMELS is the founder and CEO of both the Education Alliance and the Samels Group, a full-service higher education consulting firm. He is also the founding partner of Samels Associates, a law firm serving independent and public colleges, universities, and nonprofit and for-profit higher education organizations. Samels has served on the faculties of the University of Massachusetts and Bentley College and as a guest lecturer at Boston University and Harvard University. Prior to his appointment at the University of Massachusetts, Samels served as the deputy and acting state comptroller in Massachusetts, special assistant attorney general, Massachusetts Community College counsel, and general counsel to the Massachusetts Board of Regents.

Samels holds a bachelor's degree in political science, a master's degree in public administration, a juris doctor degree, and a doctor of education degree. He has written and cowritten a number of scholarly articles, monographs, and opinion editorials appearing in the *Chronicle of Higher Education, AGB Trusteeship, Christian Science Monitor, London Guardian, Boston Globe, Boston Herald, Boston Business Journal, Journal of Higher Education Management,* and *Planning for Higher Education.* He is the coauthor, with James Martin, of *Merging Colleges for Mutual Growth* (1994), *First among Equals: The Role of the Chief Academic Officer* (1997), *Presidential Transition in Higher Education: Managing Leadership Change* (2005), *Turnaround: Leading Stressed Colleges and Universities to Excellence* (2009), and *The Sustainable University: Green Goals and New Challenges for Higher Education Leaders* (2012), all from Johns Hopkins University Press. Samels has previously consulted on projects and presented research papers at universities, colleges, schools, and ministries of education in Canada, China, France, Great Britain, Korea, Sweden, Thailand, and Turkey.

—

KRISTINE CLERKIN is the executive director of College for America at Southern New Hampshire University. College for America is the first accredited degree program in the United States to offer a low-cost ($2,500 per year), competency-based degree with no courses, credits, or grades. The program is targeted at working adults with no prior college experience and is sponsored by employer partners.

Clerkin believes that partnerships based on and driven by educational technology are creating new opportunities for social mobility and economic development. She has over thirty years of experience in the higher education industry. Previous roles include president of Houghton Mifflin's Higher Education Division and general manager of Wolters Kluwer Legal Education. Clerkin has a BA from the University of Wisconsin and an MPA from the Kennedy School at Harvard University.

PHILLIP DICHIARA is managing director for the Boston Consortium for Higher Education. His career began in healthcare administration, concluding as vice president for operations at Boston's Beth Israel Hospital, since merged as Beth Israel Deaconess Medical Center. Having had divisional responsibility at several major institutions during a period of great change in healthcare, he was exposed to the need for developing leadership capacity at all levels of an organization.

DiChiara has been an instructor at Northeastern University and has spoken at numerous conferences, including the Association for Governing Boards, the Association for Consortium Leadership, and the Academy of Management, of which he is a member. His research interests focus on organizational behavior and specifically adult developmental psychology as applied to real-world operations. He has utilized these tools within both the collaborative enterprise and traditional organizations undergoing rapid changes including merger or acquisition.

Since joining the Boston Consortium in 1998 as its first chief executive, he has worked closely with the administration of the sixteen member schools to create trustful and productive relationships across every non-academic discipline. With the consortium as a vehicle for change, many productive communities of practice have been created. In addition, engaged senior managers among the consortium board have driven numerous large-scale projects. These initiatives, both "bottom–up" and "top–down," have validated the importance of mutual learning and systems thinking within the workplace. The result has been that member colleges and universities have benefited from cost reductions and service enhancements, exceeded only by the fresh enthusiasm and new insights that managers bring to their responsibilities.

PAMELA EIBECK became the twenty-fourth president of the University of the Pacific in July 2009. She is Pacific's sixth president since the university moved to Stockton in 1924 and the first woman to hold the office. Pacific has seen its endowment investments more than double since President Eibeck took office, and she has also made connecting with the community a major priority through her Beyond Our Gates campaign.

Eibeck received her bachelor's, master's and doctoral degrees in mechanical engineering from Stanford University. She joined the faculty at the University of California, Berkeley, where she earned tenure and served from 1985 to 1995. In 1995, she became a professor and chair of mechanical engineering at Northern Arizona University, where she later served as director of the honors program and then vice provost for undergraduate studies. From 2004 to 2009, Eibeck served as dean of the Edward E. Whitacre Jr. College of Engineering at Texas Tech University.

An expert in heat transfer, Eibeck conducted experimental research related to electronics cooling and thermal tiles used by NASA on the space shuttles. Her later work focused on engineering educational reform, including early use of multimedia in the classroom, curriculum development, and, most recently, ways to attract young people and women to the profession. She has authored or coauthored nearly fifty articles and papers.

Eibeck became a fellow of the American Society of Mechanical Engineers in 2008. She received the Distinguished Engineering Educator Award from the Society of Women Engineers in 1996 and the Boeing Outstanding Educator Award in 1999.

KENNETH ENDER became Harper College's fifth president in July 2009. Under his leadership, Harper has become a national leader in student success by increasing graduation, transfer, and certificate completion rates; aligning the college's curriculum with high schools; training students for new economy jobs; and implementing new accountability and transparency standards. The college has also implemented a growing group of partnerships and strategic alliances with regional businesses and manufacturers to fill the shortage of skilled workers in key industries in the Chicago area. In 2015, Harper announced the Harper College Promise Scholarship program, where every high school student in Harper's district can earn up to two years of free Harper tuition if they maintain solid grades, have good attendance, do not repeat classes, graduate on time, and perform community service.

Before coming to Harper, Dr. Ender served as president of Cumberland County College in New Jersey. In March 2006, Dr. Ender was selected as the National President Pacesetter of the Year by the National Council for Marketing and Public Relations. In March 2007, Dr. Ender was chosen as the recipient of the eighth annual Community College Alliance Leadership award, given by Franklin University in Ohio.

LYNSI FREITAG currently is the chief of staff for EdPlus at Arizona State University.

J. MATTHEW HARTLEY is a professor of education and associate dean at the University of Pennsylvania Graduate School of Education. His research focuses on academic governance and the social and democratic purposes of higher education. Hartley is also executive director of the Alliance for Higher Education and Democracy (AHEAD). He serves on the editorial boards of *Educational Researcher*, the *Review of Higher Education*, and the *Journal of Higher Education Outreach and Engagement*. He earned his master's and doctoral degrees from Harvard University's Graduate School of Education and his baccalaureate degree from Colby College.

Hartley has also worked with the Council of Europe in Strasburg, France, exploring partnerships between universities, schools, and civil society organizations aimed at promoting education for democratic citizenship. In 2011, he completed a Fulbright Fellowship in Bratislava, Slovakia, in partnership with the Slovak Governance Institute, studying the launch of community-based learning efforts at several universities. His book *To Serve a Larger Purpose*, coedited with John Saltmarsh, examines the roles of universities in democratic societies.

MICHAEL HOYLE is vice president for business and finance at Lasell College. He was the final president of McIntosh College in New Hampshire, which closed in 2009 after more than a century of service.

MICHAEL JACKSON is emeritus vice president for student affairs and executive director of international advancement at the University of Southern California. He also teaches in the Rossier School of Education.

Jackson served as USC's vice president for student affairs for eighteen years, and oversaw the construction of the International Residential College at Parkside, the Arts and Humanities Residential College, the Ronald Tutor Campus Center, and the Engemann Student Health Center. As well as working on the development of various international partnerships, he supervised the expansion of the USC Career Center and helped add the Lesbian, Gay, Bisexual and Transgender Center, the Office of Veterans and Transfer, and the Office of Parent Programs.

LIAM LAIR is a visiting assistant professor in gender studies at the College of St. Benedict/St. John's University.

JAMES LARIMORE's professional background includes dean of student positions at Swarthmore, Dartmouth, and New York University Abu Dhabi, as well as several student-life appointments, including acting dean of students and assistant to the provost, at Stanford University.

Larimore majored in criminal justice with a concentration in sociology at Texas A&M University–Commerce, and earned an AM in higher education from Stanford, where he also has completed all but his dissertation in higher education administration and policy analysis.

Earlier in his career, he served the Bill and Melinda Gates Foundation as its deputy director for student success.

PAUL LEBLANC is president of Southern New Hampshire University. Under the ten years of his direction, SNHU has more than tripled in size and is the largest provider of online higher education in New England, one of the five largest in the country, and the first to have a full competency-based degree program (untethered to the credit hour or classes) approved by a regional accreditor and the US Department of Education. In 2012, the university was number twelve on *Fast Company* magazine's "World's Fifty Most Innovative Companies" list and was the only university included. Paul won a New England Higher Education Excellence Award in 2012 and was named one of "New Hampshire's Most Influential People" by *New Hampshire Business Review*. In 2012, *Forbes Magazine* listed him as one of its fifteen "Classroom Revolutionaries," and he was featured on Bloomberg TV's *Innovators* series.

Paul immigrated to the United States as a child, was the first person in his extended family to attend college, and is a graduate of Framingham State University (BA), Boston College (MA), and the University of Massachusetts (PhD). From 1993 to 1996 he directed a technology start-up for Houghton Mifflin Publishing Company, was president of Marlboro College in Vermont from 1996 to 2003, and became president of SNHU in 2003.

CHARLES MIDDLETON served as the president of Roosevelt University from 2002 to 2015. Middleton was one of the founders of the organization LGBTQ Presidents in Higher Education in 2010.

JOHN OTTENHOFF is vice president for academic affairs and dean of faculty at the College of Idaho. Prior to this position, Ottenhoff served as vice president for the Associated Colleges of the Midwest, and prior to that, Ottenhoff worked at Michigan's Alma College for nearly twenty years, serving as a professor of English, an English Department chair, and an associate provost.

Ottenhoff received a bachelor's degree in English from Calvin College in Michigan in 1972. He went on to receive his master's and doctoral degrees in English language and literature from the University of Chicago.

SUSAN RESNECK PIERCE is the president of SRP Consulting, LLC, and president emerita of the University of Puget Sound, where she served from 1992 to 2003. Under her leadership, Puget Sound entered the ranks of the national liberal arts colleges. The endowment grew from

$68 million to $213 million. From 1990 to 1992, she served as vice president for academic affairs at Lewis and Clark College, and from 1984 to 1990 as dean of the College of Arts and Sciences at the University of Tulsa. As assistant director of the Division of Education Programs at the National Endowment for the Humanities, she directed the three federal programs that supported undergraduate education in the humanities. She also has served as chair of the English Department at Ithaca College and as visiting associate professor at Princeton University.

Today, as president of SRP Consulting, Pierce advises colleges and universities on such matters as effective board and presidential performance, governance, board development, and strategic planning. She coaches presidents; advises board chairs; and facilitates focused retreats for boards, president's cabinets, and faculty.

Pierce writes and speaks extensively about higher education. Jossey-Bass published and *Inside Higher Ed* sponsored her two recent books: *Governance Reconsidered: How Boards, Presidents, Administrators and Faculty Can Help Their Colleges Thrive* (2014) and *On Being Presidential: A Guide for College and University Leaders* (2012). She is also the author of *The Moral of the Story: Literature, Values and American Higher Education* (1982) and numerous essays about American literature, and she is coeditor of a book on Ralph Ellison's *Invisible Man* (Modern Language Association, 1989).

Pierce received a bachelor's degree from Wellesley College in 1965, a master's degree in English from the University of Chicago in 1966, and a doctoral degree in English from the University of Wisconsin in 1972. She is a member of Phi Beta Kappa.

VITA RABINOWITZ is executive vice chancellor and university provost at the City University of New York. Her service in that role began in July 2015.

For nearly a decade prior to her current appointment, Rabinowitz served as provost and vice president for academic affairs at Hunter College, where she has been a dedicated faculty member for her entire academic career. In addition to teaching and mentoring thousands of students over the course of her thirty-seven years at Hunter, she held a variety of administrative positions before assuming the role of provost, including chairperson of the Department of Psychology, acting associate provost, and acting provost.

While at Hunter, Rabinowitz was the recipient of major grants from the National Science Foundation (NSF), including one that established Hunter's Gender Equity Project (GEP), which sought to advance women faculty in the natural and social sciences and became an incubator for faculty development at Hunter. She served as codirector of the GEP for eight years. As provost, she received an NSF award to strengthen the many science, technology, engineering, and math (STEM) enrichment programs at Hunter College and launch Hunter's Undergraduate Research Initiative. In addition to her extensive service at Hunter, since 1978 Rabinowitz has been a member of the doctoral program in psychology at CUNY Graduate Center, where she served as acting program head of the social/personality doctoral subprogram.

Rabinowitz received her master's and doctoral degrees in social psychology at Northwestern University. The range of her scholarly interests includes the study of women and achievement; methodological issues in the study of gender and memory; and coping with adverse outcomes. Her coauthored textbook on the psychology of women, *Engendering Psychology: Women and Gender Revisited*, is in its second edition.

PHILIP REGIER is responsible for Arizona State University's expansion into online learning and has been a member of the university leadership team focused on education innovation since 2009. In the first six years of his tenure as dean of ASU Online, the fully online student population grew from 400 to more than 19,000, with the number of degree programs offered growing from 6 to more than 100.

Regier helped the university develop innovative partnerships with leading education technology companies, including Pearson, Knewton and edX. Today, online programs at ASU utilize more than 150 technologies, and the university is a co-convener of the ASU + GSV Education Innovation Summit, the largest and most recognized convening of education technology entrepreneurs, investors, and users in the world.

In 2015, ASU ranked number one on *U.S. News & World Report*'s inaugural list of the most innovative universities. The university has also received recognition from the *New York Times*, the *Chronicle of Higher Education*, and the Bill and Melinda Gates Foundation for its work in adaptive learning and use of data in student advising, as well as earning the top ranking by *U.S. News & World Report* for online student services and technology. In June 2014, the university announced a groundbreaking partnership with Starbucks Corporation to provide ASU's online degree programs to eligible US Starbucks partners at no out-of-pocket cost for tuition.

In 2015, Regier was named university dean for educational initiatives and chief executive officer of EdPlus at ASU for the purpose of expanding upon the university's successful digital-immersion programs and extending online teaching and learning globally. He earned his undergraduate degree in philosophy and mathematics from St. John's College and his doctoral degree in accountancy from the University of Illinois at Urbana-Champaign.

ALAN RUBY has had a long career in government, business, philanthropy, and education, ranging from schoolteacher to Australian deputy secretary of education to scholar. At the University of Pennsylvania, Ruby, as a senior scholar in the Alliance for Higher Education and Democracy, focuses on globalization's effects on universities.

JAMES STELLAR earned a biology degree at Ursinus College in 1972 and a psychology PhD from the University of Pennsylvania in 1976. After two years of postdoctoral fellowship in the Department of Anatomy at the Penn Medical School, in 1978 he joined Harvard University as an assistant professor of psychology, becoming an associate professor in 1983. In 1986, Dr. Stellar moved to Northeastern University, where he became a full professor. His professorial neuroscience research and teaching centered on the anatomical and molecular biological basis of reward and motivational processes in laboratory animals as a model for human cocaine addiction, and his curriculum vitae lists over 150 scientific papers, chapters, books, and presentations. Although he had previous administrative positions as associate dean and department chair, Dr. Stellar began his administrative career in earnest in 1998 when became the dean of the College of Arts and Sciences during a remarkable ten-year period of rapid rise in Northeastern University's reputation. In 2009, Dr. Stellar moved to the publics at Queens College, City University of New York, to become provost. In 2013, Stellar transitioned at Queens to a specially focused vice presidential position to develop an Office of Academic Innovation and Experiential Education. In February of 2015, he became provost and senior vice president at the University at Albany, State University of New York, his current position.

Outside the university, Stellar cofounded and codirects the Planning Institute on Experiential Education that since 2005 has helped more than eighty colleges and universities create on-campus experiential education plans. The institute operates under the World Association of Cooperative Education (www.waceinc.org), where Stellar is a board member. Since 2009, Stellar and a team have been writing a blog (www.otherlobe.com) about experiential education, its management by colleges and universities, and the personal transformation such an approach can achieve for students when properly combined with classical academic excellence. A lay book on this general subject showing its fundamental grounding in neuroscience, *Education That Works: The Neuroscience of Building a More Effective Higher Education*, is forthcoming from Ideapress in 2016.

R. MICHAEL TANNER is senior academic counsel at the Association of Public and Land-Grant Universities. In this position, Tanner leads the association's academic affairs activities, including the Voluntary System of Accountability/College Portrait project. He also serves as senior staff liaison to the association's Council on Academic Affairs, composed of the provosts and chief academic officers from each of the 215 member universities and university systems. In 2015, he was named a National Academy of Inventors Fellow.

Tanner previously served as provost and vice chancellor for academic affairs at the University of Illinois, Chicago, one of the top US universities as ranked by federal research expenditures and including fifteen colleges and schools enrolling almost 17,000 undergraduate and 10,000 graduate students. Prior to joining the UIC faculty and administration in July 2002, Tanner had spent thirty-one years at the University of California, Santa Cruz, as computer and information sciences faculty member and administrator, including six years as executive vice chancellor and three years as academic vice chancellor.

Through his engineering and computer sciences research, Tanner has produced four patents; more than ten refereed journal articles; and almost thirty conference papers, book chapters, proceedings, and technical reports. His research has focused on codes that protect digital messages against errors introduced in transmission.

R. OWEN WILLIAMS served as president of Transylvania University from 2010 to 2014, following a twenty-four-year career as a Wall Street investment banker (director, Salomon Brothers Inc.; managing director, Goldman Sachs Group Inc.; chairman, Bear Stearns Asia).

He earned a bachelor of arts in philosophy from Dartmouth College and then studied at the University of Cambridge in England, earning a master of arts in intellectual history. In 1999, Williams left the business world to study at Yale University and Yale Law School, where he earned a doctorate in American history and a master's of studies in law.

Williams was awarded the Raoul Berger Fellowship at Harvard Law School, the Samuel Golieb Fellowship at the New York University School of Law, the Fletcher Jones Fellowship at the Huntington Library, the Legal History Fellowship at Yale Law School, and the Cassius Marcellus Clay Postdoctoral Fellowship in History at Yale. He has published in several magazines, journals, and encyclopedias. He edited *The Encyclopedia of Antislavery and Abolition* and was an articles editor for the *Yale Journal of Law and the Humanities*.

NANCY L. ZIMPHER has served as the first female chancellor of the State University of New York since 2009. Prior to this, she served as the first female president of the University of Cincinnati and, before that, as the first female chancellor of the University of Wisconsin, Milwaukee.

Index

Academically Based Community Service (ABCS), 98
Accelerated Study in Associate Programs (ASAP), 83–84
accountability, 102, 107, 181, 234; and CBE, 128, 132; legal, 30; at SUNY, 56, 57
accreditation, 4, 14, 16, 21; and closure, 24–26, 28, 31, 201, 203–5; for international partnerships, 146; and mergers, 107, 189, 192, 193; for public-private partnerships, 150–52; and Sweet Briar, 202
administration: in Collaboration Continuum, 175; consolidation of, 67–69, 71, 73; in consortia, 174–76; costs of, 187; duplication of, 64; and international partnerships, 146; and mergers, 207; mergers of, 186, 207; and scale, 44, 48; of SUNY, 52, 54, 60; and UOP alliance, 65
affiliation, xii, 4–5, 6, 19, 72; deep, 80; program-based, ix, 7. *See also* alliances, strategic; collaboration; consolidation; consortia; co-ventures; mergers; partnerships
Affordable Care Act, 71, 150
Agatston Urban Nutrition Initiative, 99
agreements, contractual, 7, 8, 16, 22, 31, 78, 85; in CBE partnerships, 128, 132, 134; in community college partnerships, 108; in elite-college partnerships, 94, 95, 100; with faculty, 24, 26, 29, 75,

152; international, 94, 216, 217, 218; international free trade, 138–39; joint operating, 72; for joint ventures, 10, 16, 17, 19, 20; memoranda of understanding (MOUs), 152, 153; nondisclosure, 21, 164, 188; in public-private partnerships, 11, 151, 152, 153; purchasing, 43, 187; real estate, 27, 82; with staff, 26, 29; with students, 24, 29, 83; on teach-outs, 25; on transfer policies, 22, 61, 153
Albany State University (Georgia), 210
Alliance for Health Sciences (Rosalind Franklin and DePaul universities), 17–18
Alliance for Higher Education and Democracy (AHEAD; U. Pennsylvania), xii, 92–97, 217–18
alliances, strategic, ix, xii, xiii, 4, 33, 37–182, 216, 218; vs. consortia, 169; vs. mergers, 5; systemness, 52; and technology, 112–22; typology of, x; and UOP, 64–65. *See also* affiliation; collaboration; consolidation; consortia; co-ventures; mergers; partnerships
Alliant International University, 70, 209
Alphabet (Google), 38
Altbach, Philip G., 138
alumni, 13, 21; of Antioch, 203; and closure, 26, 27, 28, 33, 203–4; and international partnerships, 137, 139–40, 142, 143, 146; and mergers, 186, 190, 194, 196; of Sweet Briar, 201, 202

243